INSTRUCTOR'S RESOURCE MANUAL

John Marshall Carter

A HISTORY OF WORLD SOCIETIES

Fourth Edition

John P. McKay
University of Illinois at Urbana-Champaign

Bennett D. Hill
Georgetown University

John Buckler
University of Illinois at Urbana-Champaign

HOUGHTON MIFFLIN COMPANY   Boston   Toronto
Geneva, Illinois   Palo Alto   Princeton, New Jersey

Senior Sponsoring Editor: Patricia A. Coryell
Senior Associate Editor: Jeffrey Greene
Marketing Manager: Clint Crockett

Acknowledgments

To Pam and Aelfgyva

A special note of thanks to the Thomasville, North Carolina, City Schools, and especially to Judy Dorety, Linda Roberts, Rick Jones, and Joanne Guy for sharing their office space, equipment, and expertise. Without their help, this project could not have been completed.

Printed in the U.S.A.

ISBN: 0–395–74079–7

123456789–H–99 98 97 96 95

CONTENTS

TEACHING A HISTORY OF WORLD SOCIETIES

This Instructor's Resource Manual, which accompanies the fourth edition of McKay, Hill, and Buckler's *A History of World Societies*, has many new features for instructors. There are more inquiry-approach activities and more attention has been given to pedagogy than in the previous edition of the manual. The section entitled Doing History emphasizes methods used by historians and other researchers to uncover the past: reading and analyzing primary sources; writing from primary sources; using art and literature as historical sources; historiography; and relating geography to historical developments.

Because writing can be an important way to know the past, this Instructor's Resource Manual encourages different kinds of writing assignments: short reflective essays; the traditional term paper; book reviews; interpretive essays based on primary sources; and other types of writing. These different kinds of writing are suggested in the section Doing History.

Each chapter of this manual includes the following: instructional objectives, a chapter outline of the corresponding text chapter, and lecture suggestions. This edition includes several changes and new material. For example, the classroom discussion suggestions and the section Doing History have been grouped with a section on Cooperative Learning Activities under the heading Activities for Discovering the Past. In addition, there is a new section on Using Primary Sources. There is also a new section called Map Activity. The audiovisual bibliography has been updated to include many new videodisc and CD-ROM offerings. Many primary source selections have been included at the back of the instructor's resource manual. Finally, a list of addresses of audiovisual material suppliers has been added to the manual.

The audiovisual bibliography has been prepared with a view toward utilizing full-length feature films, videodiscs, and CD-ROMs in the world civilization curriculum. Although most class periods are too short to show an entire full-length movie, many feature films, videodiscs, and other audiovisual materials can be a valuable resource for history courses. Furthermore, a broad selection of films is available at video stores across the country, and many university and college libraries are amassing valuable video collections. Moreover, many university and college libraries now have sizable videodisc and CD-ROM collections.

Instructors are encouraged to investigate the following slide program to add to their own collections for further course enrichment:

Instructional Resources Corporation
1819 Bay Ridge Avenue
Annapolis, MD 21403
301-263-0025

This slide program includes more than 2,000 slides covering the history of world civilizations. A text accompanies the program.

TEACHING LARGE SECTIONS OF WORLD HISTORY

The best thing for the instructor of large sections of world history courses is an army of teaching assistants. In such a situation, like those in major universities where world history courses are from 200–400 students, teaching assistants can review and fine tune the lecture given two or three times a week by the professor. Unfortunately, many instructors have to teach extremely large sections without the help of a T.A. army. What do they do?

Team-taught world history courses can lessen the workload somewhat; yet, even in team-taught situations, two or three professors still have to divide up the grading of exams and research papers or other written projects—good but probably not ideal. Of course, many professors at small colleges or community colleges have no help with large classes. Some legitimate shortcuts are available.

Although machine-scored multiple-choice tests help to ease the workload, students in a world history course need to write in order to process the material, improve their writing abilities, and develop higher-order thinking skills. Therefore, the instructor of large sections is still pressed to make writing assignments and give essay tests. In large sections, the instructor can use a combination of multiple-choice tests and essay tests, as well as term papers and/or shorter written papers. For one thing, multiple-choice tests do tell us if the students are learning the material (maybe memorizing at first, but learning has to begin somewhere). However, if students are going to learn about how the historical process works, writing should be assigned. For large classes, two short interpretive papers or one traditional research paper per semester would give students opportunities to write about history, sharpen their research and thinking skills, and engage in the historical process. I highly recommend Professor William L. Chew's research and writing system delineated in his article "Clio's Quadrivium: New Rigor in Undergraduate History" in the February, 1995 issue of *The History Teacher* (Volume 28: Number 2, pp. 161–181). In the article, Professor Chew states: "In my freshman courses I give four written assignments, for a total of some twenty-five typed pages. . . . The assignments are themselves organically interrelated and build up to a culminating piece of work, the term paper. First comes an abstract of a journal article; second a biographical sketch; third a source analysis; finally, the term paper. Each paper may be revised once, one week for revision being allotted for the first three papers, two weeks for the term paper."

Another pedagogical help was suggested to me by Professor Emory Maiden of the Appalachian State University English Department. This is the "admit card." Admit cards provide the instructors of large sections with a relatively simple, time-saving way to monitor student comprehension of course lectures and readings. On a regular basis, students are allowed to turn in to the instructor index cards with no more than one side filled with summaries of text chapters or lectures, or with questions and ideas about a specific subject in the course. Admit card grades can be used to supplement other course grades.

Cooperative learning can be an effective way to help reduce the workload of the instructor while aiding in student learning. Cooperative learning research projects, presentations, and even exams can considerably reduce the instructor's workload while enhancing student learning. In a large section of, say, 100 students, an instructor might employ the JIGSAW approach (described in the section on cooperative learning). By organizing the class into teams of five or six students each, the instructor would then be faced with grading twenty or so presentations instead of 100. And, according to a mountain of research on the subject, students will probably learn a great deal from the team approach.

THE WRITING PROCESS IN THE WORLD HISTORY COURSE

Over the past several years, writing-intensive world civilization courses (as well as courses in Western civilization and other fields) have begun appearing in colleges and universities throughout the country. The activities included in this manual in the section Doing History are aimed at all college and university world civilization courses, not just the writing-intensive ones, for writing in history class helps students to learn their subject.

A practical way to improve student writing is the writing process approach. Developed by the Bay Area Writing Project of 1973, the writing process approach has been included in hundreds of secondary and university curricula. Writing across the curriculum has been suggested as a way to provide opportunities for students to write in many or all of their courses. The world history class can provide important and exciting opportunities for students to think and write about the past.

The writing process approach stresses that the conceptualization, research, and writing of the paper are as important as the finished product. Instructors can help students improve their writing by planning writing conferences into the course schedule and reserving time for the writing, rewriting, and editing of papers. Using writing to learn history can improve students' thinking, as well as their writing skills.

The writing process includes the following steps:

1. **Prewriting Activities.** Reading books, discussing topics, taking field trips, viewing art works, dramatizing a historical event, and brainstorming are activities that can help elicit ideas for writing assignments.

2. **"Playing" with a Topic.** Thinking about the subject and discussing the subject with the instructor, another student, or a friend often helps writing ideas evolve and crystallize. Notes should be taken during this stage of the process.

3. **Outlining and Clustering.** Ideas that grow out of playing with a topic are organized at this step of the writing process.

4. **Writing.** The composing process comes next.

5. **Scheduling a Conference.** As time permits, the instructor might schedule short conferences with students to talk about their papers.

6. **Submitting a First Draft.** The writing process includes submitting a first draft of the paper to the instructor. After reading a first draft, the instructor provides feedback and suggests how the paper might be improved before it is turned in for a grade.

7. **Peer Review.** Class time may be scheduled to allow students the opportunity to read and comment on classmates' papers.

8. **Revising and Rewriting.** After the instructor has read the first draft and suggested improvements, and after peer review, students should revise their first drafts.

9. **Evaluating the Final Paper.** Some papers may be evaluated and assigned a grade that is part of the course grade. Other papers may not be assigned a grade.

10. **Starting Over.** Depending on the instructor's time, students may be asked to write two, three, or more short papers over the course of a semester or quarter. The instructor may opt for the traditional term paper, a marvelous way to involve students in the writing process: conceiving a topic; doing the initial reading; conducting research; writing an outline; compiling a bibliography; writing a first draft; making revisions; and composing a final draft.

Suggested Reading for the Writing Process

Barzun, Jacques, *Simple and Direct: A Rhetoric for Writers* (1976).

Barzun, Jacques, and Henry F. Graff, *The Modern Researcher* (1970).

Braine, John, *Writing a Novel* (1975).

Britton, James, *Language and Learning* (1970).

Carter, John Marshall, "The Bayeux Tapestry in the Social Studies Class," *Social Education* (December, 1986), 31–32.

Carter, John Marshall, "The Social Studies Teacher As Writing Coach," *The Clearing House* (May/June, 1991), 346–349.

Elbow, Peter, *Writing Without Teachers* (1973).

Elbow, Peter, "Reflections on Academic Discourse: How It Relates to Freshmen and Colleagues." *College English* 53:2 (February, 1991), 135–155.

Emig, Janet, "Writing As A Mode of Learning," *College Composition and Communication* (May, 1977), 122–128.

Flower, Linda S., and John R. Hayes, "Problem-Solving Strategies and the Writing Process," *College English* 40:1 (February, 1989), 11–22.

Fulweiler, Toby, *Language Connections: Reading and Writing Across the Curriculum* (1983).

Highet, Gilbert, *The Art of Teaching* (1950).

Moffett, James, *Active Voice: A Writing Program Across the Curriculum* (1981).

Murray, Donald, *A Writer Teaches Writing* (1968).

Olson, Carol Booth, *Practical Ideas for Teaching Writing as a Process* (1987).

Rothenberg, Albert, *The Emerging Goddess: The Creative Process in Art, Science, and Other Fields* (1979).

Shuman, R. Baird, "Toward Redefining the Humanistic Perspective," *Journal of Aesthetic Education* (July, 1980), 91–103.

Shuman, R. Baird (with Eric Hobson), *Reading and Writing in High Schools* (1990).

Steward, Joyce S., and Marjorie Smelstor, *Writing in the Social Sciences* (1984).

Turabian, Kate L., *A Manual for Writers of Term Papers, Theses, and Dissertations* (1973).

Vonnegut, Kurt, "Teaching the Unteachable," *Wampeters, Foma, and Granfallons* (1976), 25–30.

Vonnegut, Kurt, "Triage," *Palm Sunday* (1981), 73–81.

Wolfe, Denny, and Robert Reising, *Writing for Learning in the Content Areas* (1983).

Zinsser, William, *On Writing Well* (1976).

Making the Transition from Western Civilization to World History

Many instructors who have taught a history of Western civilization now find themselves with the challenge of teaching world history. With the ever-decreasing size of the world, it is imperative that students gain from their instructors a large view of world history and societies. McKay, Hill, and Buckler's *A History of World Societies* offers a unique, creative approach to the teaching of world societies—a truly world historical approach that attempts to put the world, not just the West, into vivid historical context. A considerable amount of new material has been added to this edition, enhancing the discussion of non-Western areas of the world.

A very useful way of making the transition from Western to world history is to help students see similarities and contrasts between the non-Western societies and the Western ones. Instructors should encourage their students to develop ways of making comparisons between the non-West and the West without arbitrarily holding the non-Western world to a Western standard. Instructors should point out that various factors have facilitated growth and decline at different speeds in different parts of the world.

Needless to say, instructors who have taught only about Western societies should concentrate their efforts on the non-Western areas of the world. Collecting materials on non-Western areas and building files of journal articles, newspaper clippings, and other print media should help enrich the teaching about non-Western societies.

Information on teaching about non-Western societies can be obtained from the following organizations:

1. American Historical Association
    400 A Street, SE
    Washington, DC 20003

2. The Social Studies Development Center
    Indiana University
    2805 East Tenth Street
    Bloomington, IN 47405

3. National Council for the Social Studies
    3501 Newark Street, NW
    Washington, DC 20016

4. Society for History Education
    c/o California State University
    Long Beach
    1250 Bellflower Blvd.
    Long Beach, CA 90840

COOPERATIVE LEARNING IN THE WORLD HISTORY CLASS

Cooperative learning is not a new idea, although the systematic application of the concept has received considerable attention and analysis in the past fifteen years. Historians can point to any number of historical illustrations of people doing and accomplishing things cooperatively. Indeed, to cite one or more would be condescending and pointless. Furthermore, there is a hesitancy to suggest to instructors the idea that they should allow "group work" in their classrooms. A semester system or quarter system provides only a minimum number of meetings and instructors must budget their time wisely to cover all the material set before them. However, the daring instructor who decides to give cooperative learning a whirl may find that it has the potential to reduce the workload and, if advocates of cooperative learning are correct, it has the potential to increase student learning.

D. Johnson and R. Johnson, two contemporary scholars of cooperative learning, define the term thusly: "cooperative learning means instructionally using small groups so that students work together to maximize their own and each other's learning." According to Johnson and Johnson, instructors may employ cooperative learning in three ways: (1) formal cooperative learning groups, where the instructor organizes the class into groups or teams of from two to six, makes an assignment, allows the teams time to do the work, intervenes in the groups whenever necessary, and evaluates both individual and team outcomes. Formal cooperative learning groups are somewhat permanent and the semester's workload is done cooperatively by the teams; (2) informal cooperative learning groups are temporary groups or teams used as a part of the total learning program, along with instructor's lectures and other approaches; (3) cooperative learning base groups are permanent, semester- or year-long groups with stable team memberships throughout the term.

Stahl suggests the following steps or principles in his informative overview of cooperative learning:

1. Each cooperative learning group is as heterogeneous as possible.
2. Instructor and students set clear, specific individual and group goals.
3. Group/team members are held individually accountable.
4. Instructor provides group rewards. In the cooperative learning activities in this instructor's resource manual, team grades averaged with individual grades has been suggested as a reward that might be suitable for college and university classrooms.
5. Division of required individual tasks is necessary. In the cooperative learning activities that follow in the manual, depending on the particular task/presentation assigned, instructors may assign specific roles for members of the groups/teams: (1) team leader, (2) scribe, (3) presenter, (4) researcher, and so forth.
6. A positive interdependence among group members.
7. Attitude and abilities of civility. (Here Stahl emphasizes the socialization aspect of cooperative learning.)
8. Group-processing abilities. (Here is where the cognitive success of the idea is evaluated.)
9. Equal opportunity for success.
10. Sufficient time for learning. (To overcome logistical problems, more class time than usual is spent on the processing of information.)

Slavin discussed the cooperative learning strategies that have been empirically compared to traditionally taught control groups:

1. **Student Teams Achievement Divisions.** Groups of four get assignments from instructor and complete task in the group. Instructor gives individual quizzes and compares STAD scores with students' past averages. Those scoring higher because of the STAD receive additional points.

2. **Teams-Games-Tournament.** This approach uses the same instructor presentation and team organization as STAD but replaces quizzes with weekly tournaments. Winning teams receive team points.

3. **Jigsaw.** Six-member teams work on material that the instructor has organized into sections. Each member reads an assigned section and becomes an expert on that section. "Experts" from all teams meet to discuss their respective section. Then, experts return to their teams to teach their particular section.

4. **Group Investigation.** Here the class studies a particular subject (the Crusades, for example). Two- to six-member teams study subtopics and make reports to the class.

The cooperative learning activities that follow in this manual use a variety of strategies (and variations on them). Instructors are encouraged to try one or more. A reminder: Much of the research on cooperative learning has been done in an elementary school environment. What are the possibilities for cooperative learning in the college and university classroom?

Suggested Reading

Aronson, Elliot, et al., *The Jigsaw Classroom* (1978).

Devries, D. L., and R. E. Slavin, "Teams-Games-Tournament (TGT): Review of Ten Classroom Experiments," *Journal of Research and Development in Education* 12 (Fall, 1978), 28–38.

Johnson, D. W., and R. T. Johnson, *Learning Together and Alone: Cooperative, Competitive, and Individualistic Learning* (1987).

Schmuck, R. A., and P. A. Schmuck, *Group Processes in the Classroom* (1992).

Slavin, R. E., *Introduction to Cooperative Learning* (1983).

Slavin, R. E., *Cooperative Learning: Theory, Research, and Practice* (1990).

Stahl, R. J., and R. L. van Sickle, *Cooperative Learning in the Social Studies Classroom* (1992).

SOME PRELIMINARY QUESTIONS
FOR ANALYZING PRIMARY SOURCES

Getting students to think and act like a historian are worthwhile goals of the world history class. The primary sources that are appended to this manual are included to give students opportunities to read and analyze the words that were written by people in past societies. Indeed, it is their words that form the basis of the historian's undertaking. Having students read, analyze, interpret, and synthesize primary sources is having them do what historians do. The following questions are intended to serve as preliminary questions for attacking the primary sources.

I. Reading (or observing, or listening to, in the cases of visual or sound-recorded sources).
   A. Read the source(s) carefully.
   B. Reread the corresponding text chapter to see how the primary source fits within the broader historical context.
   C. Try to get a preliminary understanding of the sources.
   D. Circle words that are not clear and look them up or ask the instructor for help.
   E. Reread the sources after you have looked up the words that were not clear.
   F. Write a brief summary of what the document said to you.

II. Analyzing
   A. For subsequent sources, use the same procedure described above.
   B. Compare the evidence of the sources (in the case of multiple sources on one subject).
      1. Do the sources agree on the subject they describe?
      2. If not, how do they differ?
      3. When were the sources composed?
      4. Were the authors of the sources equally close in time to the historical event they are describing?
      5. Who were the authors of the sources?
      6. Were the authors eyewitnesses to the events they are describing?
      7. If they were not eyewitnesses, did they know an individual (or individuals) who participated in the event(s) they are describing?
      8. How do your answers to questions 1–7 aid in your choice of what you consider to be the most reliable source?
      9. What criteria did you use to determine which of your sources is most reliable?
      10. After you have read, reread, and analyzed the primary sources, write out brief summaries of the authors' main ideas.
      11. What biases might the authors have toward the subject about which they wrote?
      12. List these possible biases.
      13. How might these biases have affected their interpretation of what happened in the histories they wrote (or created, in the case of visual sources)?
      14. How did the textbook authors of *A History of World Societies* employ these sources?

TRANSITION GUIDE TO THE FOURTH EDITION

Overall

Length   The length has been reduced. The two Rome chapters have been combined into one chapter (7); the three chapters on medieval Europe have been combined into two (12 and 13); and the three chapters on nineteenth-century Europe have been combined into two (25 and 26).

More non-Western coverage   The reduction in text length has been accomplished through cuts in Western material, while important revisions have been added to non-Western coverage. Thus the proportion of non-Western material has been increased.

More cultural history   Cultural history has been increased throughout.

Women's history   Coverage of women has been better integrated into the main narrative.

Listening to the Past   This addition to the fourth edition is a lengthy primary source excerpt at the end of each chapter that extends and illuminates a major historical issue considered in the chapter. It opens with a problem-setting introduction and closes with Questions for Analysis that invite students to evaluate the evidence as historians would.

Chapter-by-Chapter Revisions

The following is a chapter-by-chapter guide to the most significant changes in the fourth edition.

Chapter 1   Origins

- The updated treatment of Neolithic society draws on recent archaeological evidence.
- The section on Mesopotamian culture has been reorganized to clarify the chronology and the role of writing in Sumerian civilization.
- New archaeological evidence on the spread of Sumerian culture has been incorporated.
- The discussion of Akhenaten's legacy has been revised to reflect current scholarly opinion.
- The treatment of Hittite cultural contacts with Egypt and Mycenaean Greece has been updated.
- New material has been added on Ramses II.
- Listening to the Past—A Quest for Immortality (*The Epic of Gilgamesh*)

Chapter 2   Small Kingdoms and Mighty Empires in the Near East

- The evolution of Jewish religion has been expanded and updated. It includes added coverage of Babylonian Captivity, the evolution of Hebrew law and the Torah and the Talmud, and the role of women in Hebrew religion and society.

- New material has been added on Assyrian art.
- Listening to the Past—The Covenant Between Yahweh and the Hebrews (*Book of Samuel*)

Chapter 3   Ancient India to ca A.D. 200

- There is added clarification of the Bhagavad Gita.
- Coverage of the Brahmi alphabet has been added.
- Added explanation of the spread of Buddhism is provided.
- Listening to the Past—An Account of the Gods and the Creation of the World (the *Mahabharta*)

Chapter 4   The Rise and Growth of China to ca A.D. 200

- The treatment of neolithic culture in China has been updated.
- Listening to the Past—The Daoist Approach to Administering the Empire (The *Dao De Jing*)

Chapter 5   The Legacy of Greece

- An expanded discussion of the Lyric poets emphasizes their political and social setting.
- The treatment of democracy in the classical period has been updated and revised to examine the impact of Athenian ideology on social order and life.
- The discussion of Athenian women has been revised for greater clarity.
- Material has been added on popular religion in classical Greece.
- The revised and expanded discussion of Plato and Aristotle clarifies the social and political context for their ideas.
- Listening to the Past—A Veteran's Account of the Battle of Salamis (Aeschylus, *The Persians*)

Chapter 6   Hellenistic Diffusion

- The treatment of Hellenistic women has been updated and integrated into discussions of economy and politics.
- A discussion of Jews in Hellenistic cities has been added.
- Listening to the Past—A Queen's Sacrifice to Her Society (*Plutarch's Lives*)

Chapter 7   The Glory of Rome

- This chapter reduces and consolidates the third edition's Chapters 7 and 8 into a single chapter, reducing the text in the third edition chapters by approximately 30 percent. It also incorporates the following improvements:
    - A new discussion of Ovid illuminates the artistic response to political developments.
    - The coverage of pagan/Christian relations has been revised based on new research.
    - A discussion of the later Roman period's consequences for agriculture and agricultural labor has been added.
- Listening to the Past—Popular Roman Views of Religion and Magic (Roman Curse Tablets)

Chapter 8   The Making of Europe

- The treatment of the growth of the Christian church has been revised to clarify sources of Christian doctrine and the nature of Arianism.
- There is added discussion relating Christianity with the development of Western attitudes toward women and sexuality.

- The treatment of the Germanic peoples and German life has been revised and updated.
- A discussion of Eastern monasticism has been added to the section on the Byzantine East.
- Coverage of the "Justinian plague" and Byzantine health and medicine also has been added to the Byzantine section.
- Listening to the Past—The Conversation of Clovis (Gregory of Tours, *History of the Franks*)

Chapter 9   The Islamic World, ca 600–1400

- New material has been added on the issue of divorce in Islam.
- A new discussion compares the experiences of Jews living under Islam with those living in Christian Europe.
- Greater prominence is given to trade and commerce, the backbone of Islamic culture.
- A new discussion compares educational objectives of medieval Islam with education in western Europe in the high and late Middle Ages and in Ming China.
- The treatment of women in Islam has been revised to reflect new scholarship.
- Listening to the Past—The Endowment of a Madrasa

Chapter 10   Africa Before European Intrusion, ca 400–1500

- This chapter has been repositioned from its former location following the chapters on Europe in the Middle Ages.
- The introduction on African geography has been revised for more clarity.
- The discussion of Ethiopia has been moved to precede the discussion of the east African coastal states.
- The bibliography has been entirely rewritten to incorporate fresh material.
- Listening to the Past—The Epic of Old Mali (self-description of the griot Djeli Mamoudou Kouyate)

Chapter 11   Tradition and Change in Asia ca 320–1400

- More concise treatment of Guptan politics.
- Added discussion of how the Guptas encouraged the spread of Hinduism for political reasons at the expense of Buddhism.
- Listening to the Past—Women in Chinese Society (poems from *The Book of Songs*)

Chapters 12 and 13 on the Middle Ages

These chapters reduce and consolidate former Chapters 12, 13, and 14, reducing the text contained in the third edition chapters by approximately 30 percent. In addition, several changes have been incorporated.

Chapter 12   Europe in the Early and High Middle Ages

- The discussion of Kievan Russia has been relocated to this chapter (from third edition Chapter 19) to reinforce chronology and Russia's integral role in early medieval Europe.
- The treatment of the origins of feudalism has been revised to reflect current scholarship.
- The discussion of economic revival incorporates new material on women in commerce.
- Discussion of the Crusades' impact on women has also been added.
- Listening to the Past—An Arab View of the Crusades (Ibn Al-Athir's history of the First Crusade)

Chapter 13   Creativity and Crisis in the Central and Later Middle Ages

- A new section on troubadour poetry has been added.
- The introduction to the social section has been revised to qualify medieval social divisions.
- The coverage of women's role and work in agriculture has been increased.
- A new section has been added on medieval health care, based on current research.
- The revised, updated section on popular religion clarifies the influence of the sacramental system of religious belief.
- The updated discussion of peasant marriage incorporates new research.
- Listening to the Past—A Medieval Noblewoman (*The Autobiography of Guibert of Nogentsous-Coucy*)

Chapter 14   The Americas Before European Intrusion, ca 400–1500

- The coverage of Aztec religion and culture has been expanded with the object of showing that Aztec religion was in fact the basis of all facets of the society's culture.
- A new explanation, based on new research, has been provided for the practice of human sacrifice and the Mexica collapse.
- Information has been added on new archaeological discoveries about the Moche peoples in northern Peru.
- Based on new research, the text offers a fresh interpretation of Inca society emphasizing the cult of the royal mummies and the role of religion in the empire's problems.
- Listening to the Past—The Installation of the Inca

Chapter 15   European Society in the Age of the Renaissance and Reformation

- Discussion has been added on the impact of the Renaissance on the lives of ordinary women.
- Recent research on the political uses of pornography has been incorporated.
- There is a new discussion of the influence of hymns and Luther's catechisms in spreading the Reformation's ideas.
- The discussion of how the spread of Luther's message affected women has been expanded.
- The section on Calvin's Geneva has been refined.
- The treatment of the origins of the English Reformation has been updated and tightened for improved topical balance.
- New material has been added on social legislation issued by the Council of Trent.
- The discussion of the Jesuit order has been revised to reflect current scholarship.
- Listening to the Past—Grievances of the Peasants of Stuhlingen and Lupfen (article of peasant demands presented to the Imperial Chamber Court)

Chapter 16   The Age of European Expansion and Religious Wars

- Throughout this chapter, an effort has been made to clarify the relationship of social and cultural material to political and religious unrest.
- A new section on Columbus's motives and legacy has been added.
- The section on changing attitudes has been revised to interpret social and cultural change as a reflection of political and religious uncertainty and conflict.
- The section on literature and art has been tightened and revised to stress the political and social conditions for artistic developments.
- A new discussion on gender roles in early modern European arts and letters has been added.
- Listening to the Past—Columbus Describes His First Voyage (Columbus's letter to Isabella and Ferdinand)

Chapter 17   Absolutism and Constitutionalism in Europe, ca 1589–1725

This chapter has been greatly tightened to reduce the text by approximately 20 percent. The following changes have also been incorporated:

- The discussion of Louis XIV's relations with the French nobility has been updated.
- The treatment of the development of the Kievan principality, which was in this chapter in the 3/e, has been relocated to Chapter 12 for better chronology.
- Listening to the Past—A Foreign Traveler in Russia (Olearius, *Travels in Russia*)

Chapter 18   Toward a New World-View in the West

- The updated treatment of the philosophes examines the social origins and impact of their ideas.
- The discussion of Rousseau has been revised to clarify the social and political impact of his thought.
- A new treatment of eighteenth-century cultural transformation incorporates recent scholarship on the "reading revolution," the diffusion of Enlightenment thought, the emergence of "public opinion," and the impact of the Enlightenment on the lives of elite and ordinary women.
- The section on the Enlightenment and absolutism has been revised to compare Eastern and French forms of absolutism, to clarify the origins of revolution in France.
- Listening to the Past—Voltaire on Religion (Voltaire, *Philosophical Dictionary*)

Chapter 19   The Changing Life of the People in Europe

- This chapter has been updated and revised throughout to reveal the widening cultural divide between rich and poor in the eighteenth century.
- The section on marriage and the family has been revised to illustrate the influence of collective attitudes on individual behavior and family organization.
- New material has been added on popular literature.
- An explanation of "just price" has been added, including popular reaction to market grain prices.
- The discussion of diet and medical practice has been tightened for clarity and topical balance.
- The treatment of religion and popular culture has been reorganized to stress the growing tensions between elites and the common people.
- A new section on popular leisure and recreation has been added.
- Listening to the Past—A New Way to Educate Children (Rousseau, *Emile*)

Chapter 20   Africa, 1400–1800

- The section on Swahili city-states has been entirely rewritten to reflect current scholarship.
- The discussion of the slave trade has been revised to reflect new research.
- Listening to the Past—A Discussion on the Abolition of the Slave Trade (report by Captain Robert Craigie)

Chapter 21   The Middle East and India, ca 1450–1800

- New material has been added to the discussion of Mehmet II.
- The discussion of health and medical care in the Ottoman world has been expanded and a comparison with Western Europe added.

- There is a new section on women in the Ottoman world incorporating material from the diaries of Lady Montague.
- New material has been added on Persia under Mongol domination.
- The treatment of the institutions of the Mughal state under Akbar has been revised to reflect new research.
- Listening to the Past—Culture Shock (from *The Commentary of Father Monseratte, S.J., On His Journey to the Court of Akbar*)

Chapter 22 China and Japan, CA 1400–1800

- A broader discussion of Chinese attitudes toward merchants and material consumption has been included.
- A new section covers Qing foreign relations policies and includes discussion of the Macartney Mission of 1788–1792, emphasizing cultural contacts and clashes.
- New material on women in Japan includes coverage of farm women of the Tokugawa period, as well as a focus on the role and social status of the bride at marriage and afterward and discussion of divorce.
- Listening to the Past—The Macartney Mission to China (Letter from Emperor Qian Long to George III)

Chapter 23 The Revolution in Western Politics, 1775–1815

- Consideration of gender differences has been added to the discussion examining the concept of equality.
- The treatment of liberalism has been revised and updated to clarify popular attitudes.
- In "The French Revolution, 1789–1791," the discussion of bourgeois objectives and attitudes has been revised.
- New material on Republican political culture, based on recent research, has been added.
- The integrated treatment of women in Republican France has been expanded.
- The discussion of Napoleon's social legislation includes added emphasis on the consequences for women.
- Listening to the Past—Revolution and Women's Rights (Olympe de Gouges, "Declaration of the Rights of Women")

Chapter 24 The Industrial Revolution in Europe

- The examination of the role of banks in promoting industrial development in Continental Europe has been revised and clarified.
- New material on the rise of class consciousness has been added to the section "Capital and Labor."
- A new section expands coverage of the early labor movement.
- Listening to the Past—The Testimony of Young Mining Workers (Parliamentary testimony, 1841–1842)

Chapters 25 and 26 on nineteenth-century Europe

These chapters reduce and consolidate former Chapters 27, 28, and 29, reducing the text contained in the third edition by approximately 20 percent. The following changes have also been incorporated:

Chapter 25 Ideologies and Upheavals, 1815–1871

- The updated treatment of early socialism stresses its debt to the French Revolution.

- Coverage of Walter Scott has been added to the tightened section on the romantic movement.
- The coverage of national development has been condensed and divided, with "Nation Building" in this chapter and "The Responsive National State" in Chapter 26. In addition to being condensed the coverage has been revised to help clarify the role of class issues.
- Listening to the Past—Faith in Democratic Nationalism (Joseph Mazzini, *The Duties of Man*)

Chapter 26   European Life in the Age of Nationalism

- New material on popular urban culture has been added.
- An updated section in "The Changing Family" interrelates urbanization with changes in family life and practices.
- The discussion of women's changing roles in urban society has been updated.
- Listening to the Past—Middle-Class Youth and Sexuality (Stephan Zweig, *The World of Yesterday*)

Chapter 27   The World and the West

- The treatment of the causes of imperialism has been updated to stress technology and domestic political and social conflicts.
- Listening to the Past—A Scholar's Defense of Imperialism (Arminius Vambery, *Western Culture in Eastern Lands*)

Chapter 28   Nation Building in the Western Hemisphere and in Australia

- A new section examines the nature of racial identity in the United States and how it developed.
- The treatment of the black family in the United States has been consolidated and repositioned.
- A revised discussion of attitudes toward women in Australia stresses the brutality and hypocrisy of a colonial administration that simultaneously punished women severely while exploiting them sexually.
- Listening to the Past—Separate But Equal

Chapter 29   The Great Break: War and Revolution

- The discussion of European alliances has been tightened and clarified.
- Listening to the Past—German War Aims and the Treaty of Versailles (Bethmann-Holweg's memorandum on German war aims; the Treaty of Versailles)

Chapter 30   Nationalism in Asia, 1914–1939

- Some discreet updating has been done to reflect recent scholarship.
- Listening to the Past—Nonviolent Resistance in India (Webb Miller, *I Found No Peace: The Journal of a Foreign Correspondent*)

Chapter 31   The Age of Anxiety in the West

- The coverage of Nietzsche's thought and influence has been increased.
- The discussion of Einstein has been expanded.
- Listening to the Past—A Christian View of Evil (C. E. M. Joad, *God and Evil*)

Chapter 32   Dictatorships and the Second World War

- The discussion of the totalitarian model has been rewritten and updated.
- The treatment of Mussolini has been updated to reflect current scholarly opinion.
- The coverage of the political culture of Nazi Germany also has been updated.
- Listening to the Past—Witness to the Holocaust (Marco Nahon, *Birkenau: The Camp of Death*)

Chapter 33   Recovery and Crisis in Europe and the Americas

- This chapter has been revised and updated from a post–Cold War perspective that interrelates the political, economic, social, and cultural developments of the period.
- A new section on the counterculture has been added.
- Listening to the Past—The Marshall Plan for European Recovery (1947 address by George C. Marshall)

Chapter 34   Asia and Africa in the Contemporary World

- New, up-to-date material has been included on Muslim fundamentalism.
- The coverage of South Africa has been revised to include recent political events and their effects on society.
- Coverage of other regions also has been updated to reflect significant recent developments.
- Listening to the Past—The Struggle for Freedom in South Africa (Nelson Mandela's opening statement at the 1964 treason trial)

Chapter 35   The Changing Lives of Third World Peoples

- A new section has been added on the growing diversity in the Third World since 1980.
- The rise of East Asia is chronicled and the near collapse of sub-Saharan Africa (excluding South Africa) is noted.
- Listening to the Past—Voices from the Village (Interview excerpts from Perdita Huston, *Third World Women Speak Out*)

Chapter 36   One Small Planet

- This chapter has been updated to cover recent developments and their significance for perspectives on the future.
- Listening to the Past—One World and a Plan for Survival (Brandt Commission, *North-South: A Program for Survival*)

CHAPTER 1

ORIGINS

Instructional Objectives

After reading and studying this chapter, students should be able to describe briefly the historian's craft. Then, students should be able to comprehend the evolution of mankind from the Paleolithic Age to the highwater marks of Sumero-Babylonian and Egyptian societies. They should have a grasp of Mesopotamia's and Egypt's contributions to world history.

Chapter Outline

I. What Is History?
   History is humankind's effort to reconstruct the past. It is a uniquely human endeavor that involves the study and analysis of primary sources. Historians piece together sources of primary information to create a believable picture of the past. The study of history has led almost inevitably to the study of civilization: What is a civilization? What is a citizen? The study of history provides students with answers to these and other questions.

II. The First Human Beings
   A.   Origins
        Since the nineteenth century, scholars have been influenced by the idea that humankind evolved from some lower order. Historians, as well as other scholars, have worked in the wake of the Darwinian Revolution. More recently, anthropologists have pointed to the need to study the broadest possible array of prehistoric remains in an effort to understand the origins of humankind. Although considerable uncertainty exists about the origins of humankind, a somewhat clear picture can be painted of two early periods: the Paleolithic, or Old Stone, Age and the Neolithic, or New Stone, Age.
   B.   The Paleolithic Era
        Lasting from about 400,000 to 7,000 B.C., the age takes its name from the primitive stone tools and weapons produced by the people. The epoch was characterized by hunter-gatherer societies, typically organizing themselves into family units.
   C.   The Neolithic Age
        Around 7,000 B.C., an obvious transformation began: some hunter-gatherer societies began to rely chiefly on agriculture for their subsistence. Neolithic peoples contributed greatly to the development of human society: systematic agriculture, writing, sedentary living, and improved tools and weapons.

III. Mesopotamian Civilization
   Most historians trace civilization back to the land between the Tigris and Euphrates rivers. Geography provided irrigation for surplus food supplies and Sumerians and Babylonians

built cities along these two rivers. These cities became independent political states that shared a common civilization.

A. Sumerian society

    The demanding environment of Sumer fostered a grim people who sought to please the pantheon of gods and goddesses. The temple, or ziggurat, was the center of Sumerian life and religion. The temple priests oversaw the agricultural work and the distribution of the agricultural yield. The lugal (king) exercised political power over the landowning populace. Sumerian society was organized into four classes of people: nobles, free clients of the nobility, commoners, and slaves.

B. Assimilation of Sumerian culture

    The third millennium witnessed the growth and spread of Sumerian culture, by the Sumerians themselves and by the Semites. Sargon I's "world empire," although lasting only a few generations, spread Sumerian civilization to the Mediterranean area. The Ebla find is evidence of the Semitic-Sumerian assimilation process.

C. The Babylonian phase

    Several reasons, such as war, migration, and drought, have been given for the demise of Akkadian Civilization in the late third and early second millennia. The Babylonians, a Semitic people, were geographically suited to dominate Mesopotamia. Babylon's best-known king, Hammurabi (r. 1792–1750 B.C.) set out to insure Babylon's leadership in Mesopotamia. Through conquest and assimilation Hammurabi forged a vibrant Sumero-Babylonian culture.

D. Writing and education

    Writing (as well as history) appears to have begun at Sumer. The Sumerian pictographic form evolved by the fourth millennium into cuneiform ("wedge-shaped") writing. The signs in the cuneiform system later became ideograms and an intricate system of communication. The writing system was so complicated that only professional scribes mastered it. Scribal schools flourished throughout Sumer. Although practical, scribal schools were also centers of culture and learning. These schools set the standard for all of Mesopotamia.

E. Thought and religion

    Mesopotamians made great strides in mathematics, medicine, and religion. Mesopotamian religion was polytheistic. Gods and goddesses existed to represent almost everything in the cosmos. The gods were much like human beings, only with supernatural powers. In Mesopotamian religion, we find attempts to explain the origins of mankind. There are numerous myths woven into the Mesopotamian religious tapestry. Additionally, there is the Sumerian epic of creation, *The Epic of Gilgamesh.* Its hero, Gilgamesh, is a wandering king who discovers many of the meanings of life and life after death.

F. The Rule of law

    One of the greatest accomplishments of Sumero-Babylonian Civilization was Hammurabi's Code. Not only is it a giant step forward from earlier Sumerian legal codes, it is a mine of information for the social and legal history of Sumero-Babylonian society.

IV. Egypt

A. Egyptian society

    Egyptian society revolved around the life-giving waters of the Nile River. By ca. 3100 B.C., there were some forty agricultural communities along the Nile. Geography isolated Eygpt: the Nile, deserts, and the Mediterranean Sea. This isolation afforded centuries of peace for Egypt. During this pacific period, Egypt developed a vital civilization.

B.   Egyptian religion and government
Pharaoh (king) was perceived as a god on earth. This was the central feature of Egyptian life. Many Egyptians believed that a mythic king, Menes, unified Egypt around 3100 B.C. Subsequently, Egyptian history was divided into dynasties or families of kings.

Egyptian religion was a complex polytheism rooted in the environment. Central to the religion was pharaoh's place in the pantheon of gods and goddesses—his presence assured the people that the gods cared for them. The pharaoh's ostentation reflected his power. The famous pyramids attest to the power and prestige of the pharaoh.

V.   The Hittite Empire
The Hittites, according to recent Anatolian archaeological evidence, entered peacefully around 2700 B.C. There they assimilated with the native populace.
A.   Hittite society
Although the Hittites were ruled by petty kings, a group of local officials called "Elders" handled local and regional affairs.
1.   The aristocrats were the most powerful group in Hittite society.
2.   Below the aristocrats were the warriors who met in an assembly called the "pankus."
3.   The king was the supreme commander of the army, chief judge, and supreme priest.
4.   Hittite kings created law codes.
B.   Hittite greatness
1.   From about 1475 to 1200 B.C., the Hittites reached their zenith.
2.   The Hittites formed alliances with the Egyptians and Babylonians.

VI.   The Fall of Empires
The so-called Sea Peoples destroyed both Egyptian and Hittite empires.

Lecture Suggestions

1.   "Love in the Ancient World." What were the courting habits of people in Mesopotamia and Egypt in the third and second millennia? How can we know? Did lovers think and talk as lovers do today? Use slides portraying Egyptian couples and poetry from Mesopotamia and Egypt to help students understand that ancient peoples were very much like us—with desires, fears, plans for the future, and strong feelings. Sources: W. K. Simpson, ed., *The Literature of Ancient Egypt* (1973); J. B. Pritchard, ed., *Ancient Near Eastern Texts*, 3rd ed. (1969); Ezra Pound, *Come Swiftly to Your Love: Love Poems of Ancient Egypt* (Hallmark editions). Accompanying slides can be obtained from the Louvre in Paris: Editions de la Réunion des Musées Nationaux, 10 rue de l'Abbaye, 75006 Paris, France.

2.   "The Idea of the Mythic Unifier." Egyptians believed that Menes united the southern and northern kingdoms. Was Menes a real historical character or a mythical hero? The image of the unifier appears often in Western civilization. Lycurgus the Lawgiver of Sparta, Romulus and Remus, and King Arthur of Britain are other examples of mythic unifiers. What characteristics do these mythic heroes have in common? How can we know whether they actually existed? What is their significance? Why do civilizations have myths? Sources: J. Gray, *Near Eastern Mythology* (1969); M. Bloch, *The Royal Touch: Sacred Monarchy and Scrofula in England and France*, trans. J. E. Anderson (1973); J. G. Frazer, *The Golden Bough*, (1922).

Using Primary Sources

Source: Reread the passages in "The Flood Stories of the Ancient Near East" found in the "Primary Source" section of this manual. After reading the passages, list ways in which the gods and goddesses were like human beings. Then, using the list, write a poem on anthropomorphism in which you include several human characteristics found in the flood passages.

Activities for Discovering the Past

I. Classroom Discussion Suggestions

1. Why does Mesopotamian civilization seem so grim and joyless compared to Egyptian civilization?
2. Compare the severity of the punishments for crime in Hammurabi's code with punishments found in the Old Testament.
3. Why did scribes have such high status in Mesopotamian society?
4. How did geography affect the military history of Mesopotamia and Egypt from 3000 to 1000 B.C.?
5. How did outsiders influence Mesopotamian and Egyptian civilization?

II. Doing History

1. Conduct research and write a paper on the economic functions of priests in ancient Mesopotamia.
2. Write a short paper comparing the Code of Hammurabi, the Roman Twelve Tables, and the dooms (laws) of Anglo-Saxon kings. How were they alike? How were they different? Which was most humane? Sources: J. B. Pritchard, ed., *Ancient Near Eastern Texts* (1969); N. Lewis and M. Reinhold, *Roman Civilization Sourcebook I: The Republic* (1966); C. Stephenson and F. Marcham, *Sources of English Constitutional History: A Selection of Documents from A.D. 600 to the Interregnum* (1972).
3. Have students read about sports and pastimes in ancient Mesopotamia and Egypt. Ask them to create their own versions of these games and then demonstrate them to their classmates. Sources: E. Gardiner, *Athletics of the Ancient World* (1930); V. Olivova, *Sports and Games in the Ancient World* (1984); W. Decker, "The Record of the Ritual: The Athletic Records of Ancient Egypt," in *Ritual and Record: Sports Records and Quantification in Pre-Modern Societies*, ed. J. M. Carter and A. Krueger (1990).
4. Have students investigate the roles of women as described in the legal, historical, and fictional literature of the ancient Near East. Sources: J. B. Pritchard, ed., *Ancient Near Eastern Texts* (1969); B. S. Lesko, *The Remarkable Women of Ancient Egypt*, 2nd ed. (1987); M. Lichtheim, *Ancient Egyptian Literature*, 3 vols. (1975–1980); L. Manniche, *Sexual Life in Ancient Egypt* (1987). Have students report their findings.

III. Cooperative Learning Activities

1. Guided Imagery: A Place in Time
    Organize the class into groups of four students each. One student in each group is charged with finding a descriptive passage of an ancient Near Eastern place. Students might use the Bible, *Gilgamesh*, or other primary sources to find the passage. Or, students may wish to use a more contemporary description of a Near Eastern place. After securing the passage, the student should read it aloud to the other three students in the group. From the verbal description in

the passage, the three students should attempt to draw the particular place. Students should then share their drawings to see how their visual creations compare to the reader's verbal description.

2. Division of Labor

   One criterion for the emergence of civilization in the ancient Near East was a division of labor. Organize the class into groups of seven. Each group represents a society (or kingdom) in the ancient Near East. In each society, the students should represent the ruler (pharaoh, king, lugal, etc.); chief priest; warrior; artist; artisan; farmer; slave. Each student in the group should conduct research on his/her social class and write a brief report using the first person singular (for example, "I am Roshtar, a farmer from Ur." Then Roshtar describes his particular role in his society). In class, each society introduces its respective members and their functions.

3. "Walk like an Egyptian": Musical Geography

   Tapping into students' popular culture interests is a fun way to begin the semester and a useful way to create mnemonic devices that may increase and enhance learning over the course of the semester (and after!). Organize students into groups of five or six. Charge them with compiling a list of pop songs (*pop* here is used to mean any number of musical categories: rock, rap, country, beach, reggae, Ska, et al.) that contain geographical references. This activity would be good to use during one of the first few classes of the semester. It is widely focused and can be referred back to at any time during the semester. After the students compile the lists, allow them to share their lists in class. Each group should check to see if they have included songs from other groups' lists. Past lists have included everything from "Africa" by Toto to "Back in the U.S.S.R." by the Beatles, to "Xanadu" by Olivia Newton-John. Of course your students will use this opportunity to teach you a great deal about contemporary pop music.

Map Activity

1. Using the *Historical Atlas of the World*, have students list the primary geographical features of the area: Tigris River, Euphrates River, Nile River, Persian Gulf, Mediterranean Sea, etc.

2. On an outline map of the ancient Near East (IRM page 177), have students list the various kingdoms of the area: Sumerians, Babylonians, Egyptians, Hebrews, Assyrians, Hittites, Persians.

Audiovisual Bibliography

1. *Why Man Creates.* (29 min. Color. Pyramid Films.)
2. *The Ten Commandments.* (219 min. Available at most video stores.)
3. *Ancient Egypt.* (51 min. Color. Time-Life Films.)
4. *Mysteries of the Great Pyramid.* (50 min. Color. Wolper Productions, Inc.)
5. *Egypt: Gift of the Nile.* (29 min. Color. Coronet Films.)
6. Slides of the Egyptian Collections in the Louvre: Editions de la Réunion des Musées Nationaux, 10 rue de l'Abbaye, 75006 Paris, France.
7. R. D. Barnett and D. J. Wiseman, *Fifty Masterpieces of Ancient Near Eastern Art* (1969).
8. J. B. Pritchard, *The Ancient Near East in Pictures*, 2nd ed. (1969).
9. Egyptian Pyramids. (CD-ROM. Learning Services.)
10. Time Traveler CD. (CD-ROM. National Geographic.)

CHAPTER 2

SMALL KINGDOMS AND MIGHTY EMPIRES IN THE NEAR EAST

Instructional Objectives

After reading and studying this chapter, students should be able to describe the factors that led to the dissolution of Egypt and the creation of small kingdoms in the wake of Egypt's decline. Then, students should be able to distinguish Hebrew life and thought from that of the other peoples of the ancient Near East. Students should be able to describe the factors that led to Assyrian dominance in the ninth and eighth centuries B.C. Finally, students should be able to explain how Zoroastrian beliefs influenced both Judaism and Christianity.

Chapter Outline

I. Decline of Egypt and the Hittite Empire
   A. Invaders from Africa and the Near East shattered power of Egypt and the Hittites.
      1. Long wars weakened Egypt, causing political and economic chaos.
      2. Central government disappeared and was replaced by petty administrators and local strongmen.
      3. Nubians extended power northward.
      4. Kingdom of Kush grew up in the area of modern Sudan.
      5. Egyptian ideas and beliefs made their way, through Palestine and Syria, to Europe.
   B. There evolved a cluster of smaller kingdoms: Phoenicians, Syrians, Hebrews.

II. The Hebrews established a kingdom in Palestine.
   A. South of Phoenicia arose the small kingdom of the ancient Jews.
      1. Origins of Hebrews are uncertain.
      2. Hebrews came to Palestine through the Sinai Peninsula from Egypt.
   B. Political stability was established by the kings Saul, David, and Solomon.
      1. Saul warred against the Philistines and established a monarchy over the twelve tribes.
      2. David carried on Saul's work.
         a. Captured and fortified the city of Jerusalem.
         b. Made Jerusalem the political and religious center.
      3. Solomon organized the collective tribes into twelve territorial districts.
         a. Temple at Jerusalem was part of his overall building program.
         b. Dedicated temple and made it the home of the Ark of the Covenant.
      4. Hebrews broke into two political halves upon Solomon's death.

a. Southern kingdom defeated by Babylonians in 587 B.C.
b. Cyrus the Great of Persia permitted exiles to return to Jerusalem.
C. Jewish Religion
1. Old Testament was the key sacred writing.
2. The Covenant was a formal agreement between Yahweh and the Hebrews.
3. Yahweh was the Jews' only god (monotheism).
4. Ten Commandments
a. The Torah, or Mosaic Law, was very harsh.
b. Later custom and law was more humanitarian.

III. The Assyrians developed a political state with their efficient military organization.
A. Many Near Eastern kingdoms fell to Tiglath-pileser III (774–727 B.C.) and Sargon II (721–705 B.C.)
B. Assyria's success was attributed to sophisticated military organization.
1. The Assyrians developed a wide variety of siege machinery and techniques.
2. Royal roads and mounted messengers linked the Assyrian Empire.

IV. The Persians created one of the ancient world's great empires.
A. Iranians were Indo-Europeans from central Europe and southern Russia.
B. Cyrus the Great (559–530 B.C.) threw off the control of the Medes and created his first satrapy, or province.
1. Cyrus viewed Iran as a state.
2. He had an enlightened view of empire.
3. He united the Medes and the Persians.
C. Zoroastrianism
1. Zoroaster preached a new concept of divinity and human life.
2. Described cosmos as a battle between opposing forces.
3. Taught that individual must decide whether to choose Ahuramazda or Ahriman.
4. Zoroaster preached a Last Judgment.
5. Persian royal family adopted Zoroastrianism.

Lecture Suggestions

1. "Perceptions of Black People in Antiquity." What was the role of blacks in ancient societies such as Egypt and Persia? How were blacks perceived? Was there extreme racial prejudice in antiquity? Sources: M. I. Finley, *Ancient Slavery and Modern Ideology* (1980); F. M. Snowden, *Before Color Prejudice* (1983); L. Bugner, ed., *The Image of the Black in Western Art*, Vol. I (1983).
2. "Women in the Ancient Near East." What were the roles of women in Egypt, Palestine, Assyria, and Persia in the first millennium? How can we know? Sources: A. Cameron and A. Kuhrt, *Images of Women in Antiquity* (1983); H. W. F. Skaggs, *Everyday Life in Babylonia and Assyria* (1987); R. N. Frye, *History of Ancient Iran* (1984).

Using Primary Sources

"God and Man in the Ancient Near East"
Have students read the selection from "The Epic of Gilgamesh" in the "Primary Source" (Flood Stories of the Ancient Near East) section of this manual and the "burning bush" segment of the Old Testament. Have students list the ways that each man (Utanapishtim and Moses) communicated with deities (Gilgamesh and Yahweh). What were the deities' instructions for mankind? What

topics of "conversation" went on between them? What do these "conversations" tell us about what the Sumero-Babylonians and Hebrews believed about the relationship between God and humankind? After students compile lists of conversation topics, have them write a short paper in which they elaborate their ideas. Completed papers might be read in class and used to initiate a discussion about the relationships of gods, goddesses, and people in the ancient Near East.

Activities for Discovering the Past

I.   Classroom Discussion Suggestions

1.   How was Hebrew monotheism different from the religion espoused by the Egyptian pharaoh Akhenaten?
2.   What was family life like in the Hebrew culture?
3.   How was Assyrian art influenced by the militaristic nature of its society?
4.   What Zoroastrian influences can be found in later religions?

II.   Doing History

1.   Have students browse through books of the Old Testament and record passages in which women are mentioned. Then have them use this data as the basis for a term paper on women in Hebrew society.
2.   Have students write short papers on the kinds of food eaten by various classes of people in one of the civilizations mentioned in this chapter.
3.   Have students conduct research and write term papers on the views of "hell" described in Judaic and Zoroastrian beliefs.

III.   Cooperative Learning Activities

1.   Jigsaw: Experts on the Ancient Near East
     Employ the Jigsaw approach to cooperative learning discussed in the section on using cooperative learning in the Western Civilization class. To apply this approach, organize the class into six-member teams. Team 1 is charged with learning about the Hebrews; Team 2, the Assyrians; Team 3, the Persians (for larger classes, instructors may want to reassign the societies studied in Chapter 1); Team 4, the Sumerians; Team 5, the Egyptians; Team 6, the Hittites. Each team divides up the material into six sections: 1) history; 2) location (geography); 3) governmental organization; 4) religion; 5) social classes; 6) art, education, technology. Each of the six teams should have an "expert" on each of the six subjects. Allow for the experts on all six teams to meet and discuss their sections. Then have the teams regroup and have all "experts" teach their group what they have learned about their subject. An expert on Hebrew social classes would have learned not only about Hebrew social organization but about social organization in five other societies as well. This activity should help students make generalizations about society in the ancient Near East.
2.   Using the STAD for an Examination
     You might use the Student Teams Achievement Divisions for testing the usefulness of cooperative learning. Some instructors give a minimum of three exams per academic term. Others administer more. To experiment with the STAD, Activity 1) use the teams organized in above (Coop. Learn.) as study groups. They should study lecture notes, text, and review the team work completed. After studying in their teams, they are given an exam and are not allowed to work in teams. After they have taken individual exams, they are given the same or similar exam and allowed to work in their teams to complete the cooperative learning exam. The instructor then averages the one common exam grade with the student's individual

test grade. A wealth of research confirms that cooperative learning testing improves student grades.

Map Activity

Using the map on page 3 of the *Historical Atlas of the World*, shade in the seventh-century B.C. Near Eastern kingdoms on an outline map of the ancient Near East (IRM page 177). List the following places on the map:
1. Nineveh
2. Jerusalem
3. Babylon
4. Damascus
5. Byblos
6. Sidon
7. Tyre
8. Joppa
9. Abu Simbel
10. Nippur

Audiovisual Bibliography

1. *The Bible as Literature: Part I—Saga and Story in the Old Testament.* (27 min. Color. Encyclopaedia Britannica Films.)
2. *The Bible as Literature: Part II—History, Poetry, and Drama in the Old Testament.* (24 min. Color. Encyclopaedia Britannica Films.)
3. *Israel.* (25 min. Color. National Geographic Films.)
4. *Jerusalem: Within These Walls.* (59 min. Color. National Geographic Films.)
5. *Chronicles and Kings.* (52 min. Color. Films for the Humanities and Sciences.)
6. *World Geography Series* (Interactive Videodisc. National Geographic Educational Services.)
7. The Real Picture Atlas. (CD-ROM. Learning Services.)
8. Bible Library. (CD-ROM. National Audio-Visual Supply.)

CHAPTER 3

ANCIENT INDIA TO CA A.D. 200

Instructional Objectives

After reading and analyzing this chapter, students should be able to describe how geography influenced the development of India to about 200 A.D. Students should also be able to explain how Hinduism reflected the attitudes of ancient India. Students should also be able to discuss the dynamics of the ancient Indian caste system.

Chapter Outline

I. India: The Land and the People (ca. 2500–1500 B.C.)
   A. The Role of Geography
      1. India is a geographically enclosed landmass as large as western Europe.
      2. India comprises three main areas
         a. the Himalaya Mountains in the north
         b. the great river valleys of the Indus and the Ganges
         c. the southern coastal plains and the dry and hilly Deccan Peninsula
   B. Geography has guarded India from its neighbors and divided the country into subregions.
      1. The Himalayas have protected India from invasion.
      2. The Himalayas and the southern monsoons give India most of its water.
      3. Agricultural production is best in the Indus River valley and the Punjab.
   C. The Indus Civilization (ca. 2500–1500 B.C.)
      1. Around 2500 B.C., settlers entered the Indus Valley.
      2. These peoples carried on a cultural exchange with the civilization of Mesopotamia.
   D. Mohenjo-daro and Harappa were the best-known cities.
      1. These cities were well-planned.
      2. They had citadels and tall brick houses with open courtyards.
      3. These cities seem to have had a strong central government.
      4. The peoples of Mohenjo-daro and Harappa appear to have worshiped an earth goddess.
      5. This civilization disappeared mysteriously.

II. The Coming of the Aryans (ca. 1500–500 B.C.)
   A. The coming of the Aryans, a Nordic people, was a turning point in ancient Indian history.
      1. The Hindu hymnbook, the Rigveda, provides some information about the Aryans and the native Indians they encountered.

2. The Aryans were a warlike people who were governed by a tribal chief, or raja.
3. Aryan society was composed of warriors, priests, commoners, and slaves.
4. The Aryans pushed into the jungles of the Ganges Valley.
5. They founded Delhi and assimilated with the native peoples.

B. The Social Organization of the Aryans
1. The Aryans created powerful kingdoms under absolute rulers.
2. The priests, or brahmins, were powerful allies of the kings.
3. The organized village emerged as a way to tend to the land.
4. Frequent wars allowed small states to be absorbed by stronger ones.
5. A caste system—a hereditary class of social equals—emerged to separate Aryan from non-Aryan.
6. By ca. 500 B.C., the four main groups were the priests, warriors, peasants, serfs, and outcastes.

III. Ancient Indian Religion
A. Early Indian Religion
1. The Aryan gods symbolized forces in nature such as fire, water, and trees.
2. The idea of a "Wheel of Life" evolved.
3. Samsara is the doctrine of transmigration of souls through rebirth.
4. Karma is the belief that deeds determine the status of one's next life.
5. Escape from the wheel of life was through atman and Brahman.

B. Hinduism evolved in the fifth and sixth centuries B.C.
1. Hinduism is linked to the caste system.
2. Hinduism is a guide for life; the goal is to reach Brahman through four steps.
3. Dharma is the moral law all Hindus observe.
4. Certain gods came to be thought of as manifestations of Brahman.
5. The *Bhagavad Gita* is a guide to how to live and to honor dharma.
6. Arjuna meets the god Krishna who teaches Arjuna the relationship between reality and eternal spirit.

C. Jainism also took root in the fifth and sixth centuries B.C.
1. Mahavira, the founder, taught that the doctrine of karma extended to all animate and inanimate objects.
2. A key teaching was that eternal happiness occurs when the soul rids itself of all matter.
3. Nonviolence and asceticism became key principles of Jainism.

D. Buddhism began to have an impact in India during the fifth and sixth centuries B.C.
1. Siddhartha Gautama—the Buddha—found universal enlightenment through meditation.
2. He abandoned Hinduism and prescribed the Four Noble Truths: pain, suffering, frustration, and anxiety are fundamental parts of human existence.
3. People can overcome these obstacles by adopting the Eightfold Path.
   a. First, one needs to understand the pain and misery of one's life.
   b. Freedom from pain can come through right conduct and speech, love, and compassion.
   c. With the eighth step, one achieves nirvana, a state of happiness and release from the effects of karma.

E. After Buddha's death, Buddhism split into two branches.
1. The Theraveda branch claimed to be pure and more strict; it was popular in southeast Asia.
2. The Mahayana branch, which stressed that other Buddhas may come, dominated in China, Japan, Korea, and Vietnam.

IV. India and the West (ca. 513–298 B.C.)
   A. The Indus Valley was conquered by Persia in the sixth century B.C.
      1. The conquest of Darius I extended a short distance beyond the Indus River.
      2. The Persian Conquest introduced India to the ways of other cultures.
      3. Coined money was adopted.
      4. The Aramaic language was adapted to fit Indian needs.
   B. Alexander the Great invaded the Indus valley in 326 B.C.
      1. He discovered Taxila to be a great city.
      2. He won a signal victory over an Indian leader, Porus, at the Battle of the Hydaspes in 327/26 B.C.
      3. Alexander left behind many Greek settlements and a power vacuum which was filled by Chandragupta.

V. The Mauryan Empire (ca. 322–232 B.C.)
   A. Chandragupta united much of India into the great Mauryan Empire.
      1. He took advantage of the vacuum left by Alexander.
      2. He defeated his enemies and accepted the surrender of the Seleucid monarchy.
      3. He organized India into provinces.
      4. He created an elaborate bureaucracy.

VI. The Reign of Ashoka (269–232 B.C.)
   A. Prince Ashoka became king of India and extended the borders of the Mauryan Empire.
      1. He was an efficient and content king in the early years of his reign.
      2. After a savage campaign in Kalinga, he turned to Buddhism.
      3. He adopted a highly paternalistic policy toward his people, building shrines, roads, and resting places.
      4. After Ashoka's reign, India was invaded repeatedly and became highly fragmented.
      5. The Kushan invaders put India into closer contact with the East.
      6. The Kushan invaders were assimilated into Indian society as the Kashatriyas caste.
      7. Under Kushan rule, Greek ideas and art forms influenced India.
      8. One of the most important developments during this era was the spread of Buddhism to China.

Lecture Suggestions

1. "Women and the Caste System." How did women fare in ancient India? What evidence is there that ancient attitudes toward women persist today? Sources: R. Thapar, *Ancient Indian Social History* (1978); M. M. Deshponde and P. E. Hook, eds., *Aryan and Non–Aryan in India* (1979).
2. "Alexander in Baluchistan." How did the Indians perceive Alexander of Macedon? What legacy did he leave? Sources: P. H. L. Eggermont, *Alexander's Campaigns in Sind and Baluchistan* (1975); J. R. Hamilton, *Alexander the Great* (1973).

Using Primary Sources

"The Spirit Dwells Among Us."
Have students read select passages from *The Upanishads* (trans. J. Mascaro, London: Penguin Books, 1965, especially pp. 117–118) concerning Hindu beliefs in atman. Then, encourage them to compare

their findings with explanations of the Holy Spirit in the New Testament. Use student findings for a class discussion and/or have students write short papers comparing the two.

Activities for Discovering the Past

I. Classroom Discussion Suggestions

1. What are the basic tenets of Hinduism?
2. How was Chandragupta able to forge a formidable Mauryan state in the fourth century B.C.?
3. What are some of the similarities between Krishna and Christ?
4. Was the Dravidian-Aryan social stratification based on racial prejudice?

II. Doing History

1. Have students read the following accounts of the Battle of the Hyphasis, a classic encounter between East and West and then recreate the great battle in a short paper. Sources: Arrian, *The Campaigns of Alexander* (Penguin Edition, 1976). P. H. L. Eggermont, *Alexander's Campaigns in Sind and Baluchistan* (1975).
2. Have students write a short, comparative paper on the caste system in India and the social stratification of feudalism. In what ways were they alike and how did they differ? Sources: J. Auboyer, *Daily Life in Ancient India from 200 B.C. to 700* (1965); M. Bloch, Feudal Society, 2 vols. (1961); R. Thapar, *Ancient Indian Social History* (1978).

III. Cooperative Learning Activities

1. Social Stratification in Ancient India
   Organize the class into groups of six. Give each group a photocopied sheet with instructions to do basic research on the social groupings of the Hindu caste system: priests, warriors, peasants, serfs, and untouchables. Questions might include the following:
   a. When did the caste system begin?
   b. What were the reasons for the development of a caste system.
   c. What percentage of society belonged to the _____ (priestly, warrior, peasant, etc.) caste?
   d. What were the responsibilities of the _____ caste?
   e. How did the caste system influence India's historical development?
   After research and discussion among members of the groups, each group should make a presentation to the class.

2. World Religions
   Organize the class into six groups and assign basic research projects on major world religions to each group.
   a. Selections might include: Christianity, Judaism, Islam, Buddhism, Shintoism, Daoism, etc.
   b. Each group should be responsible for presenting a historical summary of the religion's development to the class.
   c. Groups might also create posters illustrating the religion's important symbols and rituals. These posters might be displayed on the classroom walls.
   d. If the class conducts this basic research during the first three or four chapters of the text, they will be laying a foundation for comparing world religions throughout the remainder of their study of world societies (although Christianity and Islam will be introduced anachronistically).

Map Activity

Using the maps of ancient India on page 8 of the *Historical Atlas of the World*, have students list the following geographical features on an outline map of India (IRM page 178):

1. Taxila
2. Pattala
3. Surparaka
4. Ujjain
5. Sravasti
6. Kausambi
7. Kasi
8. Tamralipti
9. Tosali
10. Kanchi
11. Anuradhapura
12. Indus River
13. Ganges River
14. Thar Desert
15. Himalayas Mountains

Audiovisual Bibliography

1. *India: An Introduction.* (25 min. Color. International Film Foundation.)
2. *India and the Infinite: The Soul of a People.* (30 min. Color. Hartley Film Foundation.)
3. *India: Population 600 Million.* (13 min. Color. Sterling Educational Films.)
4. *India Today.* (17 min. Color. International Film Bureau.)
5. *The Fourth Stage: A Hindu's Quest for Release.* (40 min. Color. Center for South Asian Studies, University of Wisconsin-Madison.)
6. *Tibetan Buddhism: The Wheel of Life.* (30 min. Color. Center for South Asian Studies, University of Wisconsin-Madison.)
7. *The Ganges.* (49 min. Color. Videodisc. Films for the Humanities and Sciences.)
8. World GeoGraph. (CD-ROM. Cambridge Development Laboratory, Inc.)
9. Global Explorer. (CD-ROM. National School Products.)
10. World Religions. (CD-ROM. National School Products.)

CHAPTER 4

THE RISE AND GROWTH OF CHINA TO CA A.D. 200

Instructional Objectives

After reading and analyzing this chapter, students should be able to explain how Daoism reflected the attitudes of the ancient Chinese toward life. Students should also be able to discuss the influence that Buddhism had on ancient China. Finally, students should also be able to suggest ways in which the early Chinese confronted the geographical factors of climate, soil, and land.

Chapter Outline

I. China and Geography
   A. The Geography of China
      1. Geography isolated China from the west and north.
      2. The Himalayas separated China from India.
      3. The Gobi Desert formed China's northern border.
      4. China's avenue to civilization was through the northwest corridor through central Asia.
   B. Chinese civilization emerged along two river basins, the Yellow and the Yangtze
      1. The Yellow River provides loess (fertile land) and flooding in the north.
      2. The Yangtze valley in the south is used for rice farming.
      3. The Xi River makes up China's southern border.

II. The Shang Dynasty (ca. 1523–1027 B.C.)
   A. The Shang Dynasty rose to power in northern China.
      1. The king, through his bureaucracy, directed the people.
      2. Warfare was endemic in Shang society.
      3. King and nobility lived a luxurious life.
      4. Their houses built on platforms of earth and their sculpture set a standard for Chinese society.
      5. Writing emerged out of the Shang religion.
      6. Thousands of signs with phonetic values were created.
      7. Both the Koreans and the Japanese based their written language on Chinese writing.

III. The Zhou Dynasty (ca. 1027–221 B.C.)
   A. The Zhou of the Wei basin conquered the Shang Dynasty in the eleventh century B.C.
      1. They assimilated well with the Shang.
      2. They originated the political concept of the Mandate of Heaven.
      3. At first, strong kings ruled the dynasty.

4. As new border states emerged, they eventually defeated the Zhou King in 771 B.C.
5. The Zhou dynasty fell and in 221 B.C., the ruler of the Qin conquered all the other states.

B. Provincial aristocracy became the forerunner of China's civil service.
1. Armed camps grew into walled cities.
2. The discovery and use of iron changed warfare and agriculture.

IV. Chinese Philosophy
A. Confucianism
1. Confucius, a teacher from a poor but aristocratic family, was interested in how to attain order and to create stable human relationships.
2. Confucius was interested in human conduct.
3. A Confucian gentleman was a man of integrity, education, and culture.
4. Confucianism significantly influenced the working of the evolving Chinese bureaucracy.
B. Daoism
1. Daoist ideas are attributed to Lao Tzu and the book *Dao De Ding*.
2. Daoists argue that peace and order can only come from following the Dao, the way of nature.
3. Daoism held that the best government was the one that governed least.
C. Legalism, I Ching, and Yin and Yang
1. Fei Zu and Li Su were two of the founders of Legalism.
2. They argued that human nature is evil and the ideal state is one in which people are treated humanely but kept uneducated and are not allowed dissent.
3. The I Ching is an ethical guide to life.
4. The I Ching was based on common sense.
5. Yin and Yang concept also helped people to understand life.
6. Yin was weak, dark, moist, and womanly; Yang was strong, radiant, dry, and male.

IV. The Qin and Han Dynasties
A. The Qin Dynasty unified China.
1. The emperor and his adviser built a highly centralized state.
2. The nobility was forced to move to the capital.
3. The emperor controlled the provinces through governors.
4. Peasant land rights were expanded.
5. Increased trade led to the growth of cities.
6. The first emperor ordered the building of the Great Wall.
B. The Han Dynasty (206 B.C.–A.D. 220) was established by Liu Bang.
1. Political centralization was relaxed under Liu Bang.
2. Han Wudi drove the Huns farther north and opened relations with India.
3. Western Korea was added to the empire.
4. Under Han rule, China enjoyed unparalleled peace and prosperity.
C. Revival of Confucianism
1. During the Han era, Confucianism applied the Mandate of Heaven to dynasties.
2. The emperor was to protect China, maintain order, and not interfere in the lives of people.
3. Sima Qian the historian composed the *Records of the Grand Historian*.
D. Daily life in Han China
1. The peasant was the backbone of Chinese society.
2. All members of the peasant household worked in the fields.
3. Zhao Guo, a Han minister, introduced a new planting system.

4. A new plow, a hammer system for milling, and irrigation pumping were developed.
5. The rich lived in ornate houses in the city.
6. Gambling was popular and crime was common.
E. The Decline of the Han Dynasty
    1. Imperial extravagance and war weakened Han China.
    2. Agricultural production declined.
    3. Landlords shifted the tax burden to peasants.
    4. During the era of the Three Kingdoms (A.D. 221–280) disorder and barbarism flourished.
    5. In the fifth century, the Toba assumed control of northern China.
    6. They adopted Chinese political and social organizations.

Lecture Suggestions

1. "The Buddha in China." Lead students to an understanding of the Buddhist impact on ancient China. How was the impact of Buddhism on China similar to its impact on India? Source: E. Zurcher, *The Buddhist Conquest of China*, 2 vols. (1959).
2. "Confucius and Socrates." Discuss the similarities of these two monumental philosophers and their effect on their respective civilizations. Sources: H. G. Creel, *Confucius and the Chinese Way* (1966); I. F. Stone, *The Trial of Socrates* (1989).

Using Primary Sources

Students should try to understand how the ancient Chinese perceived the true gentleman's demeanor by reading selections from the *Analects* of Confucius (trans. A. Waley, London, 1938, 4.18) and the *I Ching* (Virginia Beach, 1971, p. 1). For comparison with the West, students might compare these ancient Chinese views of gentlemanly conduct with those of the Renaissance writer Baldasar Castiglione's *The Book of the Courtier.*

Activities for Discovering the Past

I. **Classroom Discussion Suggestions**

1. What are the basic tenets of Confucian philosophy?
2. How did Zhou political organization resemble that practiced by lords in medieval Europe?
3. What role did geography play in China's development?

II. **Doing History**

1. "War and Work During the Ch'in Dynasty." How did the Ch'in (Qin) Dynasty transform China? What advances did it make in work and war? Sources: D. Bodde, *China's First Unifier: A Study of the Ch'in Dynasty as Seen in the Life of Li Ssu* (1958); P. Nancarrow, *Early China and the Wall* (1978); J. Needham, *Science and Civilization in China*, vol. 4, pt. 3 (1970).
2. "Everyday Life in Ancient China." What was life like for the ordinary people of ancient China? What did their daily grind consist of? Sources: M. Loewe, *Everyday Life in Early Imperial China* (1968); W. Zhongshu, *Han Civilization* (1982).

III. **Cooperative Learning Activities**

1. Organize the class into five groups. Assign each group the task of researching and writing short reports on the following Chinese philosophies: (1) Confucianism, (2) Daoism, (3) Legalism, (4) I Ching, and (5) Yin and Yang. After each group has presented its findings, students might discuss the similarities and differences of these systems of belief. Students might also be encouraged to consider how these beliefs have penetrated areas beyond China.
2. Organize students in class into five groups. Assign each group the task of doing basic research on the following eras in ancient Chinese history: (1) Shang Dynasty, (2) Zhou Dynasty, (3) Qin Dynasty, (4) Han Dynasty, and (5) Three Kingdoms Era.

    Groups should make presentations to the class. They should be encouraged to provide chronological charts and emphasize the major contributions of each era. They should make charts/posters to use in their presentations. The charts/posters might be displayed on the classroom walls.

Map Activity

Using the map on page 9 of the *Historical Atlas of the World,* have students list the following geographical features on an outline map of China (IRM page 179):

1. Eastern Sea
2. Southern Sea
3. Chiang (Jiang)
4. Ch'ao Hsien (Chao Xian)
5. Shuofang
6. Chinch'eng (Jincheng)
7. Ch'angsha (Changsha)
8. Honei
9. Yuan
10. Yen
11. Yangtze River
12. Wei River
13. Ho River
14. Han River
15. Chiang River (Jiang)

Audiovisual Bibliography

1. *China: A Portrait of a Land.* (18 min. Color. Britannia Films.)
2. *The China Tea Pot Story.* (10 min. Color. Sterling Educational Films.)
3. *China: The Beginnings.* (19 min. Color. Indiana University AV Center.)
4. *China: The Enduring Heritage.* (19 min. Color. Indiana University AV Center.)
5. *China: The First Empires.* (19 min. Color. Indiana University AV Center.)
6. *Taoism.* (23 min. Color. Hartley Film Foundation.)
7. *Taoism: A Question of Balance—China.* (52 min. Color. Time-Life Video.)
8. Countries of the World Encyclopedia. (CD-ROM. National School Products.)
9. The First Emperor of China. (CD-ROM. National School Products.)

CHAPTER 5

THE LEGACY OF GREECE

Instructional Objectives

After reading and analyzing this chapter, students should be able to explain how geography influenced the development of ancient Greece, the distinguishing characteristics of the Greek polis, and the differences between the city-states of Athens and Sparta. Students should also be able to discuss the impact of the Persian War and the Peloponnesian War on ancient Greek civilization. Finally, students should be able to describe many of the achievements of the Greeks in the so-called Classical Age.

Chapter Outline

I. Greece and geography were intimately connected.
   A. Geography played a major role in the development of Greek city-states.
      1. The islands of the Aegean served to link the Green peninsula and Asia Minor.
   B. Created rugged individualism in Greeks.
      1. The mountains inspired the Greeks and isolated them.

II. The Homeric Period gave the Greeks a heroic past.
   A. Homer's *Iliad* and *Odyssey*
      1. The poems of Homer idealized the Greek past.
      2. The *Iliad* describes the expedition against the Trojans.
      3. The *Odyssey* tells of the adventures of Odysseus.
   B. Hesiod's *Theogony* and *Works and Days*
      1. The *Theogony* traces the origins of Zeus.
      2. The *Works and Days* tells of Hesiod's own village life.
   C. Fall of Minoan-Mycenaean civilization inaugurated a "Dark Age"
      1. Minoan society had been wealthy and peaceful.
      2. Minoan and Mycenaean contacts had been peaceful until the fifteenth century B.C.

III. The Polis was the center of Greek life.
   A. The term *polis* (city-state) designated a city or town and its surrounding countryside.
      1. By the end of the "Dark Age" the city-state was the common social entity.
   B. The polis could be governed as a monarchy, aristocracy, oligarchy, tyranny, or democracy.
      1. Athens, Sparta, Thebes, and Corinth were leading Greek city-states.
   C. The agora of a polis was its public square or marketplace.
      1. The agora witnessed the unfolding of daily life in the Greek world.
   D. The acropolis housed the temples, altars, and public monuments.

1. The acropolis witnessed the day-to-day state business and the performance of public religion.

IV. Sparta and Athens dominated politics.
A. Both increased their power during the so-called Archaic Period.
B. Sparta became an oligarchy, with the political power held by two kings and 28 elders.
1. Real power resided in five ephors.
2. All citizens owed allegiance to the state.
C. Cylon, Solon, Pisistratus, and Cleisthenes developed legal and social reforms that improved the lives of Athenians.
1. Cleisthenes was the founder of Greek democracy.
2. Central government was based on a political unit called a *deme*.

V. The Persian and Peloponnesian Wars engulfed the Greek world.
A. Greeks and Persians spread into each other's spheres of influence.
1. Battle of Marathon (490 B.C.)
2. Battle of Thermopylae (480 B.C.)
3. Battle of Salamis (480 B.C.)
B. The struggle against Persians forced Greeks into military alliances.
1. The Delian League was established as a naval alliance against the Persians.
2. The Athenians turned the league into a vehicle for empire-building.
C. Alliances triggered a conflict between Sparta and Athens.
1. Athens' attempt to gain hegemony disturbed the Spartans.
2. Athens' conflict with the Corinthians brought Sparta into the fray.
D. The Peloponnesian War weakened Greece and allowed for Macedonian invasion and conquest.
1. Even after the Peace of Nicias (421 B.C.), cold war conditions continued.
2. Lysander and the Spartans defeated the Athenians in 405 B.C.

VI. The flowering of art and literature came during the Classical Period.
A. Herodotus and Thucydides became the founders of the study of history for later generations.
1. Herodotus chronicled the events of the Persian War.
2. Thucydides wrote of the Greek suicide in the Peloponnesian War.
B. Arts in the Periclean Age
1. Pericles made Athens a cultural center.
2. The Parthenon became the prototypical example of classical architecture.
3. Aeschylus, Sophocles, and Euripides created enduring dramas.
4. Thales, Anaximander, and Heraclitus laid the foundations of science.
5. Socrates' method of questioning left a lasting impact on the Western world.
6. Plato believed that truth lay in the world of ideas.
7. Aristotle advocated a philosophy that put emphasis on the material world.

VII. The Macedonian Conquest came in the wake of the Peloponnesian War.
A. Philip II, King of Macedon
1. Thebes petitioned Macedonians to liberate Delphi.
2. Philip defeated the combined armies of Thebes and Athens in 338 B.C. at Chaeronea.
3. The victory at Chaeronea led to Macedonian hegemony of the Greek world.

Lecture Suggestions

1. "Greeks and Outsiders." How did the Greeks view foreigners? Did they readily include them in their city-states? How did their attitudes toward foreigners affect their continued growth as a civilization? Sources: H. D. F. Kitto, *The Greeks* (1973); W. H. Auden, "The Greeks and Us," in *Forewards and Afterwards* (1973).

2. "What Sports Meant to the Greeks." What role did sports play in ancient Greece? Was there a distinction between amateurs and professionals? How did sports reflect Greek society? Was there any difference between aristocratic sports and sports for the common folk? Sources: E. N. Gardiner, *Athletics of the Ancient World* (1930); M. I. Finley and H. W. Pleket, *The Olympic Games: The First Thousand Years* (1976); V. Olivova, *Sports and Games in the Ancient World* (1984); D. Sansone, *Greek Athletics and the Genesis of Sport* (1988).

3. "Greek Ideas of Education: Their Impact on Modern Society." What kind of education did the Greeks pursue? What made an educated man or woman? What Greek ideas continue to influence educational systems in the West? Sources: W. Jaeger, *Paideia*, 3 vols. (English translation, 1944–1945); E. B. Castle, *Ancient Education and Today* (1961); H. I. Marrou, *A History of Education in Antiquity* (1964).

Using Primary Sources

Have students read Book XXIII of Homer's *Iliad*. Have students list the games the Greek warriors engaged in. Then, have them draft a short paper in which they discuss the significance of these games for Greek society. What did the "playing" of the games mean to the Greeks? How did they commemorate the slain Patroclus?

Activities for Discovering the Past

I. Classroom Discussion Suggestions

1. Who was Homer? Was he a fictional character or the greatest poet of all time? What is the evidence for his existence and his authorship of the *Iliad* and the *Odyssey*?
2. What were some of the major factors in the Greeks' victory over the Persian Empire?
3. What is the real significance of Athenian democracy? Was Athens democratic in the modern sense?
4. What was life in the polis like? Describe a day in the life of the polis.

II. Doing History

1. Have students compare the schools of thought promoted by Greek historians Herodotus and Thucydides. Have them read excerpts from Herodotus and Thucydides in M. I. Finley, *The Portable Greek Historians: The Essence of Herodotus, Thucydides, and Others* (Viking Edition, 1960); and H. E. Barnes, *A History of Historical Writing* (Dover Edition, 1963).
2. Have students read Book XXIII of the *Iliad* and list the different kinds of sports played by the Greeks at the funeral games for Patroclus. According to Homer, what was this warrior society like in the thirteenth century B.C.?
3. Students can be assigned term paper topics on women's roles in Sparta and Athens. Which city-state provided the most opportunities and freedom for women? Sources: R. Just, *Women in Athenian Law and Life* (1988); and D. M. Schaps, *Economic Rights of Women in Ancient Greece* (1984).

III.   Cooperative Learning Activities

1. Governing the Polis
Organize students into Jigsaw Teams (explained in Activity 1 above). Each team should be responsible for learning about a different Greek polis: (1) Athens, (2) Sparta, (3) Thebes, (4) Corinth, (5) Lesbos, (6) Byzantium. Team members are responsible for learning how the polis was organized and governed and for teaching what they have learned to the other teams. One member of each team should list key points on the chalkboard, on an overhead transparency, or on a handout.

2. Polis Sweet Polis
Using the Jigsaw Teams from Activity 1 above, have each group learn about the geography and culture of its polis. Then have teams write letters to other teams describing the life and culture of their particular polis. You may wish to allow a series of letter-writing among the various poleis and to have someone from each team read the letters aloud in class. This activity should encourage students to pay closer attention to geographical and cultural detail and stimulate them to focus on clear, descriptive writing.

Map Activity

Using an outline map of Greece and the eastern Mediterranean area (IRM page 180) have students list the following places:
1. Macedonia
2. Mt. Olympus
3. Epirus
4. Thessaly
5. Marathon
6. Lesbos
7. Troy
8. Lydia
9. Athens
10. Sparta
11. Corinth
12. Thebes
13. Pylos
14. Crete
15. Rhodes
16. Aegean Sea
17. Mediterranean Sea
18. Ionian Sea
19. Thrace
20. Delos

Audiovisual Bibliography

1. *Athens: The Golden Age.* (30 min. Color. Encyclopaedia Britannica Films.)
2. *The Greek Myths: Myth as Fiction, History, and Ritual.* (27 min. Color. Encyclopaedia Britannica Films.)
3. *The Greek Myths: Myth as Science, Religion, and Drama.* (25 min. Color. Encyclopaedia Britannica Films.)

4. *The Trojan Women.* (111 min. Color. Films for the Humanities and Sciences.)
5. *Greek Epic.* (40 min. Color. Films for the Humanities and Sciences.)
6. *The Rise of Greek Tragedy—Sophocles: Oedipus the King.* (45 min. Color. Films for the Humanities and Sciences.)
7. *Aristophanes: Women in Power.* (58 min. Color. Films for the Humanities and Sciences.)

CHAPTER 6

HELLENISTIC DIFFUSION

Instructional Objectives

After reading and analyzing this chapter, students should be able to discuss Alexander the Great's ideas of a political state. Students should also be able to explain how the meeting of Greek and Eastern ideas impacted upon philosophy, religion, science, and society. Finally, students should be able to compare the role of women in Hellenic and Hellenistic times.

Chapter Outline

I. The Age of Alexander saw the expansion of Greek ideas and customs.
   A. Alexander defeated the mighty Persian Empire.
      1. Alexander proclaimed the invasion of Persia a great crusade.
      2. Alexander won three major battles at the Granicus River, Issus, and Gaugamela.
   B. He led his forces as far east as the Indus River.
      1. After hard fighting at the Hyphasis River, his troops refused to go farther.
      2. Alexander died in Babylon in 323 B.C.

II. The Alexandrian Conquest had a tremendous impact on the Eastern world.
   A. Hellenistic cities became links in a great communications network.
      1. Greek culture spread throughout Asia Minor and even into India.
      2. Greek theaters, temples, and libraries sprang up throughout the Mediterranean world.
   B. Production of goods increased and international commerce was facilitated by new communications networks.
   C. Eastern mystery cults found favor with Greek citizens during this period.
   D. Alexander's successors could not hold the empire together after his death.
      1. By 275 B.C., three of Alexander's officers had divided the empire into large monarchies.
      2. Monarchy's resurgence came as a result of the division of Alexander's empire.

III. East-West relations resulted in increased international trade.
   A. The East was brought into the Greek sphere of economics.
      1. Alexander's conquests developed trade routes with India and Italy.
      2. The slave trade flourished.
   B. People's needs remained basically the same as those of fifth century B.C. Athens.
      1. The existence of inexpensive labor left little motivation for innovation.
   C. The real achievement of Alexander and his successors was linking East and West in a broad commercial network.

      1.   The Greeks sent their oil, wine, and fish to the East in return for eastern grain.

IV. Hellenistic agriculture and industry underwent significant changes.
    A.   Hellenistic kings paid special attention to agriculture.
        1.   Much of their revenue was derived from the produce of royal lands.
        2.   Some kings sought out and supported agricultural experts.
    B.   Few industrial innovations were made in the Hellenistic Ages.
        1.   The inventions of mathematicians and other thinkers failed to produce corresponding technological innovations.

V. Philosophy and science flourished in this period.
    A.   Three main schools of philosophy emerged:
        1.   Cynicism advocated rejection of the world.
        2.   Epicureanism encouraged a focus on material things and political passivity.
        3.   Stoicism demanded that individuals accept their lot in life and resign themselves to their duty.
    B.   Science was the greatest achievement of the Hellenistic period.
        1.   Aristarchus of Samos propounded the heliocentric theory.
        2.   Euclid created a system of geometry still in use today.
        3.   Medicine also made signal advances in the work of Herophilus and Erasistratus.
        4.   The Empiric School emphasized the prescription of medicine and drugs.

VI. Women in the Hellenistic ages exercised more power than in the previous era.
    A.   The Hellenistic period witnesed a return of royal women to politics.
        1.   The philosophies of the day emphasized differing opinions of women: the Stoics believed women to be inferior to men; the Cynics believed them equal to men.
        2.   Women made economic gains during this period.

Lecture Suggestions

1.   "Great People and How They Get That Way: Alexander the Great." What special qualities did Alexander possess that made him appear larger than life and superior to his fellow men? Are these qualities ones that he shares with other great men and women of history? How does one become great? Sources: J. R. Hamilton, *Alexander the Great* (1973); U. Wilcken, *Alexander the Great* (English translation, 1967).
2.   "Alexander's Homosexuality: Fact or Fiction." Was Alexander the Great a homosexual? How was homosexuality viewed by the Greeks of the Classical and the Hellenistic periods? Sources: M. Renault, *The Persian Boy*; Arrian, *The Campaigns of Alexander* (Penguin Edition, 1976).
3.   "The Cults and Their Followers." Why did the Greeks turn to Eastern mystery cults for spiritual fulfillment in the Hellenistic period? What in those cults was most appealing to the West? Sources: R. E. Witt, *Isis in the Graeco-Roman World* (1971); S. K. Heyob, *The Cult of Isis Among Women in the Graeco-Roman World* (1975); W. Burkert, *Ancient Mystery Cults* (1987).

Using Primary Sources

Have students read passages in Arrian's *The Campaigns of Alexander* (1976) that describe Alexander's tactics and strategy. Have students generalize about Alexander's tactics and strategy based on Arrian's primary account in a class discussion. Then, have students write short papers further developing their ideas.

Activities for Discovering the Past

I. **Classroom Discussion Suggestions**

1. How did life in Macedonia prepare Alexander for success in the cosmopolitan world of Greece and Asia Minor?
2. Why has Alexander been remembered so vividly?
3. How did the role of women change from the Hellenic period to the Hellenistic period?
4. What scientific innovations were made during the Hellenistic period?

II. **Doing History**

1. Give students an outline map of the eastern Mediterranean region that also includes Asia Minor and India. Have them plot the route of Alexander's conquests. Discuss with them the importance of certain ancient cities, such as Babylon and Alexandria. Some attention might be given to the importance of these cities in today's world.
2. Alexander the Great is a lasting example of a person who can influence historical developments. Do great people make history or does history make great people? Have students do research and write short papers on the hero approach to history. Sources: S. Hook, *The Hero in History*; W. W. Tarn, *Alexander the Great* (1956).
3. Have students look at art books that contain pictures of wall paintings and sculpture from the Hellenistic period. Have them comment on whether they feel that the art in any way reflects the changes that occurred in the Hellenistic world. Source: H. Gardner, *Art Through the Ages* (many editions).

III. **Cooperative Learning Activities**

1. Organize the class into four teams. Assign them the task of learning about the battles of Alexander the Great (this can be a followup activity to the primary source activity described above). Each group should become expert on a particular Alexandrian battle: Granicus, Issus, Gaugamela, and Hyphasis. Each team should present an overview of the battle, listing troop placements on the chalkboard, overhead, or handout. Finally, it might be useful to have students "re-enact" an Alexandrian battle, on the quad or somewhere on campus. Instructors may wish to give extra credit to students who create facsimiles of armor and weapons of the period.
2. Dramatizing Philosophy
   Organize the class into three groups. Each group is assigned the task of writing a short one-act play illustrating the philosophies of Cynicism, Epicureanism, and Stoicism. The play might be set in the Hellenistic era or in modern times. Each group might discover and elect a director, scriptwriter(s), scenery maker, actors, etc. Finally, the students should present their plays in class.

Map Activity

The World When Alexander Died.
Using an outline map of the world (IRM page 181), have students do brief research reports on a select number of world locations for the time of Alexander the Great. What was going on in each of these places? Have students list these places on a large wall map of the world and tell the class what was happening at these places at the time of Alexander's death. Students should consult page 4 of the *Historical Atlas of the World*.

Audiovisual Bibliography

1. *Greek and Roman Legends.* (35 min. Color. Films for the Humanities and Sciences.)
2. *Alexander the Great.* (135 min. Color. Films, Inc.)
3. *Games and Festivals.* (27 min. Color. Media Guild Films.)
4. *Coins of the World: History in Metal.* (18 min. Color. Centron Corporation.)
5. The Jason Voyage: The Quest for the Golden Fleece. (Videodisc. Films for the Humanities and Sciences.)
6. Time Table of History. (CD-ROM. National Audio-Visual Supply.)

CHAPTER 7

THE GLORY OF ROME

Instructional Objectives

After reading and studying this chapter, students should be able to describe the factors that contributed to Rome's conquest of the Italian Peninsula and explain the challenges Rome faced in its conquest of the Mediterranean world. Students should also be able to discuss the impact that Greek culture had on Roman society. Finally, students should be able to analyze the problems that Rome acquired as the result of its acquisition of empire.

Chapter Outline

I. The land and the sea played significant roles in Rome's development.
   A. Italy had a lack of navigable rivers but relatively fertile soil.
      1. Latium and Campania are two of Italy's most fertile areas.
      2. The Romans built their city on seven hills along the Tiber River.

II. The origins of the Roman Republic are shrouded in mystery.
   A. The Regal Period (753–509 B.C.) witnessed the assimilation of Roman and Etruscan customs and traditions.
      1. Historians are divided in their opinions about Etruscan origins.
      2. They may have been one of the many peoples who moved into Italy from the thirteenth to the eighth century B.C.
   B. The Republic, according to tradition, was established in 509 B.C. when the Romans drove out their Etruscan rulers.
      1. Much of the history of this early period is based on myths and legends.
      2. A series of legal, economic, military, and political reforms helped to create the Roman state.
      3. The Roman army subdued the peoples of the Italian Peninsula by 290 B.C.
      4. Rome moved into south-central and southern Italy in three wars against the Samnites.
      5. Rome defeated neighboring Carthage in the three Punic Wars and became master of the western Mediterranean world.
      6. Rome then turned her attention to the Greek world, defeating Macedonia and other Greek states.
      7. Pergamum, Egypt and other states became provinces of Rome.

III. Roman Government was a complex, yet efficient human mechanism.
   A. The Republic was governed by two consuls, elected magistrates, and ruled by people's assemblies.

B. The senate was an advisory body whose advice had the force of law.
1. The experience and wisdom of the senators provided public stability.
2. The *comitia centuriata* actually decided Roman political policy.
3. The plebeians finally won their own representative body in 471 B.C., the *concilium plebis*.
C. The patrician class dominated the offices of the Roman priesthood.
1. The *pontifex maximus* wielded considerable authority in Roman society.
D. The so-called Struggle of the Orders was a significant social conflict in the Roman Republic.
1. The Struggle of the Orders was the attempt by the plebeians to win political representation and to protect their rights from patrician domination.
2. The patricians formed the land-owning aristocracy that could trace its ancestry back to the founding of the city.
3. The plebeians were the artisans, small farmers, and landless urban dwellers.
4. Rome's need for plebeian soldiers led to early reforms.
5. The *lex Canuleia* made it legal for patricians and plebeians to marry.
6. The Law of the Twelve Tables was codified as a result of plebeian agitation.
7. Licinius and Sextus agitated further for plebeian rights.
8. The struggle ended in 287 B.C. with the passage of the *lex Hortensia*.

IV. Political disturbances in the last centuries of the Republic stemmed from the acquisition of empire.
A. Cato the Elder represented the traditional values of Rome.
1. The paterfamilias was the most powerful force in the Roman family in the traditional scheme of things.
2. Religion played a significant role in Roman life.
B. Scipio Aemilianus represented the new Roman of wealth and leisure.
1. Roman military victories brought the bounty of the East back to Rome.
2. Hellenism had a great impact on Roman art, literature, and leisure activities.
C. Factional politics and civil wars resulted from Rome's acquisition of empire.
1. Political leaders such as Marius, Sulla, Pompey, and Julius Caesar acquired enormous power.
2. Powerful generals jeopardized republican government.
3. Rome's Italian allies sought full citizenship.
4. A growing number of urban poor led to further problems for the Roman state.
5. The Gracchi Brothers sought land reform for the Roman poor and full citizenship for Rome's Italian allies.
6. The Social War resulted from the agitation of the Italian allies for full Roman citizenship.
7. The reforms of powerful leaders like Marius and Sulla had dangerous implications for the republican constitution.
8. Cicero urged a "concord of the orders."
9. Two political alliances, called the First and Second Triumvirates, undermined the power of the republican constitution.
10. Rome was plagued by civil war in the last century of the republic.
D. Order restored by Caesar's grand-nephew Octavius in 31 B.C.
1. Octavian defeated his last rival, Marc Antony, at the Battle of Actium in 31 B.C.
2. Octavian began the process of restoring the republic.

V. Octavian restores order after the period of civil wars.
A. Octavian used the guise of restoring the Repubic.
1. In reality, Octavian created a constitutional monarchy.

2. He called himself princeps civitatis ("first citizen of the state").
3. Octavian assumed most of the important civil and religious offices of Rome.
4. Much of his power resided in his role as commander of the army.
   B. Literary flowering under the Pax Romana
      1. This period is generally referred to as the golden age of Roman literature.
      2. This age produced well-known writers such as Horace, Virgil, Livy, and Ovid.
      3. Roman writers celebrated the dignity of humanity.
   C. The early first century witnessed the rise and spread of Christianity.
      1. Christianity was born in Palestine, but later it found great success in the western Mediterranean world.
      2. It appealed to the downtrodden.
      3. It evolved into a religion that appealed to the upper classes.
      4. Christianity was in competition with eastern mystery cults such as those of Isis, Cybele, Mithra, and Sol.
      5. Paul developed a brand of Christianity that was nonexclusionist.
      6. Christianity gave a promise of salvation and forgiveness.
      7. It also had a sense of belonging and community.

VI. Augustus' successors were named for two clans: the Julians and Claudians.
   A. The Julio-Claudian emperors were a diverse lot.
      1. Claudius created an efficient bureaucracy.
   B. Imperial personage assumed greater powers under the Antonines.
   C. Population of Rome approached one million during the Pax Romana.
   D. The army and the Praetorian Guard assumed greater power in political affairs and set a negative precedent in the Roman state.
      1. The year of the Four Emperors proved that the Augustan settlement was a failure.
   E. The period of the Antonine Emperors (A.D. 96–180) truly deserved the title Pax Romana.
      1. Hadrian reformed the bureaucracy.
      2. During this period, the government provided the citizens of Rome with "bread and circuses" to prevent riots in the city.

VII. The reforms of Diocletian and Constantine attempted to thwart the decline of Rome.
   A. Diocletian reorganized the administration and fixed prices and wages.
   B. Constantine made tax-collecting positions into a hereditary class.
      1. Small farmers were reduced in status.
   C. Constantine recognized Christianity as a legitimate religion.
      1. Constantine also built a new capital, called Constantinople (on the site of the Greek city of Byzantium).
   D. Despite reforms, decline could not be checked.

VIII. The Pax Romana gave way to civil wars and invasion in the third century A.D.
   A. Commodus' reign was the harbinger of evil things to come.
      1. Between 235 and 284 over twenty emperors ascended the throne.
      2. The army was playing a dangerously greater role in political affairs.
      3. Rome was wracked by instability in politics and government.
   B. Migrating barbarians penetrated gaps in the frontier defenses.
      1. The Goths marched into Europe in A.D. 258.
      2. The Franks, Saxons, Alemanni, and other tribes invaded the empire and created serious problems.
      3. The collapse of order led to crime and corruption.

IX. The decline and fall of Rome has long fascinated scholars.
  A. Edward Gibbon composed the classic on the fall of Rome.
    1. Gibbon believed that the empire declined due to a loss of strength and prosperity.
    2. Gibbon saw Christianity as the chief culprit in the fall of Rome.
  B. Marxists argue that Rome fell because the economy was built on slave labor.
    1. Others have argued that Rome declined because of racial mixing.
    2. The variety of reasons for Rome's fall underscores the complexity of the problem.

Lecture Suggestions

1. "Romans and Aliens." How did Romans view foreigners? Was the Romans' view of foreigners similar to that of the Greeks? What institutions did the Romans develop to incorporate noncitizens into the "Roman family"? Sources: J. P. V. D. Balsdon, *Romans and Aliens* (1979); E. Badian, *Foreign Clientelae, 264–70* (1958); A. N. Sherwin-White, *The Roman Citizenship* (1939).
2. "Roman Imperialism: Fact or Fiction?" Did Rome pursue a policy of aggression or merely "back into empire"? Historians have long debated this aspect of Roman history. Sources: E. T. Salmon, *Samnium and the Samnites* (1967); J. Heurgon, *The Rise of Rome to 264 B.C.* (English translation, 1973); W. V. Harris, *War and Imperialism in Republican Rome, 327–70 B.C.* (1979).
3. "The Gracchi: Radical Reformers." Why were the Gracchi brothers perceived as radicals? What were their real intentions in seeking social reform in the second century B.C.? Were the Gracchi brothers genuinely interested in the plight of the disadvantaged of Rome, or were they self-seeking opportunists plotting personal gain and increased political power? Sources: P. A. Brunt, *Social Conflicts in the Roman Republic* (1971); A. W. Lintott, *Violence in the Roman Republic* (1968); H. C. Boren, *The Gracchi* (1968).
4. "Games Romans Played and Watched." What did the citizens of Rome do for entertainment? What entertainments did the state provide? Did Roman sports reflect Roman society? Sources: R. Auguet, *Cruelty and Civilization: The Roman Games* (English translation, 1972); H. A. Harris, *Sport in Greece and Rome* (1972).

Using Primary Sources

1. "How to win an election—Roman Style"
   Have students read part, or the whole of *The Handbook of Electioneering* by M. T. Cicero's brother Quintus. The book provides graphic insights into the details of Roman politics in the late Republic. Use the reading as the basis for a discussion of Roman political life. Then have students write a short paper on comparing Roman political techniques in Quintus Cicero's book with those of contemporary American society. Finally, have students discuss their insights in class.
2. Reread the funerary inscription of Encolpus in this chapter. What does his personal philosophy tell you about his view of an afterlife? How does this view compare with other Romans of the middle to late imperial period? How does this view compare with the followers of Christ or some of the other Eastern mystery cults?

Activities for Discovering the Past

I. Classroom Discussion Suggestions

1. How did the Romans win battles against such able commanders as Pyrrhus of Epirus and Hannibal the Carthaginian?
2. What was a "new man" in Roman politics and what implications did this designation have for an individual entering the Roman political arena?
3. How were conquered peoples assimilated into the Roman system?
4. What do historians mean by the term Struggle of the Orders?
5. How does Livy's *History of Rome* differ in approach from modern works of history?
6. What were some of the major reasons for the destruction of the Roman Republic?
7. How did Christianity spread throughout the empire?
8. Why did Constantine accept Christianity as a legitimate religion?

II. Doing History

1. Have students read selections from the literature of the Roman Republic and find descriptions of daily life in ancient Rome. Use these descriptions as the basis for a class discussion and/or a term paper about Roman social life. Sources: Livy, *History of Rome,* 3 vols. (Penguin paperback edition); Plutarch, *Lives of the Noble Romans* (Penguin paperback edition); Virgil, *Aeneid* (Penguin paperback edition); R. M. Ogilvie, *Roman Literature and Society* (1980).
2. Although the historicity of characters like Aeneas, Dido, Romulus, Remus, Horatius, and Cincinnatus is in doubt, Romans of the mid- to late Republic seemed to believe in these "Fathers and Mothers of the Republic." What role did myth play in the development of the Roman state? Do myths usually have some basis in historical fact? Have students read some of the Roman myths as preparation for a class discussion or for a short paper. Sources: H. H. Scullard, *A History of the Roman World,* 753–146 B.C. (1961); M. Morford and R. J. Lenardon, *Classical Mythology* (1971); N. Lewis and M. Reinhold, *Roman Civilization: Sourcebook I: The Republic* (1966); *Larousse Encyclopedia of Mythology* (1960).

III. Cooperative Learning Activities

1. The Republic Creates an Empire.
   Organize the class into the Jigsaw Teams of six students each. Charge each team with learning about the wars that Rome fought that led to the creation of an empire: (1) the Latin Wars; (2) the Samnite Wars; (3) the Punic Wars; (4) the wars against the Greek and Macedonian world; (5) the conquests of Gaul and Britannia. Each team should answer the following questions: (1) Who were Rome's significant military leaders at the time? (2) What were the strategy and tactics employed? (3) Whom did Rome fight? (4) What battles were decisive in the war? (5) What outcomes resulted from the war(s)? Each group should create a chart in which they present their answers to the questions. Each group should present its findings in class. Charts might be affixed to the classroom wall or a bulletin board.
2. The Ever Lovable Toga Party?
   If fraternities and sororities are going to maintain this tradition, why not make sure they make their parties historically accurate? Try to give each student a particular Roman of the Republic (either a real character like Julius Caesar or a semifictional one such as Horatius). Their task is to learn about the character and come to class (on an appointed day) dressed as the character. You might also ask students to decorate the classroom and bring refreshments (based on students' understanding of what Romans of the Republic ate and drank). The

students' tickets to the toga party are their costumes and oral presentations on their particular characters.

3. Historiography: Why Did Rome Fall?
Have students investigate the reasons for the demise of Rome. Organize students into teams of six each. Assign each team the task of becoming experts on a particular school of thought on Rome's decline and fall: (1) Edward Gibbon, (2) Arnold Toynbee, (3) Oswald Spengler, (4) A Marxist interpretation, (5) the view expressed in A. Ferrill, *The Fall of Rome* (1985). After the teams have completed their research, have them present their findings in class. After a class discussion, have the class write a paper summarizing the major interpretations for Rome's fall.

Map Activity

1. Using the map of the Roman World on page 6 of the *Historical Atlas of the World*, have students shade in the Roman provinces on an outline map of the Mediterranean world (IRM page 182). Instructors may wish to have students compare this map with the map of the Persian Empire in Chapter 2 of the textbook.

2. Using the map of the Roman Empire on page 7 of the *Historical Atlas of the World*, have students prepare an itinerary of a two-week tour of cities of the Roman Empire. Organize the class into four teams. Each team is to be responsible for one of the four Roman Prefectures. The team then decides on which cities of the old prefecture would be most interesting and informative to visit. When the teams have completed their work, the whole class then has to decide how to work the tour into the two-week time limit. The teams should finally decide on a workable two-week tour, explaining why they want to visit the places chosen.

Audiovisual Bibliography

1. *Julius Caesar: The Rise of the Roman Empire.* (22 min. Color. Encyclopedia Britannica Films.)
2. *Julius Caesar.* (116 min. Color. Republic Pictures Home Video.)
3. *The Etruscans.* (27 min. Color. Films for the Humanities and Sciences.)
4. *Pompeii: Daily Life of the Ancient Romans.* (45 min. Color. Films for the Humanities and Sciences.)
5. *Cleopatra.* (186 min. Color. Films, Inc.)
6. *Life in Ancient Rome.* (Videodisc. Color. Britannica Videos.)
7. *Thine Is the Kingdom.* (52 min. Color. Films for the Humanities and Sciences.)
8. *The Robe* (135 min. Color. Films, Inc.)
9. *Life in Ancient Rome* (Videodisc. Color. Britannica Videos.)
10. *Claudius: Boy of Ancient Rome* (Videodisc. Color. Britannica Videos.)
11. *The Romans on the Rhine and the Danube.* (Videodisc. Color. Britannica Videos.)
12. *The Roman Empire: Growth and Development* (Videodisc. Color. Britannica Videos)

CHAPTER 8

THE MAKING OF EUROPE

Instructional Objectives

After reading and studying this chapter, students should be able to discuss the foundations of the medieval period. Students should also be able to explain how Christianity assimilated pagan culture. Finally, students should be able to discuss how both Byzantine and Islamic culture influenced western Europe in the Middle Ages.

Chapter Outline

I. The growth of Christianity dominated the early Middle Ages.
   A. The words *Christian church* originally applied to the officials who administered to Christians.
      1. Rome provided the bureaucracy for the church's organization.
      2. The church assimilated many diverse peoples.
      3. In the early Middle Ages, the church was led by creative, literate thinkers.
   B. Caesar and Christ
      1. Constantine legalized Christianity in A.D. 312.
      2. He embarked upon an extensive church-building project.
      3. Theodosius made Christianity the religion of the state.
   C. The Arian Heresy challenged the foundation of the church.
      1. The Council of Nicaea was held in 325 to combat the Arians.
      2. The council produced the Nicene Creed—the doctrine that Christ was of the same substance as God.
      3. The Nicene Creed became Christian orthodoxy.
      4. Bishop Ambrose formulated the theory that the church was superior to the state.

II. Leadership in the early church was creative and inspirational.
   A. Many talented Romans, such as Ambrose, became leaders in the early church.
      1. The church adopted Rome's diocesan system.
      2. Bishops presided over the various dioceses.
   B. The Bishop of Rome became the Patriarch of the West.
      1. Other patriarchs presided over their sees at Antioch, Alexandria, Jerusalem, and Constantinople.
   C. Early medieval Christianity conducted extensive missionary work.
      1. Martin of Tours brought Christianity to Gaul.
      2. St. Patrick took Christianity to Ireland.
      3. Pope Gregory I sent Augustine to convert the English.

4. The Roman brand of Christianity won out over its Celtic rival at the Synod of Whitby in 664.
5. Germanic assimilation into Christianity was slow.
6. Priests used manuals called penitentials to teach people Christian virtues.
D. Christianity and Classical Culture
1. The early Christians were hostile to pagan culture.
2. Saint Paul and Saint Jerome incorporated pagan thought into Christianity.

III. Augustine of Hippo (A.D. 354–430) had a tremendous impact on early Christianity.
A. He was the most important leader of early medieval Christianity.
1. His *Confessions* delineated the pre-Christian struggles of the author.
2. His *City of God* established the historical/philosophical base of a new Christian world-view.

IV. Monasticism played a vital role in the development of Christian Europe.
A. St. Anthony, an ascetic monk who disdained communal, urban existence, personified the early eremitical life.
1. Cassiodorus began the connection between monasticism and scholarship and learning.
B. St. Benedict of Nursia developed the guide for all Christian monastic life.
1. The *Rule of St. Benedict* was influenced by earlier monastic codes.
2. Benedict's rule outlined a life of discipline and moderation.
3. Monks made a vow of stability, conversion of manners, and obedience.
4. Benedictine monasticism succeeded because of its emphasis upon the balanced life and because it suited the social circumstances of the early Middle Ages.

V. Germanic societies created an important foundation of the early Middle Ages.
A. Germanic tribesmen entered the empire as army recruits, refugees, prisoners of war, or free barbarian units of soldiers.
1. The war chieftain led the tribe.
2. The *comitatus* (warband) that fought with the chief gradually become a warrior nobility.
B. Tribal customs seemed primitive to the sophisticated Romans of the late imperial period.
1. Tacitus, in his *Germania*, gives us a glimpse of Germanic tribal customs.
2. Visigoths, Burgundians, Lombards, Anglo-Saxons, and Franks had written codes of legal custom.
3. Anglo-Saxons created an exemplary Germanic state.
4. The Germanic tribes lived in small villages.
5. Warfare was endemic in this kind of society.
6. Males engaged in animal husbandry and women grew grain.
7. Some royal women exercised considerable political control.
8. Germanic law aimed at the reduction of violence.
C. The Anglo-Saxons achieved a model Germanic state.
1. After Roman withdrawal from Britannium, Germanic invaders drove out the native Britons.
2. By the seventh and eighth centuries, there were seven Germanic kingdoms: the Anglo-Saxon Heptarchy.
3. They were united under Alfred the Great in the ninth century.

VI. Byzantine and Islamic institutions also influenced the development of the medieval West.
A. Byzantium created a buffer state between East and West.

B. The Legal Code of Justinian was a significant contribution to the early Middle Ages.
   1. The *corpus juris civilis*, consisting of the Code, the Digest, and the Institutes, is the foundation of European law.
C. Byzantine intellectual life was a stimulant for the West.
   1. The Byzantines kept learning alive in the East.
   2. They passed Greco-Roman culture on to the Arabs.
D. Islam had a tremendous impact on the West.
   1. The religion of Islam united the rural Bedouins and urban Hejazi.
   2. By 711, Islamic armies were threatening Europe.
   3. The Frankish victory at Tours (Poitiers) in 733 halted Islamic advance in Europe.
   4. Islamic scientific and mathematical advances had great influence on Western thought.
   5. Muslim scholars developed algebra and made other mathematical contributions such as the concept of zero.
   6. They excelled in medical knowledge and preserved Greek philosophy.

Lecture Suggestions

1. "The Clash of Cultures in the Early Middle Ages." How were the Christian, German, and Roman elements assimilated in the fourth and fifth centuries? What happened to pagan literature? What was the role of the early church in the assimilation process? Sources: J. B. Bury, *A History of the Later Roman Empire, 395–800* (1889); C. Cochrane, *Christianity and Classical Culture* (1940); F. Lot, *The End of the Ancient World and the Beginnings of the Middle Ages* (1961).
2. "The Impact of Monasticism." How did monasticism influence the development of medieval civilization? What role did monks and nuns play in the revitalization of literature and culture? Why was Benedictine monasticism such a success? Sources: D. Knowles, *Christian Monasticism* (1969); T. Fry et al., *The Rule of St. Benedict in Latin and English with Notes* (1981); H. W. Workman, *The Evolution of the Monastic Ideal* (1962).
3. "Women in Germanic Society." What was the role of women in the early Germanic societies? Did they share equally with men? Was their position better than that of their Roman counterparts? Sources: S. Stuard, *Women in Medieval Society* (1977); V. Bullough, *The Subordinate Sex* (1973); R. Bridenthal and C. Koonz, eds., *Becoming Visible: Women in European History* (1987); S. Wemple, *Women in Frankish Society: Marriage and the Cloister* (1981).

Using Primary Sources

Reread the excerpt from the penitential prepared by Archbishop Theodore of Canterbury. List what you consider to be the most striking punishments for crimes. How do these penitentials compare with other legal or moral codes? Further, how do they compare with contemporary secular codes (for example, the dooms of Anglo-Saxon kings)? Write a paper in which you analyze the ecclesiastical and secular codes of an early medieval state.

Activities for Discovering the Past

I.   Classroom Discussion Suggestions

1. What was the significance of the Arian heresy and the final solution of the controversy?
2. Why is the term "Dark Ages" no longer deemed appropriate to describe the early Middle Ages?
3. What were the appealing features of Islam?
4. Why did Roman Catholicism finally win out over Celtic Catholicism?

II.   Doing History

1. Have students read selections from Tacitus's *Germania* and take notes on the descriptions of food, clothing, marital customs, sports, and pastimes. Use the collected data as the basis for a class discussion of early Germanic social history.
2. Have students read selections from the Qur'an and look specifically for descriptions of Islamic social life. Students might use their information in a short paper on Islamic social history.
3. When did Rome fall and when did the Middle Ages begin? Fifty years ago, most teachers taught that the empire fell in A.D. 476 when the last Roman emperor in the west, Romulus Augustulus, was deposed by the Germanic king Odoacer. More recent scholars have pushed the date back earlier. Is there a plausible argument for a later date? Students reading the following sources should come to the conclusion that historical interpretations change over time and from one scholar to another. Sources: B. Lyon, *The Origins of the Middle Ages: Pirenne's Challenge to Gibbon* (1972); F. Lot, *The End of the Ancient World* (1965).

III.   Cooperative Learning Activities

1. The Foundations of the Middle Ages: Christian, Islamic, Jewish, Byzantine, Roman, Germanic influences. Organize the class into six teams. Charge each team with learning about one of the above foundations of the Middle Ages. After research is completed, allow each team to present findings in class. Discuss the contributions of each.
2. Medieval in the Modern
   Organize the class into teams of six each. Assign each team the task of looking into medieval society's influence on modern institutions: (1) literature, (2) law, (3) love, (4) science fiction, (5) education. Have teams make presentations on their findings and insights. Have students make lists of the medieval influences on modern society.

Map Activity

1. Using Map 8.1 in the text, have students list the following on an outline map of Europe (IRM page 183):
   Canterbury
   Cologne
   Paris
   Reims
   Toledo
   Hippo Regius
   Milan
   Rome

      Alexandria
      Constantinople
      Athens
      Ephesus
      Antioch
      Jerusalem

2. Using the map on page 8 of the *Historical Atlas of the World*, have students trace the major barbarian invasion routes on a blank outline map of Europe.

Audiovisual Bibliography

1. *The City of God.* (39 min. Color. Films for the Humanities and Sciences.)
2. *The Birth of the Middle Ages.* (43 min. Color. Films for the Humanities and Sciences.)
3. *Medieval Manuscripts.* (30 min. Color. Films for the Humanities and Sciences.)
4. *The Five Pillars of Islam.* (30 min. Color. Films for the Humanities and Sciences.)
5. *Islamic Science and Technology.* (30 min. Color. Films for the Humanities and Sciences.)
6. *The Brendan Voyage.* (Videodisc. Color. 54 min. Films for the Humanities and Sciences.)
7. *Christians, Jews, and Moslems in Medieval Spain.* (Videodisc. Color. 33 min. Films for the Humanities and Sciences.)
8. *Byzantium: From Splendor to Ruin.* (Videodisc. Color. 43 min. Films for the Humanities and Sciences.)

CHAPTER 9

THE ISLAMIC WORLD, CA 600–1400

Instructional Objectives

After reading and analyzing this chapter, students should be able to explain the origins and development of the Arabs. Students should also be able to delineate the main tenets of the Muslim faith. Then, students should be able to discuss how the Muslims governed their vast territories. Finally, students should be able to discuss features of Islamic society such as the position of women, Islamic interaction with Western society, and the effect the Sh'ite/Sunni split had on Islam.

Chapter Outline

I. The Origins of Islam
   A. In the sixth century A.D. Arabia was inhabited by Semitic tribes in the interior and agricultural-urban people, the Hejazi, in the southern valleys and towns.
      1. The Hejazi, who were wealthy, were polytheistic.
      2. Pre-Islamic societies in Arabia were governed by tribal custom and ritual.
   B. Little is known of Muhammad's life.
      1. He was a merchant who married a rich widow.
      2. He had a moving religious experience at age 40.
      3. According to Muhammad, God (Allah) sent him messages through his angel Gabriel.
      4. These messages became the Qur'an after Muhammad's death.
      5. The main beliefs of Islam were submission to God, Muhammad's teachings, and the last judgment and an afterlife.
      6. Islam united the peoples of Arabia.

II. The Expansion of Islam
   A. The Muslim Drive West
      1. Muhammad fled Mecca to Medina (the Hegira).
      2. By 632 A.D., Muhammad had brought all of Arabia under Islam.
      3. Within a hundred years, Syria, Egypt, North Africa, and Persia came under Muslim domination.
      4. In 711, the Muslims took Spain.
      5. In 733, Muslim inroads into Europe were halted at the Battle of Tours.
   B. The Muslim Drive East
      1. By 751, the Muslims had driven east into Afghanistan and central Asia.
      2. In 713, the Muslims founded a colony in the Indus Valley.
   C. Reasons for Muslim Expansion

1. The Muslims believed in the Holy War (jihad) which they used to bring non-Muslim areas under Muslim control.
2. The Muslims required Christians and Jews to submit to Muslim rule, whereas they forced atheists to convert to Islam.
3. Muslim success was also based upon economic reasons and superior military organization.

III. The Organization of the Islamic State
   A. Upon Muhammad's death, Islam was in danger of decentralizing into separate tribal groups.
      1. The umma (community) was stabilized by establishing Abu Bakr as khalifa (caliph), or leader.
      2. Abu Bakr's successors were elected by their peers.
      3. Under Mu'awiya, the caliphate exercised greater control over the tribal chieftains and the army.
      4. The assassination of the caliph Ali in 661 gave rise to a theological split within Islam between the Sh'ites and Sunnis.
      5. The Sh'ite-supported Abbasid faction ultimately set up a rival dynasty with its capital at Baghdad.
   B. The Administration of the Islamic State
      1. The Muslims appointed emirs (governors) to administer the various parts of the empire.
      2. The diwan (financial organization) became the center of Muslim administration.
      3. Sacred law was interpreted by a group of scholars called the ulema.
      4. A relay network called barid was used for communication within the empire.

IV. Islamic Decentralization
   A. During the Abbasid period, independent local dynasties emerged in Spain, North Africa, Korasan, and elsewhere.
      1. In the ninth century, the Turkish guards reduced the power of the caliphate.
      2. Rebellions, agricultural decline, hostile commercial interests, and other problems led to the decline of the caliphate.
      3. The Seljuk Turks took Baghdad in the tenth century and made the caliph a puppet of the Turkish sultan.
      4. There emerged three centers of Islam: Cordoba, Cairo, and Baghdad.

V. Social Organization in Islamic Society
   A. Social Stratification
      1. Muhammad's teaching emphasized social equality.
      2. His teachings opposed the pre-Islamic tribal code of family membership and birth as the center of Islamic life.
   B. There were four classes of Muslim society.
      1. The caliph's household and the ruling Arab Muslims made up the aristocracy.
      2. Converts constituted the second class.
      3. The dhimmis ("protected people"), largely Christians and Jews, made up the third class.
      4. Slaves constituted the fourth class.
   C. The Qur'an attempted to improve the status of women in Islamic society.
      1. The Qur'an gave women spiritual and sexual equality.
      2. In the early Umayyad period women enjoyed considerable economic, religious, and political rights.
      3. In the later Ummayad period, the status of women declined.

4. Society began to view women as subordinate to men.
5. Women's sexual instincts were distrusted.

Lecture Suggestions

1. "The Spread of Islam." Give students an outline map of the eastern hemisphere. For a starting point for a lecture on Islam, have them trace the movement of Islam into both the East and the West. Sources: E. von Grunebaum, *Medieval Islam* (1961); B. Lewis, *The Arabs in History* (1960).
2. "Crusade Against the Christians." How did the Muslims view the Christians' attempt to liberate Palestine? Did the Muslims perceive themselves as crusaders? Sources: S. Runciman, *A History of the Crusades*, 3 vols. (1955); R. Finucane, *Soldiers of the Faith* (1985).

Using Primary Sources

Have students compare social restrictions in the Qur'an and those in the Old Testament. Have students make charts showing similarities and differences between the social codes of the Muslims and Jews. Allow students to share and discuss their findings in class.

Activities for Discovering the Past

I. Classroom Discussion Questions

1. What separated the Sunni and the Shi'ites? How has this rift continued in the modern world?
2. In what ways was the Qur'an a guide for daily living?
3. What kind of a man was Muhammad?
4. How did the Franks defeat the Muslims at the Battle of Tours in 733?
5. What did the Muslims learn from the medieval Europeans?

II. Doing History

1. Did the Mediterranean civilization collapse around A.D. 476, or did it remain basically intact until the Islamic advances of the seventh and eighth centuries? Can one reach other legitimate conclusions? Have students read selections from the following source about the variety of explanations for the collapse of the West. Have them write short essays on their conclusions. Source: B. Lyon, *The Origins of the Middle Ages: Pirenne's Challenge to Gibbon* (1974).
2. Ask students to consider the problems that would have persisted if the zero had not made its way into the Western world. Have them do some problems of addition and subtraction using Roman numerals.
3. Have students review a recent book on Islamic history, asking them to use the format in the Book Review Preparation Guide at the beginning of this Manual.

III. Cooperative Learning Activities

1. Classical Islamic Literature
    Organize the class into five groups and assign them the task of reading and reporting on five classics of Islamic literature:

(1) *A Thousand and One Nights,* (2) Ibn Sina, al-Qanun, (3) Omar Khayam, *Rubiyat,* (4) al-Khwarizmi, al-Jabr, and (5) *The Adventures of Ibn Battuta: A Muslim Traveler of the Fourteenth Century* (trans. R. E. Dunn, 1987). After reading and discussing the works, each group should make a "book report" to the class, including not only a summary and analysis of the book's content, but a discussion of the process through which the book was translated and made its way into Western society. Groups might also discuss the historical and social contexts in which the books were produced.

2. Islamic Art
   Organize the class into five groups and assign each group the task of presenting and explicating an Islamic artwork. Students can find an admirable selection in A. Talbot Rice, *Islamic Art,* rev. ed. (1985). Each group should make its presentations to the class. Class time might be used to discuss the five artworks and the differences in Islamic and Western perspectives.

Map Activity

Using Map 9.1 in the text, have students list the following geographical features on an outline map of Europe and the Middle East (IRM page 184):

1. Mecca
2. Medina
3. Arabian Desert
4. Arabian Sea
5. Red Sea
6. Nile River
7. Cairo
8. Baghdad
9. Jerusalem
10. Tripoli
11. Damascus
12. Cordoba
13. Saragossa
14. Sicily
15. Tours

Audiovisual Bibliography

1. *Islam and the Sciences.* (23 min. Color. Phoenix Films and Video.)
2. *Islam: The Prophet and the People.* (34 min. Color. Texture Films.)
3. *Islamic Art.* (30 min. Color. Films for the Humanities.)
4. *Islamic Mysticism: The Sufi Way.* (27 min. Color. Hartley Film Foundation.)
5. *Moslems in Spain.* (30 min. Color. International Film Bureau.)
6. *Islam.* (30 min. Color. Films for the Humanities.)
7. *Arabian Seafarers: In the Wake of Sinbad.* (44 min. Color. Videodisc. Films for the Humanities and Sciences.)
8. *Middle East Diary.* (CD-ROM. National School Products.)

CHAPTER 10

AFRICA BEFORE EUROPEAN INTRUSION, CA 400–1500

Instructional Objectives

After reading and analyzing this chapter, students should be able to discuss what patterns of social and political organization prevailed among the peoples of Africa. Students should also be able to explain the various types of agriculture and commerce in medieval Africa. Finally, students should also be able to discuss the values that African art, architecture, and religion impart.

Chapter Outline

I. The Land and Peoples of Africa
   A. Five geographical zones divide Africa.
      1. The Mediterranean and southwestern coasts have fertile land, good rainfall, and dense vegetation.
      2. The dry steppe country of the north inland has little plant life.
      3. The Sahara Desert is in the north and the Namib and Kalahari in the south.
      4. The equatorial regions of central Africa have dense, humid, tropical rain forest.
      5. The savanna lands extend from west to east across the widest part of Africa.
      6. The climate of Africa is tropical.
   B. Africa was one of the sites where agriculture began.
      1. It spread down the Nile Valley and then to West Africa.
      2. Agricultural development led to the establishment of settled societies.
      3. Ironworking was introduced in ca. 600 B.C.
   C. Several kingdoms emerged in the area encircled by Egypt, the Red Sea, Ethiopia, Uganda, Zaire, Chad, and Libya.
      1. A key feature of early African society was a strong sense of community.
      2. Religions were largely animistic and centered around cults.
   D. The trans-Saharan Trade
      1. The camel had a significant impact on the economic and social life of West Africa.
      2. Between A.D. 700 and 900, a network of caravan trade routes developed between the Mediterranean and the Sudan.
      3. The introduction of Islam was the most significant consequence of the trans-Saharan trade.
      4. The coming of Islam to West Africa marked the beginning of written documents.

II. African Kingdoms and Empires
   A. The kingdom of Ghana (ca. 900–1100) was a wealthy state.
      1. The Soninke people called their ruler ghana, or war chief.
      2. The king was considered semisacred and his power was absolute.

3. The court was run by a bureaucracy situated at Kumbi.
4. Royal estates, the tribute from chiefs, and trade duties enabled the king to maintain an elaborate court.

B. Ghanaian Social Organization
1. Ghanaian society consisted of several orders.
   a. The governing aristocracy occupied the highest rank.
   b. The other classes were merchants, the middle classes, and a slave class.
2. There was also the army.

C. The Kingdom of Mali (ca. 1200–1450)
1. The kingdom of Ghana split into smaller kingdoms, one of which was Mali.
2. Mali became great because of successful agriculture and the West African salt and gold trade.
3. Sundiata transformed his capital, Niani, into an important financial and trading center.
4. He conquered Ghanaian areas and dominated Gao, Jenne, and Walata.
5. Mansa Musa continued the policies of Sundiata.
6. His empire grew to eight million people.
7. Musa became a Muslim.
8. Timbuktu became known as "Queen of the Sudan" as it was transformed into a commercial, intellectual, and artistic center.

D. The East African City-States
1. Commercial activity created great city-states along the East African coast.
2. Many of the natives were called "Ethiopian" or black.
3. Arab, Persian, and Indonesian immigrants to Africa intermarried with Africans.
4. The East African coastal culture was called "Swahili."
5. Ibn-Battuta left a written account of the great cities of Mombasa, Kilwas, and Mogadishu.
6. By 1300, a sheik (ruler) had arisen and Kilwa was the most powerful city on the coast.
7. Slaves were exported from East Africa for a multiplicity of duties.

E. Ethiopia
1. The kingdom of Ethiopia had close ties with early Christian rulers of Nobatia, a Nubian state, and the Roman and Byzantine worlds.
2. Axum was the center of Ethiopian civilization.
3. Coptic Christianity was the most significant feature of Ethiopian civilization between 500 and 1500.

F. South Africa
1. This region is bordered on the northeast by the Zambesi River and varies from desert to temperate grasslands.
2. South Africa remained isolated from the rest of the world.
3. Great Zimbabwe was the capital of a vast empire.
4. The empire's wealth was based primarily on gold mining.

Lecture Suggestions

1. "Slavery in Africa Before the Intrusion of Europeans." What was the basis of slavery in Africa prior to 1400? How did the intrusion of white Europeans affect the nature of slavery? Sources: M. Klein and P. Lovejoy, "Slavery in West Africa," in *The Uncommon Market*, ed. H. A. Gemery and J. S. Hogendorn (1979); R. S. Smith, *Warfare and Diplomacy in Precolonial Africa*.

2. "Islam in Africa." What was the impact of Islam? To what extent was Islam assimilated into African animism? Sources: J. Kritzeck and W. H. Lewis, eds., *Islam and Africa* (1969); M. Lombard, *The Golden Age of Islam* (1975).

Using Primary Sources

Have students compare the twelfth-century biographer William Fitzstephen's description of the city of London with al-Bakri's description of the city of Kumbi in the kingdom of Ghana. Have each student write a short paper comparing the two medieval cities.

Activities for Discovering the Past

I.   Classroom Discussion Suggestions

1. In what ways were European kingdoms more advanced than the Malian and Ghanaian kingdoms?
2. Why were the societies in Africa far in advance of the societies in pre-Columbian North America?
3. What role did Mansa Musa play in the development of Africa?
4. What kind of economic activity did the East African city-states engage in?
5. What was the role of women in African societies before 1400?

II.   Doing History

1. Have students read translations of primary accounts about the civilizations of Africa and America in the medieval period. Ask students to draw their own conclusions about those societies based on their readings of the sources, and have them discuss these conclusions in class. Sources: R. Oliver and C. Oliver, eds., *Africa in the Days of Exploration* (1965); E. J. Murphy, *History of African Civilization* (1972); B. Diaz, *The Conquest of New Spain* (1978).
2. Ask students to assume the character of one of the travelers (Ibn Battuta, Díaz, or others) from the sources listed above, and have them write a letter back home describing the places visited.

III.   Cooperative Learning Activities

Organize the class into three groups. Assign each group the task of researching and reporting on the judicial "systems" of England, France, and Ghana in the High and Later Middle Ages. One group should consult C. A. F. Meekings, *Crown Pleas of the Wiltshire Eyre 1249* for England. Another group should read N. Z. Davis's *Fiction in the Archives* (which interprets the French letters of remission). The third group should consult the Spanish Muslim geographer al-Bakri's *Description de l'Afrique Septentrionale* (1965). Each group should focus on the judicial systems: (1) how the alleged criminal is tried; (2) the type and severity of punishments for specific crimes. After students have completed their reading, analyzing, and discussion of the works, have each group make a presentation to the class.

Map Activity

Using the map on page 24 of the *Historical Atlas of the World,* have students list the following places and features on an outline map of Africa (IRM page 185):

1. Mediterranean Sea
2. Arabian Sea
3. Atlantic Ocean
4. Indian Ocean
5. Nile River
6. Congo River
7. Timbuktu
8. Gao
9. Atlas Mountains
10. Tagheze
11. Awlil
12. Kingdom of Mali
13. Awdaghost
14. Kingdom of Ghana
15. Nubia

Audiovisual Bibliography

1. *Africa.* (120 min. Color. Home Vision.)
2. *Africa: An Introduction.* (22 min. Color. BFA Educational Films.)
3. *Africa Calls: Its Drums and Musical Instruments.* (23 min. Color. Carousel Films and Video.)
4. *Africa—Chopi Village Life.* (17 min. Color. AIMS.)
5. *Africa: Historical Heritage.* (9 min. Color. Britannia Films.)
6. *African Carving: A Dogon Kanaga Mask.* (19 min. Color. Phoenix Films and Video.)
7. *Benin: An African Kingdom.* (Videodisc. 5 Discs. Each disc 15 min. Color. Films for the Humanities and Sciences.)
8. *Dance, Voodoo, Dance.* (Videodisc. Color. 15 min. Films for the Humanities and Sciences.)

CHAPTER 11

TRANSITION AND CHANGE IN ASIA, CA 320–1400

Instructional Objectives

After reading and analyzing this chapter, students should be able to explain what effect the mass migrations had on the traditional societies of Asia. Students should also be able to explain how new religions and cultural ideas were assimilated into the traditional societies of the east.

Chapter Outline

I. Indian, ca. 320–1400
   A. The founder of the Gupta Empire was Chandragupta.
      1. His son, Samudragupta, centralized the Gupta state.
      2. He ruled according to the idea of a just king (dharma).
      3. During Samudragupta's reign, India made contact with the Middle Eastern trade and culture.
      4. The Hun invasion ended the Gupta dynasty.
      5. The Gupta period was a golden age in literature and drama.
      6. Advances were made in mathematics and science.
   B. Daily Life
      1. Indian life stressed stability and tradition.
      2. Agricultural life dominated Indian society.
      3. Indian merchants held a respected place in society.
      4. A typical Indian village was organized into quarters: two main streets intersected at the center.
      5. The old caste system continued during the Gupta period.
      6. Education of boys of the aristocracy was based on religious initiation.
         a. Gurus taught boys the Veda.
         b. After their education, marriage came next for boys of the aristocracy.
      7. An Indian wife had two main duties, managing the household and producing children (preferably male).
   C. India and the Outside World
      1. Three groups pushed toward India.
         a. The Vietnamese settled on the east coast and were least influenced by Indian culture.
         b. The Thais lived to the west.
         c. The Burmans migrated in the eighth century.
      2. Foreign invaders swept into India.
      3. Muslim Arabs attacked the Indus Valley.
      4. The Turks eventually took the Punjab and the Valley of the Ganges.

5. The most lasting influence of the Muslim attack was religious.
6. Islam replaced Hinduism and Buddhism in the Indus Valley.
7. Buddhism was driven out of India, while Hinduism flourished.

II. China's Golden Age (580–ca. 1400)
   A. Buddhism comes to China.
      1. A wide variety of merchants, sailors, and others brought Buddhism from India.
      2. Chinese scholars were interested in Buddhist concepts.
      3. Buddhism's promise of eternal bliss appealed to many.
      4. China changed Buddhist concepts to conform to their way of life.
      5. Buddhism was incorporated into Chinese art.
   B. The Tang Dynasty (618–907)
      1. This dynasty was probably the greatest in Chinese history.
      2. Its founder was Tai Zong.
      3. Zong's land reforms benefited peasants.
      4. He organized China into departments.
      5. His bureaucracy gave China the world's most sophisticated political system.
      6. The Han method of the Mandarin system was revived.
      7. The Tang conquered Turkestan, allied Tibet with China, and spread Chinese culture throughout East Asia.
   C. The Song Dynasty (960–1279)
      1. After the fall of the Tang Dynasty, China was decentralized.
      2. Zhao Guangyin founded the Song Dynasty.
      3. The population increased to 100 million.
      4. Coal and iron production increased because of technological advances.
      5. Communications improved and trade increased.
      6. Gunpowder was invented.
      7. Scholarship flourished.
      8. Women suffered a decline in status.
      9. In 1126, the Jurchen drove the Song out of northern China.
      10. The Song Dynasty remained in the south, with its capital at Hangzhou.
   D. The Culture of the Tang and Song Dynasties
      1. Porcelain production flourished.
      2. Poetry became a medium of expression for the mandarins and Buddhist scholars.
         a. Tang poetry was formal in composition but humorous and emotional in subject.
      3. The invention of printing encouraged scholarly activity.
      4. Zhu Xi, the historian, explained how evil develops and how it can be corrected.
   E. The Mongol Conquest (1215–1368)
      1. Jenghiz Khan invaded northern China in 1215.
      2. He captured Beijing and all of northern China.
      3. Kublai Khan annexed southern China by 1279 and founded the Yuan Dynasty.
      4. The Mongols organized Chinese society into four classes: the Mongols, the foreign administrators, the northern Chinese, and the southern Chinese.
      5. Marco Polo's writings introduced Europeans to the East.
      6. By 1368, Hong Wu, a former monk, and his rebels had pushed the Mongols out of China.
      7. He established the Ming Dynasty and became its first emperor.

III. Japan
   A. The heart of Japan is its four major islands.
      1. Japan's climate ranges from subtropical to cold winters.
      2. The Korea Strait and the Sea of Japan protected the Japanese from outsiders.

B. The Yamato State
1. Agriculture dominated early Japanese society.
2. Japan was dominated by a warrior aristocracy.
3. The Yamato chieftain proclaimed himself emperor.
4. The Shinto religion emerged out of the Yamato hierarchy of gods at Honshu.
5. Buddhism came to Japan in 538.
6. The pro-Buddhist Japanese reformed the state based on Chinese practices.
7. Prince Shotoku was the main leader of the political reform.
8. He began a professional civil service.
C. The Heian Era (794–1185)
1. Buddhism thrived under the Tendai and Shingon sects.
2. Chinese writing was modified with the adoption of phonetic syllables.
3. This led to a literary flowering, including the writing of history and the birth of the novel.
4. The Heian era witnessed a decentralization of political power.
5. Using the samurai, the Taira and Minamoto clans defeated the emperor and established the Kamakura Shogunate in 1192.
6. The economic base of the samurai was the village and its land, the shoen.
D. The Kamakura Shogunate (1185–1333)
1. Yoritamo's victory over the emperor meant the establishment and power of feudalism.
2. The Bakufu (government) officials became hereditary.
3. Kublai Khan's armies invaded Japan but were defeated by the samurai.
4. The samurai came to dominate Japanese society for centuries.

Lecture Suggestions

1. "The More Things Change, the More They Are the Same: The Eternal Sameness of Daily Life in India." What was life like in an Indian village between 320 and 1400? How important were religion and schooling? Sources: A. L. Basham, *The Wonder That Was India* (1954); J. Auboyer, *Daily Life in Ancient India from 200 B.C. to 700* (1965).
2. "The Buddha in India and China." Lead students to a comparison of the impact of Buddhism in India and China. In what ways was the impact different—and similar? Sources: G. S. Pomerantz, "The Decline of Buddhism in India," 2 vols. (1959).

Using Primary Sources

Social Life Depicted in Indian Literature.
Have students read selected verse from medieval India and list the poets' views of social life: children, marriage, women, etc. Students might read *The Wonder that Was India* (trans. A. L. Basham, New York, 1954), and *Sutrakritanga* (in the above selection). After students compile their lists, a class period might be devoted to discussion of the social life of medieval India as portrayed in poetry.

Activities for Discovering the Past

I.   Classroom Discussion Suggestions

1.   In what ways did geography play an important role in India between 320 and 1400?
2.   Why were the Mongols unable to conquer Japan?
3.   How did Buddhism influence the religions of India, China, and Japan?
4.   How did the Mongols rule their conquered lands?
5.   By what kind of code did a samurai live?

II.   Doing History

1.   Suggest that students interview natives of India, Japan, and China, asking the natives to comment on the ways they were instructed in the history of their respective civilizations. Compile the interviewees' responses and use them for class discussions.
2.   How accurate is Samuel Taylor Coleridge's view of Mongol royalty and opulence in his classic poem "Xanadu"? Hand out copies of "Xanadu" to the students and read the poem in class. Discuss the poem, especially the elements concerning possible descriptions of Kublai Khan's ostentation. Next, distribute sections of Marco Polo's *The Travels of Marco Polo, The Venetian* (London, 1908), which describes Mongol civilization. Was Coleridge a good historian? Was Marco Polo? What other sources can students use to corroborate the work of Coleridge and Marco Polo?
3.   Have students compare the chivalric codes of the Japanese samurai and the warriors of Europe in the High Middle Ages. Sources: P. Duus, *Feudalism in Japan,* 2nd ed. (1976); R. Coulbourn, ed., *Feudalism in History* (1956), especially pp. 26–48.

III.   Cooperative Learning Activities

1.   Organize the class into three groups and assign them the task of organizing Indian, Chinese, and Japanese history from ca. 320–1400. Encourage them to focus on the following areas: social, political, scientific/technological, economic, and cultural areas. After they have completed research and organized the material, allow representatives from each subdivision of the groups (social, political, etc.) to meet with and discuss their respective area in India, China, and Japan with experts in the other two groups. After these discussions, allow the groups to present their findings in the class.
2.   Cooperative Learning Examination.
     At this juncture of the term, it might be a good idea to test the effectiveness of cooperative learning strategies. After administering a typical examination, you might follow that exam by giving a cooperative learning exam of the same material and give a group grade that can be averaged with the individual students' grades.

Map Activity

Using the map on pages 16–17 of the *Historical Atlas of the World,* have students list the following features on an outline map of Asia (IRM page 186):
1.   Green Sea
2.   Ganges River
3.   Indus River
4.   Himalayas Mountains
5.   Tibet

6. Samarkand
7. Baghdad
8. Lower Chenla
9. Nepal
10. Japan
11. Anhsi
12. Kashmir
13. Hangchow (Hangzhou)
14. Great Wall
15. Gobi Desert

Audiovisual Bibliography

1. *Asia: An Introduction.* (21 min. Color. BFA Educational Media.)
2. *China: The Golden Age.* (23 min. Color. Indiana University AV Center.)
3. *China: The Restoration.* (22 min. Color. Indiana University AV Center.)
4. *The Hindu World.* (10 min. Color. Coronet Films.)
5. *Hinduism: 330 Million Gods.* Parts 1 and 2. (26 min. each. Color. Time-Life Films.)
6. *The Great Wall of China: A Royal Geographic Society Electronic Guide.* (CD-ROM. National School Products.)
7. *Exotic Japan: A Guide to Japanese Culture and Language.* (CD-ROM. National School Products.)
8. *Astonishing Asia.* (CD-ROM. National School Products.)

CHAPTER 12

EUROPE IN THE EARLY AND HIGH MIDDLE AGES

Instructional Objectives

After reading and anyalyzing this chapter, students should be able to explain how Charlemagne acquired and governed his vast empire. After reading and studying this chapter, students should also be able to determine the accuracy of Adalberon of Laon's view of a tripartite division of society in the High Middle Ages. Students should also be able to discuss the nature of feudal society as it pertained to peasants, women, and other groups. Finally, students should be able to discuss how medieval rulers solved their problems of government, thereby laying the foundations of the modern state.

Chapter Outline

I. The early history of the Merovingians is the beginning point for Frankish history.
   A. The Coronation of Clovis was a turning point in early medieval history.

II. Charlemagne (768–814) was one of medieval Europe's greatest rulers.
   A. He established a powerful Frankish state.
      1. He continued the Carolingian tradition by building a large European kingdom.
      2. He checked Muslim advances by creating marches.
   B. He ruled the empire through a body of missi dominici, counts with hereditary power.
   C. He was crowned emperor on 25 December 800 by Pope Leo III.
      1. Charlemagne perpetuated Roman imperial ideas.
      2. He consciously identified with the new Rome of the Christian church.
   D. The Carolingian Renaissance was an intellectual awakening in medieval Europe.
      1. It was led by Alcuin of England.
      2. The Carolingian Renaissance was a revival of classical learning.
      3. It also fostered much needed monastic and educational reform.

III. The division of the empire led to instability and political chaos.
   A. In 843, Charlemagne's grandsons divided the empire into three kingdoms: West Franks, East Franks, and the Middle Kingdom.
      1. The huge empire had lacked an efficient bureaucracy.
      2. The division of the empire coincided with invasions of Carolingian lands by Magyars, Vikings, and Muslims.

IV. Feudalism became a way of life in the high Middle Ages. Although there were conditions of people outside of the feudal world order, contemporaries viewed a world of well-defined social classes, each with its role to play in the feudal scheme of things.

V. The three orders of feudal society composed the contemporary view of the world.
   A. Adalberon of Laon's view was similar to other writers of the eleventh century.
   B. Feudalism organized society into three social classes.
      1. "Those who fight" were the class of warriors (knights, miles, etc.).
      2. "Those who pray" were the monks, nuns, and priests.
      3. "Those who work" were the agricultural laborers (the many conditions of servitude).

VI. Those who work formed the largest group within feudal society.
   A. There were many conditions of servitude.
      1. Serfs often had to pay fees to their lords.
      2. Serfs were often tied to the land.
      3. Serfdom was a hereditary condition.
   B. Peasants owed obligations to their lord.
      1. Peasants tilled the lord's fields.
      2. The demesne of the manor was cultivated for the lord.
      3. The other part was held by the peasantry.
   C. Peasant religion was an important force in holding society together.
      1. Religion regulated daily life.
      2. The local church was the center of village social, religious, political and economic life.
      3. Peasants believed that God was ever-present in their affairs.
      4. The church granted indulgences to those who visited the shrines of great saints.
   D. Life on the manor was dull but secure.
      1. Peasant households consisted of a nuclear family.
      2. Women shared the agricultural duties with their husbands.
      3. Peasant diet included vegetables, fruits, beer, cheese, and occasionally meat or fish.

VII. Those who fight defended the other two classes in feudal society.
   A. Military prowess separated the warrior elite from the rest of society.
   B. Young nobles served a knightly apprenticeship before being knighted.
      1. A son of the nobility was a page beginning at about the age of seven.
      2. He then became an esquire when he learned the rules and techniques of war.
      3. Knighthood symbolized the end of formal training.
   C. The nobility, those who fight, exercised strong control over all aspects of medieval culture.
      1. The nobility was an elite class.
      2. Their function was to fight to protect the other two orders of society.
      3. The term knight connoted moral values and participation in a superior caste.

VIII. Those who pray constituted the religious community.
   A. The clergy and monastic community oversaw the spiritual existence of European Christians.
      1. Priests administered the seven sacraments to the Christian community.
      2. Literate priests were also scholars and teachers.
   B. Monasteries played a significant role in feudal society.
      1. Monasteries were houses of worship
      2. They were also educational institutions.
      3. Monasteries were also sometimes marketplaces.
      4. They served yet another function as cultural centers.
      5. They could also be banking establishments and economic corporations.

C. Monks and nuns provided many social and spiritual services.
    1. Monks provided a vital service in prayer.
    2. The daily life of monks revolved around the monastic liturgy.
    3. Monks were also teachers and scholars.
    4. Nuns performed a variety of social and spiritual duties, from religious activities to manual labor.
    5. Hildegard of Bingen represents the scholarly life of many nuns.
    6. The Cistercian order made many agricultural developments.

IX. Political revival in western Europe in the tenth and eleventh centuries returned a measure of stability to Western society.
  A. The Vikings were Christianized and assimilated into French culture.
    1. Normandy became a strong territory.
  B. Alfred's victory over the Danes in 878 slowly led to English unification.
    1. The Danish king Canute made England part of his Scandinavian empire.
  C. The nobles elected Hugh Capet dux Francorum in 987.
    1. This laid the foundation for political stability.
  D. The German king Otto halted the Magyar advance in 955 at the Lechfeld.
    1. Otto's power stemmed from his alliance with the church.
  E. There were numerous changes in population, climate, and mechanization.
    1. The population increased due to a decline in war and disease.
    2. A warmer climate made for improved agricultural production.
    3. The water mill was used on a more widespread basis.
    4. Windmills came into general use.

X. The Religious Reformation of the eleventh century also helped to revitalize Europe.
  A. Clerical abnormalities hurt the church's prestige in Europe.
    1. Simony, the buying and selling of church offices, was widespread.
    2. Pluralism, holding more than one church office at one time, also caused concern.
    3. Clerical marriage marred the celibate image of the church.
  B. Clerical reformers tried to reform the church.
    1. Leo IX made sweeping reforms.
    2. Urban II brought the crusades into the reforming program of the church.
    3. Gregory VII sought to increase the power of the papacy.

XI. Monastic reformers also played a role in the religious reformation of the period.
  A. Monastic orders aided in the general religious reformation.
    1. The Cluniac Order symbolized clerical celibacy and the suppression of simony.
    2. The Cistercians became models of piety and simplicity.

XII. The Investiture Controversy was a struggle for the mastery of medieval Europe.
  A. Gregory VII has come to symbolize the church's role in the controversy.
    1. He wanted the church to be free from lay control.
    2. He believed that the pope could hold kings accountable for their actions.
  B. Emperor Henry IV represented the lay community in the investiture struggle.
    1. He protested Gregory's position on lay investiture.
  C. Spiritual warfare brought the papacy greater prestige.
    1. Gregory excommunicated Henry IV.
    2. Henry IV finally invaded Rome in 1080.
    3. In 1122, the lay investiture controversy was settled at a conference at Worms.
  D. Innocent III's papal authority marked the zenith of the medieval church's power.
    1. Papal reform succeeded, but in the thirteenth and fourteenth centuries the papal bureaucracy became corrupt.

XIII. The Church's role in the Crusades reflected the church's influence in society.
    A. A crusade was a holy war against the Muslims to liberate the Holy Land.
        1. The Crusades gave kings the opportunity to rid their kingdoms of troublesome knights.
        2. Although successes were few, the Crusades attested to the renewed vigor of medieval Europe.
    B. There were eight crusades approved by the papacy between 1095 and 1270.
        1. Although somewhat successful, the First Crusade was marked by disputes among the leaders.
        2. Later crusades proved less successful.
        3. There were few recognizable results of the Crusades.

XIV. Medieval kingdoms in England, France, and Germany were the origins of modern European states.
    A. Anglo-Norman and Angevin kings organized England as a feudal state.
    B. Philip II and Louis IX formed a powerful kingdom in France by absorbing many smaller entities.
    C. Frederick I (Barbarossa) tried to bring recalcitrant German nobles under royal authority.

XV. A commercial revolution coincided with political stability.
    A. Trade and commerce were rejuvenated.
    B. The revitalization of towns and cities resulted from the increased political stability.

Lecture Suggestions

1. "Peasants in War." What role did peasants play in warfare? Were medieval armies made up entirely of mounted warriors from the nobility? Sources: J. Beeler, *Warfare in Feudal Europe, 730–1200* (1971); P. Contamine, *War in the Middle Ages* (1984); J. F. Verbruggen, *Warfare in Western Europe in the Middle Ages* (1957).
2. "Childhood in the Middle Ages." How were children treated by their parents? How was childhood as a developmental stage perceived in the Middle Ages? Sources: P. Ariès, *Centuries of Childhood: A Social History of Family Life* (English translation, 1962); D. Herlihy, *Medieval Households* (1985).
3. "Women's Health Care in Medieval Society." What was the state of the art of gynecology in the High Middle Ages? What did medieval physicians know about obstetrics? Sources: M. Labarge, *A Small Sound of the Trumpet: Women in Medieval Life* (1986); V. Bullough, *The Subordinate Sex* (1977); S. Rubin, *Medieval English Medicine* (1977); B. Rowland, *Medieval Women's Guide to Health* (1981).

Activities for Discovering the Past

I. Classroom Discussion Suggestions

1. What role did women of the nobility play?
2. What was life like in a medieval castle in the twelfth century?
3. Discuss the classes of people who did not fit neatly into the tripartite division of society envisioned by Adalberon of Laon.
4. Discuss infant mortality in the High Middle Ages.
5. What were the real accomplishments of the Carolingian Renaissance?

6. What was the impact of the incident at Canossa between Gregory VII and Henry IV?
7. What medieval legal ideas are still evident in modern Anglo-American law?

II. Doing History

1. Who was William Marshal? How is he an example of the existence of social mobility in the Middle Ages? Sources: G. Duby, *William Marshal: The Flower of Chivalry* (1985); J. Crosland, *William the Marshal* (1962); S. Painter, *William Marshal* (1933). Students should be asked to write a short paper on William Marshal's social climbing. They should also be asked to be on the lookout for any other examples of social mobility in the Middle Ages.
2. "Feudalism in England: When Did It Begin?" Some scholars argue that England became feudal after the Norman invasion in 1066; others suggest that it was feudal before 1066. Which view is correct? What is the evidence for such assertions? Sources: E. A. R. Brown, "The Tyranny of a Construct: Feudalism and Historians of Medieval Europe," *American Historical Review* 79 (1974), 1063–1088; F. Stenton, *The First Century of English Feudalism* (1932); R. A. Brown, *The Origins of English Feudalism* (1980); E. John, *Land Tenure in Early England* (1960).
3. Have students read pertinent selections from Andreas Capellanus's *The Art of Courtly Love*, the twelfth-century guide for the "compleat" noble lover. Students should take notes on the descriptions of interactions between lords and peasants, especially where the author suggests how the lord should treat a peasant. Their descriptions can serve as the basis of a class discussion and/or the beginning of a longer study of class relations in the High Middle Ages.

III. Cooperative Learning Activities

1. Organize your class into teams of knights who are participating in a medieval tournament (students may wish to consult J. R. V. Barker's *The Tournament in England, 1100–1400*, 1986). After researching the tournament, teams should discuss their respective nationalities (Normans, Angevins, English, Flemings, etc.), paying special attention to the arms, armor, and tournament formalities.
2. Using the team organization from Activity 1 above, have students write a "sports report" of a tournament. Teams should use the journalistic heuristic Who? What? When? Why? Where? Teams should share their newspaper reports with the class.
3. Magna Carta: Reactionary or Progressive?
   Have two student groups debate the above question. One team should research and debate the idea that Magna Carta was a reactionary document, designed to protect the traditional rights of the feudal nobility. The other team defends the idea that the Magna Carta was a progressive idea that eventually brought greater liberties to all classes of society. Allow the teams to stage their debate in class (teams may wish to consult W. L. Warren, *King John*, S. Painter, *The Reign of King John*, or other studies of the Magna Carta).

Map Activity

1. Using the map on page 10 of the *Historical Atlas of the World*, have students shade in the Kingdom of France in ca. 1140 on a blank outline map of Europe (IRM page 183). How would France look one hundred years later?
2. Using the map on page 8 of the *Historical Atlas of the World*, have students trace the routes of the barbarians on an outline map of Europe.

Audiovisual Bibliography

1. *The Medieval Manor*. (22 min. Color. Encyclopaedia Britannica Films.)
2. *The Medieval Mind*. (24 min. Color. The Humanities Series.)
3. *Medieval Society: The Villagers*. (11 min. Color. Coronet Films.)
4. *The Lion in Winter*. (131 min. Color. Films, Ltd.)
5. *The Middle Ages: Rise of Feudalism*. (Videodisc. Color. 20 min. Britannica Videos.)
6. *Time Traveler CD*. (CD-ROM. Society for Visual Education, Inc.)
7. *The Story of the Carol*. (Videodisc. Color. 52 mins. Films for the Humanities and Sciences.)
8. *Charlemagne: Unifier of Europe*. (Videodisc. Color. 13 min. Britannica Videos.)
9. *The Vatican: Fortress of Christianity*. (Videodisc. Color. 29 min. Films for the Humanities and Sciences.)
10. *Venice: Economic Power in the Middle Ages*. (Videodisc. Color. 19 min. Britannica Videos.)

CHAPTER 13

CREATIVITY AND CRISIS IN THE CENTRAL AND LATER MIDDLE AGES

Instructional Objectives

After reading and studying this chapter, students should be able to explain how universities, the Gothic cathedrals, and troubadour poetry evolved and what they reveal about medieval ideals and society. Then, students should be able to explain the process that brought the Black Death to Europe and how this disease spread throughout Europe in the later Middle Ages. Students should also be able to discuss the role of Dante, Chaucer, and Villon in the transition from Latin to vernacular languages and literature. Finally, students should be able to list factors in the demise of the later medieval Catholic Church.

Chapter Outline

I. The Central and Later Middle Ages witnessed a cultural and artistic renaissance.
  A. The university is one of medieval Europe's great gifts to civilization.
    1. Before the university, only monasteries and cathedrals existed.
    2. The first universities were at Bologna and Salerno in Italy.
    3. The cathedral school at Notre Dame in Paris became an international center of learning.
  B. Instruction and curriculum
    1. The scholastic method was used in the university.
    2. Scholastic philosophers dealt with many theological issues.
    3. The standard method of teaching was the lecture accompanied by a gloss, or interpretation.
  C. Gothic art symbolized the great cultural revival.
    1. After 1000, church construction increased dramatically.
    2. Bishops, the nobility, and the commercial classes supported cathedral construction.
    3. Cathedrals served many purposes.
    4. Tapestry-making and drama were first used to convey spiritual messages.

II. The waning of the Middle Ages witnessed disease, war, and death.
  A. The Black Death wrought havoc in Europe in the fourteenth century.
    1. Poor harvest led to famines in the years 1315–1317 and 1321.
    2. Diseases killed many people and animals.
    3. Genoese ships brought the bubonic plague to Europe in 1347.

4. The bubonic form of the disease was transmitted by rats; the pneumonic form was transmitted by people.
5. The disease continued to cause destruction as late as 1700.
B. The Black Death had many consequences.
   1. The plague was most disastrous among the poor.
   2. The disease caused widespread suffering and devastation.
   3. Priests, nuns, and monks were especially vulnerable since they ministered to the sick.
   4. The danse macabre and other gloomy artistic motifs reflected the pessimism of the times.

III. The Hundred Years' War (1337–1453) added to the gloom of the period.
   A. This struggle between England and France added to misery of the age.
   B. England's multifaceted army of warriors and yeoman archers carried the day in the first phase of the war.
      1. Crecy highlighted the new weapons of the English, the longbow and the cannon.
      2. Poitiers (1356) was also an English victory.
      3. Agincourt (1415) was the last major English victory of the war.
   C. Joan of Arc played a significant role in the ultimate French victory.
      1. She provided inspiration for the French.
      2. The French persisted and drove the English out of France.

IV. A transformation in literature was an important trend during this period.
   A. Dante Alighieri, in *The Divine Comedy*, portrayed a symbolic pilgrimage through Hell, Purgatory, and Paradise.
      1. His work embodies the psychological tensions of the age.
      2. The work contains bitter criticism of some church authorities.
   B. Geoffrey Chaucer's *The Canterbury Tales* painted a gallery of English people, focusing on their materialistic interests.
   C. Francois Villon's *Grand Testament* used the language of the lower classes.
      1. He portrayed reality, beauty, and hardship of life on earth.
   D. Vernacular dialects began to find their way into literature.
      1. The use of vernacular dialects reflected a growing national consciousness.

V. The loss of the church's prestige was symptomatic of the age.
   A. The church came under fire because of substantial corruption.
   B. Reformers argued for major changes.
      1. John Wyclif attacked papal authority and called for reform of the church.
      2. John Hus spread Wyclif's ideas to Bohemia.
   C. The Babylonian Captivity (1309–1377) was a major source of irritation.
      1. The church became a tool of the French monarchy.
      2. The pope had lived at Avignon since the reign of King Philip the Fair of France.
      3. The Babylonian Captivity badly damaged papal prestige.
      4. Pope Gregory IX moved the papacy back to Rome in 1377.
   D. The Great Schism (1378–1417)
      1. Two popes claimed to be legitimate.
      2. England and France recognized different popes.
      3. The Great Schism weakened the religious faith of many of the faithful.
   E. The conciliar movement advocated reform by a church council.
      1. Church councils with power superior to that of the pope were introduced.
      2. Marsiglio of Padua had argued that authority within the church resided with a council, not the pope.

3. The council of Constance (1414–1418) ended the schism.

VI. The life of the people
  A. Marriage usually came at age 16 or 18 for women and later for men.
    1. Legalized prostitution existed in urban areas.
    2. Economic factors usually prompted marriage.
    3. Divorce did not exist in this society.
  B. The parish was the center of daily life.
    1. Sports such as bullbaiting and bearbaiting, and drunkenness reflected the teeming violence of the age.
  C. Fur-collar crime was prolific.
    1. Nobles returning from war resorted to crime.
    2. Extortion and kidnapping by the upper classes were widespread.
    3. Outlaws were sought for protection when the governments failed.
VII. Peasant unrest escalated in this period.
  A. The Peasant Revolt of 1381 (England) resulted from the lord's attempt to freeze wages.
    1. Actually, peasants were better off in this period.
    2. Many revolts were due to rising expectations.
  B. The Jacquerie (France) revolted in France in 1358, 1363, 1380, and 1420.
    1. Most were ruthlessly put down.
  C. Similar incidents in Spain and Italy attest to the unrest of the period.
    1. In Italy, the ciompi (workers) revolted.

Lecture Suggestions

1. "The Black Death and Other Diseases and Their Impact on History." What was the lasting importance of the Black Death? Has its significance been overrated? What other diseases have had the potential to change civilization? Can the AIDS epidemic turn the late twentieth century into a period like the later Middle Ages? Sources: W. H. McNeill, *Plagues and Peoples* (1976); R. S. Gottfried, *The Black Death* (1983).
2. "Common Folk in the Fourteenth and Fifteenth Centuries." How did the common folk live in this time of transition? What was their view of what was going on at the top? Sources: J. Keegan, *The Face of Battle* (1977); D. W. Robertson, *Chaucer's London* (1968).
3. "Living on the Legal Fringe of Society." What was life like for the person living outside the law in later medieval society? Sources: M. Keen, *The Outlaws of Medieval Legend* (1961); P. Dale, trans., *The Poems of Villon* (1973); J. G. Bellamy, "The Coterel Gang: An Anatomy of a Band of Fourteenth Century Criminals," *English Historical Review* 79 (October 1964), 698–717.

Using Primary Sources

Read (or reread) the selection from *The Rule of Saint Francis* (1223) in the "Primary Sources" section of this manual. Write a short paper in which you attempt to answer the following: What kind of monk was an ideal Franciscan? Discuss (and/or read) papers in class. How did the Franciscans differ from other monastic communities such as the Benedictines or Cistercians?

Activities for Discovering the Past

I. Classroom Discussion Suggestions

1. How did medieval physicians explain the Black Death?
2. How was the Conciliar Movement a threat to papal power?
3. What were the causes of the Hundred Years' War?
4. Why did parliamentary development take different paths in France, Italy, and Spain?
5. Who were the medieval troubadours?

II. Doing History

1. If slides are available, show students the work of Hieronymous Bosch, especially the famous "Garden of Earthly Delights." How does Bosch's work reflect the flavor of the later Middle Ages?
2. Make available to students selections from the letters of the Paston family. Allow students time to read and analyze them. Then have students write short papers describing daily life in the late medieval period, based on the information they find in the letters. Sources: R. Barber, ed., *The Pastons: Letters of a Family in the Wars of the Roses* (1984).
3. What kinds of activities did later medieval people engage in for pleasure? Did the gloom and doom of the later Middle Ages keep people from having leisure time? Have students read and analyze selections from Chaucer and Villon and write short papers describing the leisure activity of common folk. Sources: N. Coghill, trans., *Chaucer's Canterbury Tales* (1977); P. Dale, trans., *The Poems of Villon* (1973).
4. Scholars still debate who Robin Hood was, whether he really existed, and where and when he lived if he really did exist. Encourage students to read some of the debates in the following sources as the basis for a class discussion and/or the writing of a short paper. Sources: M. Keen, "Robin Hood—Peasant or Gentleman?" *Past and Present* 19 (April 1961), 17–18; J. C. Holt, *Robin Hood* (1982).

III. Cooperative Learning Activities

1. Organize the class into teams charged with reading and performing (in class) one of the tales in Chaucer's *Canterbury Tales*. Each team might include a director, a scriptwriter, a set designer, costume designer, and actors. The plays of the tales might be set in fourteenth-century England or in more modern times.
2. Images of Joan of Arc
   Have students reread the section in the text on Joan of Arc, pages 381–382. Organize the class into teams of six each. Have each team write a team description of Joan. One team might write a short biographical sketch; another might draw a picture of her; another might write an editorial; still another might create a movie poster. After completing the assignment, students should share their interpretations with the class.
3. Organize your class into teams of knights who are participating in a medieval tournament (students may wish to consult J. R. V. Barker's *The Tournament in England, 1100–1400* [1986]). After researching the tournament, teams should discuss their respective nationalities (Normans, Angevins, English, Flemings, etc.), paying special attention to the arms, armor, and tournament formalities. Then, have students write a "sports report" of a tournament (either a real one they read about in the sources or one that they have created). Teams should use the journalistic heuristic: Who? What? When? Why? Where? Teams should share their newspaper reports with the class.

Map Activity

1. Use Map 13.1 in the text to list "plague cities" on an outline map of Europe (IRM page 183):
   Durham
   London
   Calais
   Paris
   Montpellier
   Aragon
   Cologne
   Würzburg
   Milan
   Naples
   Seville
   Messina
   Erfurt
   Hamburg
   Strasbourg
2. Using the map on page 12 of the *Historical Atlas of the World*, have students shade in the territory of the Kingdom of France and the Holy Roman Empire on a blank outline map of Europe.

Audiovisual Bibliography

1. *Hundred Years' War: Parts I and II.* (60 min. Color. Icarus Films.)
2. *Joan of Arc.* (100 min. Color. Sierra Pictures–Video America.)
3. *Chaucer.* (28 min. Color. Films for the Humanities and Sciences.)
4. *Christians, Jews, and Moslems in Medieval Spain.* (33 min. Color. Films for the Humanities and Sciences.)
5. *The Name of the Rose.* (100 min. Color. Films, Ltd.)
6. *Civilization: The Great Thaw.* Parts I and II. (26 min. each. Color. Time-Life Films.)
7. *Brother Felix and the Virgin Saint.* (Videodisc. Color. 78 min. Films for the Humanities and Sciences.)
8. *Europe Alive Guidisc.* (CD-ROM. Learning Services.)

CHAPTER 14

THE AMERICAS BEFORE EUROPEAN INTRUSION, CA 400–1500

Instructional Objectives

After reading and analyzing this chapter, students should be able to discuss how the geography of the Americas affected the lives of the peoples. Then, students should be able to delineate patterns of social and political organization that the Amerindian peoples developed before the coming of the Europeans. Finally, students should be able to explain the significant cultural achievements of the Mayas, Aztecs, and Incas.

Chapter Outline

I. The Geography and Peoples of the Americas
   A. Together, North and South America stretches for about 11,000 miles in length.
      1. A mountain range from Alaska to the tip of South America provides rugged terrain on the west coast of both continents.
      2. Mesoamerica is dominated by high plateaus and bounded by coastal plain.
      3. Central America is characterized by jungle, heavy rainfall, and heat.
      4. South America is a continent of varied terrain.
      5. The Amazon River bisects the north-central part of the continent.
   B. Immigrants crossed the Bering Straits as long as 20,000 years ago.
      1. These immigrants spread out to form diverse linguistic and cultural groups.
      2. By ca. 2500 B.C., they had learned how to domesticate plants and became skilled in agriculture.

II. Mesoamerican Civilizations
   A. The Olmec civilization (ca. 1500 B.C.–A.D. 300) was the first Mesoamerican civilization.
      1. Subsequent societies built on the Olmec foundation.
      2. A hereditary elite governed the mass of workers.
      3. The Great Pyramid at La Venta was the center of the Olmec religious cult.
   B. The Maya of Central America
      1. Between A.D. 300 and 900, the Maya of Central America built one of the world's most advanced cultures.
      2. The first Maya immigrated from North America.
      3. Its economic base was agriculture; trade between cities evolved.
      4. The nobility controlled the land and acted as warriors, merchants, and priests.
      5. Maya hieroglyphic writings have been deciphered.
      6. The Maya invented a calendar and devised a form of mathematics.

7. They also made advances in astronomy and wrote books of history.
C. Toltec Civilization
   1. People from the Mexico Valley built the city of Teotihuacan, which reached a population of over 200,000.
   2. The inhabitants were organized into the hereditary elite and ordinary workers.
   3. Teotihuacan society collapsed before invaders in ca. A.D. 700.
D. The Toltec confederation gained strength, assimilated with the Teotihuacan people, and attempted to preserve the latter's culture.
   1. Under Toliptzin, or Quetzalcoatl, the Toltecs came to control most of central Mexico from coast to coast.
   2. Drought, weak rulers, and invasions brought trouble to the Toltecs.
   3. The last of the Chichimec invaders were the Aztecs who absorbed the Olmec-Teotihuacan-Toltec culture.

III. Aztec Society
A. The Aztecs founded a city on the swamps of Lake Texcoco in 1325.
   1. By the time of Cortés in 1519, the Aztecs controlled all of central Mexico.
   2. The Aztecs attributed their success to their god Huitzilopochtli.
B. War and Human Sacrifice Characterized Aztec Society.
   1. War was endemic.
   2. Victim-gladiators were sacrificed to the sun god.
C. The Life of the People
   1. The early Aztecs made no sharp social distinctions.
   2. A legendary Toltec king fathered a noble class.
   3. At the time of Spanish intervention, warriors controlled the state.
   4. Provincial governors functioned much like feudal lords in medieval Europe.
   5. The maceualti, or working class, made up the backbone of society.
   6. The thalmaitl were landless workers.
   7. The emperor was selected by a small group of priests and warriors.
   8. The emperor lived in great luxury.
   9. Tenochtitlan was one of the largest cities in the world at the time of Díaz.

IV. The Incas of Peru
A. Inca civilization was established in the fertile valleys of highland Peru.
   1. The Incas built terraces along the mountain slopes to cultivate white potatoes.
   2. They also cultivated corn.
   3. Inca farms could support a large number of warriors and industrial workers.
B. Inca Imperialism and Society
   1. The Incas believed in their divine origin from their earliest king, Manco Capac.
   2. The king Pachacuti Inca and his son, Topa Inca, began the imperialistic ventures of the Incas.
   3. They extended Inca hegemony to modern Ecuador and Colombia and to the Maule River in the south.
   4. The ayllu, or clan, was the main unit of Inca society.
   5. The chief, or curacas, of the clan conducted relations with the outside world.
   6. Peasants were required to work for the lords and the state.
   7. Marriage was required of all.
   8. Polygamy was common.
   9. Inca society had several socialist characteristics.

Lecture Suggestions

1. "Everyday Life Among the Aztecs." How did the Aztecs live? What was a typical day like for the average person? Source: J. Soustelle, *Daily Life of the Aztecs on the Eve of the Spanish Conquest* (1970).
2. "Incas and Aztecs: Similarities and Differences." In what ways were the Incas and Aztecs alike and how did they differ? Sources: N. Davies, *The Aztecs Until the Fall of Tula* (1977); L. Baudin, *A Socialist Empire: The Incas of Peru* (1961).

Using Primary Sources

Have students compare the primary source description of the Toltec chieftain Toliptzin (ca. 980–1000) found in I. Bernal's *Mexico Before Cortes: Art, History, and Legend* (New York, 1975) with Einhard's description of the Frankish king Charlemagne (768–814). Have students write short papers in which they use the primary sources to compare the two rulers.

Activities for Discovering the Past

I.   Classroom Discussion Suggestions

1. Why did the Aztecs perform blood sacrifices?
2. Discuss the European conquerors Cortés and Pizarro.
3. What traces of Toltec civilization can be seen in Aztec civilization?
4. How effective a ruler was Montezuma?

II.   Doing History

1. Have students compare the Mayan calendar with our own and with the Julian calendar. Sources: J. Soustelle, *Daily Life of the Aztecs on the Eve of the Spanish Conquest* (1970); N. Lewis and M. Reinhold, *Roman Civilization: The Republic* (1966).
2. Have students read excerpts from Bernal Diaz del Castillo's *The Conquest of New Spain* (1978). Then have them write a paper in which they tell the same story from the point of view of an Aztec.

III.   Cooperative Learning Activities

1. Organize the class into five groups. Assign each group the task of researching and reporting on: (1) Olmecs, (2) Toltecs, (3) Mayas, (4) Aztecs, and (5) Incas. Each group should focus on social and political organization, religion, the economy, recreation/art, and technology.
2. As a followup to the above activity (and before the groups have made presentations to the rest of the class), allow the "experts" on social/political organization, religion, the economy, recreation/art, and technology to meet with the experts from each group. After sharing their information, have them return to their original groups to discuss what they have learned from the other groups' experts. After debriefing the experts on each of the five areas of investigation, each group should make a presentation to the class.
3. As a third activity, have each group construct charts about the five areas of their Amerindian societies. They should use the charts as visual aids in their presentations.

Map Activity

Using the maps on page 31 of the *Historical Atlas of the World*, have students list the following on an outline map of the Americas (IRM page 187):

1. Yucatan Peninsula
2. Uxmal
3. Caribbean Sea
4. Bay of Compeche
5. Isthmus of Panama
6. Andes Mountains
7. Amazon River
8. Atlantic Ocean
9. Pacific Ocean
10. Tenochtitlan
11. Teotihuacan
12. Gulf of Mexico
13. Cuba
14. Hispaniola
15. Jamaica

Audiovisual Bibliography

1. *Francisco Pizarro.* (30 min. Color. Time-Life Films.)
2. *Cortez and the Legend.* Parts I and II. (26 min. each. Color. McGraw-Hill Films.)
3. *Christopher Columbus.* (30 min. Color. Time-Life Films.)
4. *1492: Conquest of Paradise.* (137 min. Color. Films. Ltd.)
5. *The Search for the First Americans.* (Videodisc. 60 min. Color. Films for the Humanities and Sciences.)
6. *Ice Age Crossings.* (Videodisc. 28 min. Color. Films for the Humanities and Sciences.)
7. *Cannibals.* (Videodisc. 28 min. Color. Films for the Humanities and Sciences.)
8. *Before Columbus: Native Americans Tell Their Story.* (Videodisc. 6 Discs. Each disc 26–29 min. Films for the Humanities and Sciences.)
9. *Let's Visit South America.* (CD-ROM. National School Products.)

CHAPTER 15

EUROPEAN SOCIETY IN THE AGE OF THE RENAISSANCE AND REFORMATION

Instructional Objectives

After reading and studying this chapter, students should be able to discuss the meanings of the term *renaissance*. Students should also be able to compare the significant features of the so-called Italian Renaissance with other renaissances, such as the Carolingian and Twelfth-Century Renaissances. Students then should be able to explain how the Italian Renaissance affected politics, the economy, and society. Then, students should be able to elaborate on the evolution of medieval kingdoms into early modern nation-states, the spread of Renaissance humanism northward, and the effects of the Wars of the Roses. Finally, students should be able to discuss the historical context of the Protestant Reformation of the sixteenth century and explain Protestantism's impact on Western society.

Chapter Outline

I. The period known as the Renaissance coincided with the decline of medieval European civilization. It was both a political and economic movement as well as a cultural and artistic one.
    A. Origins
        1. The Renaissance was a period of commercial, financial, political, and cultural awakening, first in Italy and then in northern Europe.
        2. The northern Italian cities led a commercial renewal; especially cities such as Venice, Genoa, and Milan.
    B. The influence of communes and republics
        1. Northern Italian cities were called communes, usually associations of men seeking independence from local lords.

II. The Renaissance constituted many intellectual hallmarks.
    A. Petrarch viewed the fourteenth century as a positive break from the so-called Dark Ages, a period celebrating the return to the culture of ancient Rome.
    B. Individualism was one of the hallmarks of the Renaissance.
        1. Literature of the period was concerned with the individual and his role in the cosmos.
        2. Renaissance people seemed to have had an abiding belief in the individual.
    C. The revival of Antiquity was another hallmark of the Renaissance.
        1. Italians copied the ancient Roman way of life.
        2. Renaissance scholars studied the classics.

3. Humanism evolved as scholars sought to reconcile pagan literature with Christian thought.

D. A secular spirit emerged in the Renaissance.

1. Secularism refers to an emphasis upon materialistic things.

E. Art and artists were highlights of the Renaissance.

1. The *quattrocento* and the *cinquecento* were periods of brilliant artistic achievement.

2. The style of art changed in the fifteenth century.

III. Social effects of the Renaissance

A. Changes in education and political thought were marked.

1. Castiglione's *The Book of the Courtier* described the ideal "Renaissance Man."

B. Political theories emerged in this period.

1. Machiavelli's *The Prince* described how a ruler might acquire and maintain power.

C. The invention of movable type had a profound impact on European society.

1. Printing encouraged a wider common identity.

D. Women's roles reflected the impact of the Renaissance.

1. The status of upper-class women declined during the period of the Renaissance.

2. Poverty caused an increase in infanticide and child abandonment.

IV. The Italian Renaissance influenced a northern Renaissance.

A. The northern Renaissance stressed social reform.

1. Humanists sought to create a more perfect world.

2. Erasmus is probably the best representative of the Christian humanist.

B. Northern Renaissance art was more religious than its Italian counterpart.

1. Van Eyck painted detailed realistic works.

2. Bosch used religion and folk legends as themes.

3. Brueghel the Elder focused on the lives of ordinary people.

V. Politics and Renaissance statecraft reflected significant changes in Europe.

A. The "new" monarchs exercised considerable authority.

1. These rulers were interested in the centralization of power and authority.

2. Many seemed to act according to Machiavelli's principles.

B. France ushered in an age of recovery after the Hundred Years' War.

1. Charles VII expelled the English.

2. He made the state superior to the church.

C. In England, the Wars of the Roses created political and social problems.

1. The wars, fought between 1455 and 1471, were a civil war between the houses of York and Lancaster.

2. The English parliament continued to gain power in its struggle with the crown.

D. The marriage of Ferdinand and Isabella unified Spain.

1. Their policy was to expel Arabs and Jews and to Christianize Spain.

VI. The continued decline of the medieval church fostered an age of reform.

A. The Babylonian Captivity and the Great Schism hurt the church's prestige.

1. Critics of the church wanted moral and spiritual reform.

B. New organizations were formed to minister to the poor.

1. The Brethren of the Common Life lived simply and sought to make religion a personal experience.

2. *The Imitation of Christ* by Thomas à Kempis encouraged Christians to seek a simple life.

VII. Martin Luther spearheaded the reform of the sixteenth century.
    A. Luther was a monk and a professor who was seeking personal salvation.
        1. He believed that faith was central to Christianity and the only way to salvation.
    B. Luther's reforming ideas were summed up in his *Ninety-Five Theses*.
    C. Protestant thought was described in the Confessions of Augsburg.

VIII. The Spread of the Reformation
    A. John Calvin's beliefs were a significant part of the Reformation.
        1. Calvin believed that he was selected by God to reform the church.
        2. His *Institutes of the Christian Religion* detailed his ideas about the omnipotence of God, predestination, and the relative insignificance of humanity.
    B. Groups like the Anabaptists spread their version of Christianity.
        1. They believed in adult baptism, pacifism, and separation of church and state.
        2. Their beliefs were considered revolutionary and they were severely punished.

IX. The Reformation in England culminated in a long period of attempted reform.
    A. Wyclif and Tyndale were two English reformers who paved the way for Protestantism in England.
        1. The wealth of the clergy and the belief in the Scriptures in English were two ideas of the early reformers.
    B. Henry VIII's desire for a divorce initiated reform in the sixteenth century.
        1. Henry became head of the church of England.
        2. He dissolved the monasteries and confiscated their lands.

X. The Catholic Church attempted its own reforms by creating a new religious zeal for Catholicism.
    A. The movement within the church started as a reaction to the Protestant movement.
    B. New religious orders resulted from the attempted reform within the church.
        1. The Society of Jesus played an important role in resisting Protestant gains.

Lecture Suggestions

1. "Was the Renaissance So Light and Were the Middle Ages So Dark?" Although the view that the Middle Ages was a period of Gothic gloom between the lights of antiquity and the Italian Renaissance has been modified somewhat, the attitude that the Italian Renaissance was a burst of light out of the medieval darkness persists. Why is that so? Who began this tradition? What contrary views have been put forward? Sources: J. Burckhardt, *The Civilization of the Renaissance in Italy* (1951); J. Huizinga, *The Waning of the Middle Ages* (1933).

2. "Games Children Played in the Renaissance." What was a child's life like during the Renaissance? Was it very much different from that of a medieval child? How can we know what games and activities children engaged in at this time? Source: Pieter Brueghel the Elder, "Children's Games." If slides depicting Renaissance games are available, discuss the kinds of games that Renaissance children played.

3. "Getting an Education in the Renaissance." What were the Renaissance ideas about education and schooling? Were they superior to medieval educational ideas? Were women afforded educational opportunities? Is the idea that literacy increased significantly in the Renaissance accurate? Sources: P. F. Grendler, *Schooling in Renaissance Italy: Literacy and Learning, 1300–1600* (1989); J. H. Moran, *The Growth of English Schooling, 1340–1548: Learning, Literacy, and Laicization in Pre-Reformation York Diocese* (1985); J. Kelly-Gadol,

"Did Women Have a Renaissance?" in R. Bridenthal and C. Koonz, eds., *Becoming Visible: Women in European History* (1977), 137–161.

4.   "Women and the Reformation: How Did Their Roles Change?" S. M. Wyntjes, "Women in the Reformation Era," in R. Bridenthal and C. Koonz, eds., *Becoming Visible: Women in European History* (1977); S. Ozment, *When Fathers Ruled: Family Life in Reformation Europe* (1983); M. Wiesner, *Women in the Sixteenth Century: A Bibliography* (1983).

Using Primary Sources

1.   Have students read pertinent selections of Castiglione's *The Book of the Courtier*. Have them list the qualities described in the book for the ideal "Renaissance Man." Then, ask them to write a short paper on how the term "Renaissance Man" is interpreted today.

2.   Read the selections from Machiavelli and Luther in the "Primary Sources" section of this manual. Have students list the similarities and differences in their works. Discuss specific passages in class. Finally, have students write a short paper on how both Machiavelli and Luther represented the new order of the sixteenth century.

Activities for Discovering the Past

I.   Classroom Discussion Suggestions

1.   Discuss the impact of the *reconquista* in Spain.
2.   What was the impact of the Spanish Inquisition?
3.   How was Machiavelli's *The Prince* a product of its time?
4.   Was there a noticeable change in the way whites viewed blacks in the Renaissance compared with the Middle Ages?
5.   According to Castiglione, how was a person to become educated?
6.   Why did Protestantism and capitalism complement each other?
7.   What were Luther's views on marriage and sexuality?
8.   What role did the printing press play in the Protestant Reformation?

II.   Doing History

1.   What did Renaissance artists think of their world and themselves? Did they seem to think that they were living in a new golden age? Encourage students to read selections from the following sources and to write a short biographical sketch of one of the artists. Sources: B. Burroughs, ed., *Visari's Lives of the Artists* (1946); *Memoirs of Benvenuto Cellini: A Florentine Artist; Written by Himself* (1927); G. Bull, trans., *Aretino: Selected Letters* (Penguin edition, 1976).

2.   Was there a dramatic increase in literacy among all social classes during the Renaissance? Was it possible that there had been preconditions for increased literacy in medieval Europe before Gutenberg's movable type? After a class discussion of this topic, students should be asked to read passages from the following sources and consider the arguments of both. They might then be asked to write a short paper on literacy in early modern European society and its impact. Sources: M. T. Clanchy, *From Memory to Written Record* (1979); E. L. Eisenstein, *The Printing Press as an Agent of Change: Communications and Cultural Transformations in Early Modern Europe*, 2 vols. (1979).

3.   How did views of human sexuality change in the Renaissance? Were there problems associated with sexual deviancy in this period? Students should be encouraged to read some of the following selections as the basis for a discussion on Renaissance sexuality. Sources:

G. Ruggiero, "Sexual Criminality in Early Renaissance Venice, 1338–1358," *Journal of Social History* 8 (Spring 1975), 18–31; G. Ruggiero, *Violence in Early Renaissance Venice* (1980); R. C. Trexler, "Infanticide in Florence: New Sources and First Results," *History of Childhood Quarterly* 1:1 (Summer 1973); J. C. Brown, *Immodest Acts: The Life of a Lesbian Nun in Renaissance Italy* (1985).

4. Have students read Erik Erikson's pioneering study *Young Man Luther* (1962) as an introduction to the psychohistorical approach. This can lead to a class discussion of the uses of psychohistory and to a discussion of other psychohistorical works on other historical characters.

III. Cooperative Learning Activities

1. This activity is based on a cooperative learning idea by Cohen, Lotan, and Whitcomb "Complex Instruction in the Untracked Social Studies Classroom"; see Stahl, *Cooperative Learning in the Social Studies Classroom* in Suggested Reading under "Using Cooperative Learning in the Western Civilization Class." The authors call their method "Complex Instruction." In this method, the instructor creates activity cards for teams of students. The teams get their assignment cards and complete the assignments (much of the assignment is completed in class). The cards include chunks of material related to a larger subject—in this case, the Italian Renaissance. One card might include the problem of primary sources: "How Do Historians Know About the Italian Renaissance?" The team with this card provides the historiographical and primary source foundation for the chapter or unit on the Italian Renaissance. Another card contains questions on representative works of art. Another one includes questions on significant lives of the period. Still another asks students to answer questions on specific political, economic, and social problems of the period under investigation. As the authors of this idea state, " . . . it's the process of talking and working that produces the learning gains."

2. What is/was a Renaissance?
   To further clarify the term *renaissance*, organize students into teams and have each team explore a specific historical/artistic/literary renaissance: (1) Carolingian, (2) Twelfth-Century, (3) Italian, (4) Northern European, (5) Weimar, (6) Harlem. How has the term renaissance been used by historians, art historians, journalists, and others? How has the term been misapplied or even abused? Teams should present their reports on the various renaissances. Then, students should write papers analyzing the term.

3. Music of the Age
   Have student teams check out Reformation music from the university or college library. Each team selects a piece by composers such as Buxtehude, Pachebel, Boh, and Bach. Each team plays a selection for the class and reads or explains how they think the particular composition expresses the mood of the age.

4. Prosopography of the Reformation
   Have student teams select a specific reformer and focus research on the reformer's "power supports," his political, social, and financial backers—in essence, the networks to which he belonged that helped him make his voice heard. Teams might select Luther, Calvin, Zwingli, and Knox, among others.

Map Activity

1. Using Map 15.1 in the text, list the following on an outline map of Italy (IRM page 188):
   Duchy of Savoy
   Duchy of Milan
   Republic of Genoa

        Duchy of Modena
        Republic of Florence
        Republic of Siena
        Papal States
        Kingdom of Naples
        Corsica
        Sardinia
        Kingdom of Sicily

2. Using the map on page 13 of the *Historical Atlas of the World,* have students list the locations of schools of art, printing presses, and libraries on a blank outline map of Europe (IRM page 183).

3. Using the map on page 15 of the *Historical Atlas of the World,* have students shade in the dominions of the Spanish and Austrian Habsburgs on a blank outline map of Europe.

Audiovisual Bibliography

1. *Leonardo: To Know How to See.* (55 min. Color. National Gallery of Art.)
2. *Michelangelo: The Last Giant.* (67 min. Color. NBC News–CRM McGraw-Hill.)
3. *Boccacio: Tales from the Decameron.* (71 min. Color. Films for the Humanities and Sciences.)
4. *Chambord and the Renaissance.* (26 min. Color. Films for the Humanities and Sciences.)
5. *François I.* (22 min. Color. Films for the Humanities and Sciences.)
6. *The Age of the Medici.* (52 min. Color. Films, Inc.)
7. *Venice: Economic Power in the Middle Ages.* (Videodisc. Color. 19 min. Britannica Videos.)
8. *The Struggle for the Mediterranean in the Sixteenth Century.* (Videodisc. Color. 33 min. Britannica Videos.)
9. *The Return of Martin Guerre.* (111 min. Color. Films, Ltd.)
10. *The Last Valley.* (130 min. Color. Films, Inc.)
11. *The Dissolution of the Monasteries.* (27 min. Color. Encyclopaedia Britannica Films.)
12. *The World of Martin Luther.* (30 min. B/W. Columbia Pictures.)
13. *Paradise Lost.* (Videodisc. Color. 52 min. Films for the Humanities and Sciences)
14. *Credo: An Introduction to the Major Religious Traditions of Europe.* (Videodisc. Color. 10 Discs. Films for the Humanities and Sciences.)

CHAPTER 16

THE AGE OF EUROPEAN EXPANSION AND RELIGIOUS WARS

Instructional Objectives

After reading and studying this chapter, students should be able to discuss factors that led to the European discovery and conquest of other lands. Students should also be able to explain how Europeans influenced the peoples of other continents and how having overseas possessions affected Europe. Students should then be able to elaborate on the following topics: Portugal's role in the Age of Exploration and Discovery, the significance of advanced technology in Europe's expansion, and the consequences of the Habsburg-Valois and Thirty Years' wars.

Chapter Outline

I. The fifteenth and sixteenth centuries witnessed European discoveries of new worlds.
   A. European recovery was reflected in Europe's efforts in expanding horizons.
      1. Political centralization in Spain, France, and England paved the way for expansion.
      2. The Portuguese were the early leaders in the expansionist movement.
      3. By 1500 Portugal controlled the flow of gold to Europe.
   B. Spain challenged Portugal in the race for overseas acquisitions.
      1. Columbus sailed for Spain and gave Spain a stake in the New World.
      2. Magellan, Cortés, Pizarro, and other explorers established Spain's leadership.
   C. The Netherlands, France, and England also engaged in discovery and reconnaissance.
      1. The Dutch East India Company was the Dutch vehicle for imperialism.
      2. France and England made sporadic colonizing ventures.

II. There were many motives for discovery and colonization.
   A. Christianity was a significant motive for Europeans.
      1. They wanted to Christianize the Muslims and pagan peoples of the New World.
   B. Economic and intellectual reasons also prompted people to seek the New World.
      1. The desire for material gain was a chief impetus.
      2. Renaissance curiosity played a role.

III. Politics and war intensified in Europe during this period.
   A. The wars of religion colored the European landscape.
      1. There were religious riots and civil wars in France.
      2. Calvinism prompted the Dutch to revolt against the Habsburg Empire.
      3. Philip II of Spain was motivated by religion to send an invasion against England.

B. The Thirty Years' War (1618–1648) was an all-European religious conflict.
1. The war began with a Protestant revolt in Bohemia.
2. Catholicism won further victories in the Danish phase of the war.
3. The Swedish phase of the war ended Habsburg hopes of uniting Germany.
4. The French phase of the war ended with a devastated Germany.

IV. The age of discovery was also a vibrant period for the arts and literature.
A. Montaigne's essays anticipate the origins of modern skepticism.
1. He advocated a rejection of dogma.
B. The Elizabethan and Jacobean periods were high water marks for English literature.
1. Shakespeare became England's greatest playwright.
2. His works reflected the Renaissance ideas of classical culture, individualism, and humanism.
3. The King James Version of the Bible was composed during the period.
C. The baroque emerged in the seventeenth century.
1. Rubens symbolized the baroque style in art.
2. Bach's compositions are baroque at its best.

Lecture Suggestions

1. "The Legendary Armada." How did the English perceive the invincible Armada before English seamen actually had to face it? Did the English victory cause Spain's immediate collapse? Sources: G. Mattingly, *The Armada* (1959); G. Parker and C. Martin, *The Spanish Armada* (1988).
2. "Public Health and Public Hygiene in the Age of Exploration." How did people live in the sixteenth century? What were considered to be sanitary conditions? Was the sixteenth century a vast improvement in public health over the Middle Ages? Sources: C. M. Cipolla, *Cristofano and the Plague: A Study in the History of Public Health in the Age of Galileo* (1973); C. M. Cipolla, *Public Health and the Medical Profession in the Renaissance* (1976).
3. "Explorers and Their Thoughts." How did explorers feel about their voyages? How did they view the new lands and the new peoples they encountered? Sources: B. del Castillo, *The Discovery and Conquest of Mexico, 1517–1521* (1986); S. E. Morison, *Admiral of the Ocean Sea: A Life of Christopher Columbus* (1946).

Using Primary Sources

Have students read the excerpts from *Book of the First Navigation and Discovery of the Indies* (in S. E. Morison, *Admiral of the Ocean Sea*). Then show the film *1492: Conquest of Paradise*. Have students write a short paper describing how the movie treated the character of Christopher Columbus in light of their reading of primary source material.

Activities for Discovering the Past

I. **Classroom Discussion Suggestions**

1. What was it like to embark on a voyage like the circumnavigation of the globe by Magellan?
2. What dictated French policy in the Thirty Years' War?
3. How important was slave labor to the success of overseas empires?
4. How do we explain the tremendous success of Shakespeare?

II. Doing History

1. Have students trace the voyages of da Gama, Magellan, de Soto, Cortés, Pizarro, Cartier, and Hudson for a better understanding of the geographical context of the Age of Exploration and Discovery.

2. Historians have long debated the destructive power of the Thirty Years' War. Some historians have blamed Germany's long road to unification on the seventeenth-century conflict. Have students read selections from the following in order to understand better the nature of the historical debate: C. V. Wedgwood, *The Thirty Years' War* (1961); T. K. Rabb, ed., *The Thirty Years' War* (1981).

3. Have students examine the phenomenon of witches in sixteenth- and seventeenth-century Europe. Who were witches? What kinds of powers were they supposed to have? How do we explain the great outcry against alleged witches? Sources: J. B. Russell, *Witchcraft in the Middle Ages* (1976); H. R. Trevor-Roper, *The European Witch-Craze of the Sixteenth and Seventeenth Centuries* (1967); C. Ginzburg, *The Night Battle: Witchcraft and Agrarian Cults in the Sixteenth and Seventeenth Centuries* (1983).

III. Cooperative Learning Activities

1. Exploring. Have student teams write biographical accounts of leading explorers and share their findings with the class. Teams might choose some of the following:
   Columbus
   Da Gama
   Cabral
   Magellan
   Cartier
   the Cabots
   Vespucci
   Verrazano
   Drake
   De Soto
   Pizarro
   Cortés
   Gilbert

2. Warfare During the Thirty Years' War
   Have student teams research several aspects of warfare in the seventeenth century. What was the state of the art of war then? How had warfare changed since the Middle Ages? Teams might focus on the following: (1) fortification, (2) tactics, (3) strategy, (4) generalship, (5) arms and armor. Each team should give a historical overview with at least one illustration from a battle of the period.

Map Activity

1. Using Map 16.1 in the text, have students trace the routes of Columbus, Magellan, and da Gama on an outline map of the world (IRM page 181).
2. Using the map on page 16 of the *Historical Atlas of the World*, have students list the electors of the empire on a blank outline map of Europe (IRM page 183).

Audiovisual Bibliography

1. *The Best of Bach.* (60 min. Audiocassette. MCPS.)
2. *William Shakespeare.* (25 min. Color. Encyclopaedia Britannica Films.)
3. *The Struggle for the Mediterranean in the Sixteenth Century.* (33 min. Color. Encyclopaedia Britannica Films.)
4. *The Return of Martin Guerre.* (111 min. Color. Films, Ltd.)
5. *The Last Valley.* (130 min. Color. Films, Ltd.)
6. *Christopher Columbus.* (30 min. Color. Time-Life Films.)
7. *The Spanish Armada.* (31 min. Color. McGraw-Hill Films.)
8. *Civilization Series: Grandeur and Obedience.* Parts I and II. (26 min. each. Time-Life Films.)
9. *The Beginnings of Exploration: Why Did Europe "Discover" the Americas in 1492?* (Videodisc. Color. 11 min. Britannica Videos.)
10. *Christopher Columbus: His Voyages and His Legacy.* (Videodisc. Color. 14 min. Britannica Videos.)
11. *Europe Explores the Americas: Northern Voyages and Settlements.* (Videodisc. Color. 15 min. Britannica Videos.)
12. *Europe Explores the Americas: Southern Voyages and Settlements.* (Videodisc. Color. 16 min. Britannica Videos.)

CHAPTER 17

ABSOLUTISM AND CONSTITUTIONALISM IN EUROPE, CA 1589–1725

Instructional Objectives

After reading and studying this chapter, students should be able to discuss factors that led to the transition from feudalism to absolutism in western Europe in the sixteenth and seventeenth centuries. Students should also be able to distinguish between absolutism in England and France in the sixteenth and seventeenth centuries. Finally, students should be able to explain how Spain lost its relatively short-lived European hegemony.

Chapter Outline

I. The centralization of monarchial power and the dissolution of feudalism characterized this period.
    A. Louis XIV created the model absolutist state in France.
    B. The English Parliament restrained the absolutist tendencies of the Stuarts.

II. Louis XIV and absolutism in France provided the best model of absolutism in Europe.
    A. Louis XIV built on the work of his predecessors.
        1. He completed the construction of Versailles (begun under Louis XIII).
        2. Versailles became a pleasure prison for the French nobility.
    B. Cardinal Richelieu had begun the process that would weaken the French nobility.
        1. Richelieu made French governmental organization more efficient.
        2. He wanted to destroy Habsburg states.
    C. Mazarin succeeded Richelieu.
        1. Mazarin continued the work of his predecessor.
    D. Colbert was Louis XIV's greatest finance minister.
        1. He promoted the economic philosophy of mercantilism.
        2. His goal was self-sufficiency for France.
    E. Louis XIV's extravagant wars were a tremendous drain on the French economy.
        1. The Peace of Utrecht brought an end to his expansionist policies.

III. Spain declined during this period.
    A. Several factors led to decline.
        1. Fiscal disorder, political incompetence, and the lack of a strong middle class contributed to Spain's decline.
        2. The defeat of the Armada was a serious blow to Spain.

IV. England charted a different course in the Age of Absolutism.
  A. The Stuarts lacked the political astuteness of Elizabeth I.
    1. Although they exhibited absolutist tendencies, these were restrained by the growth of Parliament.
  B. The growth of Puritanism influenced English development.
    1. The Stuarts appeared sympathetic to Catholicism.
    2. Charles I's volatile relationship with Parliament added to the tension of the period.
  C. The English Civil War between king and parliament brought matters to a head.
    1. King Charles initiated conflict with the parliamentary forces.
    2. Parliament won the contest for sovereignty.
    3. Charles I was beheaded and Oliver Cromwell was made Lord Protector.
    4. The Glorious Revolution of 1688–89 was the final act in the struggle for sovereignty.

V. Locke's ideas reflect the changing tenor of the times.
  A. He defended ideas of the Glorious Revolution in his *Two Treatises on Government.*
  B. He argued that a government that oversteps its bounds was subject to dissolution.

Lecture Suggestions

1. "The Military Revolution of the Sixteenth and Seventeenth Centuries." How did European armies make the transition from medieval weaponry and tactics to more modern ones? What effect did this transition have on the military regimes of Europe? Source: G. Parker, *The Army of Flanders and the Spanish Road* (1976).
2. "Life at Versailles." What was life like for the French nobility as they whiled away the hours at Louis's pleasure palace? Sources: S. de Gramont, *The Age of Magnificence: Memoirs of the Court of Louis XIV by the Duc de Saint Simon* (1964); V. L. Tapie, *The Age of Grandeur: Baroque Art and Architecture* (1960).
3. "Popular Sentiment and the English Civil War." How did the common people feel about Charles I? What was the popular sentiment toward the English Civil War? Sources: K. Wrightson, *English Revel, Riot, and Rebellion* (1985); C. Hill, *Society and Puritanism in Pre-Revolutionary England* (1964).

Using Primary Sources

Have students read the quoted primary sources of the French letters of remission in N. Z. Davis's *Fiction in the Archives.* Have students use these sources to reconstruct the world of the peasant in France in the sixteenth and seventeenth centuries.

Activities for Discovering the Past

I. **Classroom Discussion Suggestions**

1. What was the role of women in the absolutist state?
2. How did absolutism fail in England?
3. How did mercantilism provide the economic structure of the absolutist state?

II. **Doing History**

1. Have students read selections from John Locke's *Two Treatises on Government* and Thomas Hobbes's *Leviathan.* Guide them in a discussion of the authors' political views and how these views are reflected in the history of the seventeenth century. The students might follow up the discussion with a short comparative paper.

2. Was Charles I a heartless absolutist? How and why have his image and impact been the subject of debate by historians? Sources: C. M. Hibbard, *Charles I and the Popish Plot* (1983); C. Hill, *The World Turned Upside Down* (1972); R. Ollard, *The Image of the King: Charles I and Charles II* (1980).

3. What role did sports play in the religious conflicts of seventeenth-century England? How did the Puritans' views of sports differ from those of the Stuart kings of England? Sources: D. Brailsford, *Sport and Society: Elizabeth to Anne* (1969); R. Lennard, ed., *Englishmen at Rest and Play* (1931).

4. What can songs and ballads tell us about the social history of an age? How do English ballads of the seventeenth century reflect English society? Sources: H. F. Brooks, *Rump Songs: An Index with Notes* (1940); B. H. Bronson, *The Ballad as Song* (1969); W. Chappell, *The Ballad Literature and Popular Music of the Olden Time,* 2 vols. (1859); W. Wilkins, *Political Ballads of the Seventeenth and Eighteenth Centuries,* 2 vols. (1860).

III. **Cooperative Learning Activities**

1. Popular Culture
Have student teams conduct research on the popular culture of England, France, the Netherlands, Germany, Spain, and Italy in the seventeenth century. Have each group focus on (1) entertainments, (2) games and sports, (3) children's games, (4) superstitions, (5) popular medical remedies, (6) food. Each team should have an "expert" on one of the six categories. Allow time for the experts of each team to meet and discuss their aspect of popular culture. Then regroup the teams for further discussion. Finally, have each team present its findings in class. Teams might make charts to display on the classroom walls.

2. Women Under Absolutism
Have student teams conduct research on the status of women under absolutist regimes in the seventeenth century. How did women's roles compare with those of women in the later Middle Ages and the Age of the Renaissance? Students might consult *Memoirs of the Court of Louis XIV by the Duc de Saint Simon* (1964), R. Thompson, *Women in Stuart England and America* (1974), and Antonia Fraser, *The Weaker Vessel* (1985). Use the teams' findings to launch a class discussion.

Map Activity

1. Using Map 17.2 in the text, have students shade in the possessions of European monarchs on an outline map of Europe (IRM page 183).
2. Using the map on page 17 of the *Historical Atlas of the World,* have students list the following rivers on an outline map of Europe:

Audiovisual Bibliography

1. *Music at the Court of Louis XIV.* (53 min. Color. Films for the Humanities and Sciences.)
2. *Cromwell.* (130 min. Color. Films, Ltd.)
3. *The Revolution of 1688.* (33 min. Color. Encyclopaedia Britannica Films.)

4. *The Sun King.* (30 min. B/W. Indiana University Audio-Visual Center.)
5. *Seven Ages of Fashion.* (Videodisc. Color. Seven 26-min. discs. Films for Humanities and Sciences.):
   a. The Elizabethans (1558–1603)
   b. The Stuarts (1603–1714)
   c. The Georgians (1714–1790)
   d. The Regency (1790–1837)
   e. The Victorians (1837–1901)
   f. The Edwardians and After (1901–1939)
   g. To the New Elizabethans (1945–)

CHAPTER 18

TOWARD A NEW WORLD-VIEW IN THE WEST

Instructional Objectives

After reading and studying this chapter, students should be able to list factors that led to the development of the Newtonian world-view and explain how the Newtonian world-view differed from the medieval world-view. Students should also be able to discuss how the Newtonian world-view affected society, religion, the economy, and politics.

Chapter Outline

I. A new view of human beings and the cosmos was developed during this period.
   A. The scientific revolution of the seventeenth century was the major cause.
   B. Scientific thought in the early 1500s was based on ancient and medieval ideas.
      1. European notions about the universe were based on Aristotelian principles.
      2. A chief feature of this view was the belief in a motionless, static earth at the center of the universe.
      3. Ten crystal spheres moved around the earth.
   C. Copernicus overturned the medieval view of the universe.
      1. He postulated that the earth revolved around the sun and that the sun was the center of the universe.
      2. This heliocentric view was a departure from the medieval view and created serious misgivings about traditional Christianity.
   D. Scholars from Brahe to Galileo contributed to the new world view.
      1. Brahe built an observatory and collected data.
      2. Galileo discovered the laws of motion using the experimental method.
   E. Newton synthesized the integral parts into a whole.
      1. Newton integrated the astronomy of Copernicus and Kepler with the physics of Galileo.
      2. He formulated a set of mathematical principles to explain motion.
   F. There were several causes of the scientific revolution.
      1. Medieval universities had provided the framework for the new view.
      2. The Renaissance stimulated science by rediscovering ancient mathematics.
      3. Better ways of obtaining knowledge about the world improved the scientific method.
      4. Bacon advocated empirical, experimental research.
      5. Descartes emphasized deductive reasoning.

II. Enlightenment ideas were the expression of the new world view.
 A. The overriding idea was that natural science and reason can explain all aspects of life.
  1. The scientific method can explain the laws of mankind.
  2. Progress is possible if the laws are understood and followed.
 B. Many scholars made Enlightenment thought accessible to a wide range of people.
  1. Fontenelle stressed the idea of progress.
  2. Skeptics such as Bayle believed that nothing can be known beyond all doubt.
  3. Locke stressed that all ideas are derived from experience.
 C. The philosophes were committed to the fundamental reform of society.
  1. Montesquieu's theory of the separation of powers was fundamental.
  2. Voltaire challenged traditional Catholic theology.
  3. The later Enlightenment writers created inflexible and dogmatic systems.

III. The philosophes believed that enlightened monarchs would create the necessary reforms.
 A. They believed that a benevolent absolutism offered the best chance for progress.
  1. Frederick II of Prussia and Catherine II of Russia were two enlightened monarchs.
  2. Frederick allowed religious freedom and promoted education and legal reform.
  3. Catherine imported Western culture to Russia and supported the philosophes.

IV. The impact of the Enlightenment
 A. By the mid-eighteenth century, Enlightenment ideas foreshadowed momentous changes.
  1. In France, the rise of aristocratic opposition and liberalism signaled the death knell of absolutism.
  2. In eastern Europe the results of the Enlightenment were modest.

Lecture Suggestions

1. "The Idea of Progress." One of the most fundamental ideas to come out of the Enlightenment was the idea of progress. How has the idea of progress become a kind of closed system for twentieth-century people? How has the idea of progress benefited Western civilization? Sources: P. Gay, *The Enlightenment: An Interpretation*, vol. I (1966); J. B. Bury, *The Idea of Progress*.
2. "How Enlightened Were the So-Called Enlightened Despots?" What reforms actually came about during the reigns of Catherine the Great of Russia and Joseph II of Austria? Were these reforming monarchs really different from their predecessors? Why? Sources: J. Gagliardo, *Enlightened Despotism* (1967); P. Bernard, *Joseph II* (1968); D. Ransel, *Politics of Catherinean Russia* (1975).
3. "Catherine the Great's Not-So-Private Life." Was this great reforming monarch as lecherous as rumors have led people to believe? What kind of woman was she really? Source: J. Alexander, *Catherine the Great, Life and Legend* (1989).

Using Primary Sources

Read (or reread) the excerpt from Voltaire's *Philosophical Dictionary* in the Listening to the Past feature in this chapter. After reading the passage, write a short analysis of the excerpt and explain what it conveys about Voltaire's religious beliefs.

Activities for Discovering the Past

I. Classroom Discussion Suggestions

1. Who were the architects of the new world-view? What did they contribute to Western civilization?
2. What were the religious views of the philosophes?
3. What impact did the Enlightenment have on political developments?

II. Doing History

1. Have students read and discuss Voltaire's *Candide*. How does literature reflect historical events and periods?
2. As an introduction to the ideas of the philosophes, have students read selections from the following sources. They might also be asked to write a paper about what they extract from these primary sources. Sources: S. Gendzier, ed., *Denis Diderot: The Encyclopedia: Selections* (1967); C. Brinton, ed., *The Portable Age of Reason* (1956).
3. What role did women play in the Enlightenment? How did the Enlightenment change attitudes toward women? Sources: S. Spenser, ed., *French Women and the Age of Enlightenment* (1984); K. Rogers, *Feminism in Eighteenth-Century England* (1982); E. Fox-Genovese, "Women in the Enlightenment," In R. Bridenthal and C. Koonz, eds., *Becoming Visible: Women in European History* (1987).

III. Cooperative Learning Activities

1. Organize the class into six teams. Charge each team with learning about one of the leading figures of the Enlightenment. Allow students to discuss their findings with one another in class. Then, have all teams make a presentation on the figure they researched. Instructors might require each team to have picture(s) of the figure, a timeline of his life, and a list of contributions he made to the thought of the Enlightenment. Teams might research Voltaire, Montesquieu, Bacon, Galileo, Newton, Diderot, or others.
2. Examining the Teams.
   At this juncture in the semester, you may wish to examine the teams once again. Teams are encouraged to study lecture notes, text, study guide, and any work prepared by the teams. Teams are encouraged to devise ways of studying for the exam. Class time might be allowed for teams to divide up individual study materials. Instructors, on exam day, will give an exam to the class. The exam is graded. Then the teams are allowed to take the exam, team members assisting each other. When team exams are graded, each student receives an average of his/her individual and team scores. Compare to see which has been more successful.

Map Activity

On a blank outline map of Europe (IRM page 183), have students identify the locations of important scientific discoveries. What were the conditions in those locations that contributed to these discoveries? Students could contrast these places with centers of absolutism in central and eastern Europe.

Audiovisual Bibliography

1. *Civilization: The Smile of Reason.* (52 min. Color. Time-Life Films.)
2. *The Majestic Clock-Work.* Parts I and II (26 min. each. Color. BBC and Time-Life Films.)
3. *Dinner at Baron d'Holbach's.* (24 min. Color. Open University, England.)
4. *Voltaire: Candide.* (Videodisc. 112 min. Color. Films for the Humanities and Sciences.)
5. *Simearth.* (Software. Learning Services.)
6. *World Atlas for Multimedia PC.* (CD-ROM. Society for Visual Education, Inc.)
7. *Time Table of History: Science and Innovation.* (CD-ROM. Society for Visual Education, Inc.)

CHAPTER 19

THE CHANGING LIFE OF THE PEOPLE IN EUROPE

Instructional Objectives

After reading and studying this chapter, students should be able to discuss living conditions, changing attitudes about marriage, pregnancy, diet, and the changing status of women.

Chapter Outline

I. The life of the common folk is discussed in this chapter.
   A. Stereotypes of people in preindustrial Europe have been shown to be false by modern research.
      1. The nuclear family was the most common in preindustrial Europe.
   B. The age at marriage was higher prior to 1750.
      1. Men and women in lower orders of society married later in life.
      2. Promiscuity was not as widespread as heretofore thought.
      3. The rising illegitimacy rates related to science, the Enlightenment, social mobility, and fewer restrictions on marriage and sex.
   C. New patterns of marriage and legitimacy emerged.
      1. The growth of the cottage industry resulted in people marrying for love.
      2. The explosion of births was caused by increasing illegitimacy.
      3. Women in cities and factories had limited economic independence.
   D. Attitudes toward children began to change during the period.
      1. They were defined by indifference and strict physical discipline.
      2. Young children were often neglected by parents.
      3. The beginnings of formal education for the masses took root.
   E. Schools and education also underwent changes.
      1. Protestantism fostered the trend toward popular education.
      2. Literacy increased in France and Scotland during the eighteenth century.

II. Nutritional and medical advances resulted in increased life spans.
   A. The life spans of Europeans increased from 25 to 35 years in the eighteenth century.
   B. Diet and nutrition underwent significant changes during the eighteenth century.
      1. The diet of ordinary people improved.
      2. Poor people's diets usually consisted of grains and vegetables.
      3. The potato improved the diet of the poor.
      4. Greater affluence meant that some people indulged in less nutritious food such as white bread and sugar.
   C. The conquest of smallpox was the greatest medical triumph of the eighteenth century.
      1. The demonic view of disease persisted.

2. Surgeons and pharmacists used questionable practices.
3. Hospital reform began in the late eighteenth century.
4. Jenner's work created the foundation for the science of immunology.

III. Religious reform continued in the eighteenth century.
   A. The emotional content of Christian faith was emphasized.
   B. Pietism and Methodism provided a challenge to established churches.
   C. Catholic piety held sway in traditionally Catholic areas.
      1. The old religious culture of ritual and superstition survived and continued to be popular.
   D. There was a Protestant revival during this period.
      1. In England, Wesley's Methodist movement rejected the Calvinist idea of predestination.
      2. There was a religious awakening, primarily among the lower classes.

Lecture Suggestions

1. "Women and Crime in the Eighteenth Century." Did women participate in crime in the eighteenth century or were they usually victims? Sources: J. M. Beattie, "The Criminality of Women in Eighteenth-Century England," *Journal of Social History* 8 (Summer 1975); M. Boxer and J. Quataert, eds., *Connecting Spheres: Women in the Western World, 1500 to the Present* (1987).
2. "The Changing Family." How did the agrarian revolution change the traditional family patterns of Europe? What role did increasing social mobility play in the changing family patterns? Sources: J. Casey, *The History of the Family* (1987); L. Stone, *The Family, Sex, and Marriage in England, 1500–1800* (1977).
3. "Changing Attitudes Toward Sexuality." How did attitudes toward illegitimacy and promiscuity change during this period? Was the eighteenth century any more promiscuous than previous or subsequent ages? Sources: R. Wheaton and T. Hareven, eds., *Family and Sexuality in French History* (1980); L. Stone, *The Family, Sex, and Marriage in England, 1500–1800* (1977).

Using Primary Sources

Have students peruse Pieter Brueghel the Elder's "Children's Games." Have them list as many games as they can find in the painting. Discuss the games. Then have students write an exploratory paper on how the Industrial Revolution might have changed the nature of children's games. After some students have discussed the hypotheses in their papers, have students read pertinent chapters in W. Baker, *Sports in Western Society* (1982) to see a scholar's interpretation of the problem.

Activities for Discovering the Past

I. **Classroom Discussion Suggestions**

1. Discuss the differences in diet between the peasants and the aristocracy.
2. Was there a tremendous advance in literacy among the lower orders of society in the eighteenth century?

3. Discuss the social, dietary, and political importance of the potato.
4. Discuss infanticide in eighteenth-century Europe.

II. Doing History

1. Did Harvey's discoveries immediately transform the world of medicine? What were doctors really like? Were there instances of quackery and shady medical practices? Sources: M. Romsey, *Professional and Popular Medicine in France, 1770–1830: The Social World of Medical Practice* (1988); H. Haggard, *Devils, Drugs, and Doctors* (1929).
2. After students read selections from the following sources, they should write a short descriptive paper on daily life in a particular European locale. Sources: A. MacFarlane, *The Family Life of Ralph Josselin* (1970); J. Knyveton, *Diary of a Surgeon in the Year 1751–52* (1937); J. C. Drummond and A. Wilbraham, *The Englishman's Food: A History of Five Centuries of English Diet* (1958).
3. Was there time for play and sports in this age of agrarian reform? What pastimes helped Europeans divert themselves from their daily drudgery? Sources: R. Malcolmson, *Popular Recreations and Pastimes in England, 1700–1850* (1979); P. Burke, *Popular Culture in Early Modern Europe* (1978); M. D. George, *London Life in the Eighteenth Century* (1965).

III. Cooperative Learning Activities

1. Organize the class into teams. Have each team research food in eighteenth- and nineteenth-century Europe. Each team should prepare a menu of a meal consumed in noble households, farmer's household, workers in industrial areas, and other socioeconomic divisions. Compare the types of food consumed by different socioeconomic groups.
2. Food in History (Class)
    As a follow-up to Activity 1 above, have teams prepare foods representing socioeconomic groups in Europe in the eighteenth and nineteenth centuries. Have each team bring samples of these foods to class. Allow students to taste the dishes. Discuss the kinds of foods and the ways that they were prepared. Also, discuss the nutritional values of these foods.

Map Activity

On the map of Europe on pages 34 and 35 of the *Historical Atlas of the World*, have students identify areas where the Protestant revival occurred as well as those areas that remained strongly Catholic. How might the differences in these areas been evident in popular culture?

Audiovisual Bibliography

1. *The London of William Hogarth.* (26 min. B/W. International Film Bureau.)
2. *Civilization: The Smile of Reason.* Parts I and II. (26 min. each. Color. Time-Life Films.)
3. *Reminders from the Past.* (Videodisc. 50 min. Color. Films for the Humanities and Sciences.)
4. *Europe Series: Southern Region.* (Videodisc. 20 min. Color. Britannica Videos.)
5. *Europe Series: Western Region.* (Videodisc. 20 min. Color. Britannica Videos.)

CHAPTER 20

AFRICA, 1400–1800

Instructional Objectives

After reading and analyzing this chapter, students should be able to discuss the kinds of economic and social structures that African societies developed. Students should also be able to discuss the impact that Islam had on African societies. Finally, students should be able to explain the role that slavery played in Africa before European intrusion.

Chapter Outline

I. Senegambia and Benin
   A. The Senegambian states of the West African coast possessed a homogeneous culture.
      1. They were a center in the trade from North Africa and the Middle East.
      2. They became an important center for the transatlantic slave trade.
   B. Ghana and Mali controlled much of Senegambia, but other states remained independent.
      1. The three Senegambian language groups were Wolof, Serer, and Pulaar.
      2. They had clearly defined social orders: royalty, nobility, warriors, peasants, artisans, and slaves.
      3. Slaves were not considered property in the Senegambian states.
      4. The Wolof nobility elected the king.
      5. Age-grades were groups of men and women who were initiated into adulthood at the same time.
      6. Age-grades cut across family ties and created communitywide loyalties.
   C. Benin (in what is now southern Nigeria) emerged in the fifteenth and sixteenth centuries.
      1. Ewuare expanded the states east to the Niger River, west to Yoruba country, and south to the Gulf of Guinea.
      2. Benin City was the capital: it was large and wealthy.
      3. Benin successfully withstood encroachments from the Portuguese and others but suffered a mysterious decline in the eighteenth and nineteenth centuries.

II. The Sudan: Songhay, Kanem-Bornu, and Hausaland
   A. Songhay dominated the Niger region of western and central Sudan.
      1. Muhammad Toure introduced political centralization and Muslim reforms into the Songhay Empire.
      2. Leo Africanus reported that Timbuktu in 1513 was a sophisticated and prosperous city.
      3. Slaves produced the main crops in Songhay.

4. Muhammad Toure's death left the country politically unstable.

B. Kanem-Bornu thrived under Idris Alooma's leadership.
  1. A strong military-feudal state was established.
  2. Agriculture and trade with North Africa was maintained.
  3. Ibn Fartua wrote about Idris Alooma's feats in *The Kanem Wars.*
  4. Alooma introduced Islam into Kanem-Bornu.

C. The Hausa were agricultural people who lived in small villages.
  1. Trade with North Africa resulted in the development of city-states such as Kano.
  2. Kano and Katsina became Muslim intellectual centers.

III. Ethiopia

A. Ethiopia faced numerous invaders.
  1. The Muslim state of Adal defeated Emperor Lebna Dengel and forced many Ethiopians to convert to Islam.
  2. Portuguese Jesuits tried to replace the Coptic Christian tradition with Roman Catholicism.

IV. The Swahili City-States

A. The Swahili city-states prospered in the fifteenth century.
  1. Mogadishu, Mombasa, Kilwa, and Sofala traded ivory, gold, and slaves with Arabian and Persian Gulf ports and the Far East.
  2. In 1498, the Portuguese under Vasco da Gama conquered many of the city-states.

V. The Transatlantic Slave Trade

A. Slavery had had a long history in Africa.
  1. Islam had heavily influenced African slavery.
  2. Portugal dominated the slave trade from 1493 to 1600, sending many slaves to Brazil.
  3. From 1690 to 1807, England was the leading carrier of slaves.

B. The four centuries of slave trade involved the exploitation of millions of people.
  1. Slaves were treated harshly in the slave ports.
  2. They were branded a number of times.

C. The Portuguese and British dominated the slave trade to the West.
  1. The Portuguese colony of Brazil provided ships, capital, and goods for the slave trade.
  2. Credit played a major role in the trade.
  3. The British slave trade was dominated by London, Bristol, and Liverpool.
  4. "Sorting" was the system of trading goods for slaves.
  5. The trade did not lead to improved economic development for Africa because the income was usually spent on luxury and consumer goods or firearms.
  6. The trade encouraged slavery within Africa, encouraged population growth, and resulted in a metis, or mulatto class.
  7. West Africa lost an enormous labor supply.
  8. Many African societies, however, suffered no significant population loss.

Lecture Suggestions

1. "Family Ties and Slavery." What happened to family and kinship among African slaves? Were families sold into slavery? Sources: E. Isichei, *The Ibo People and the Europeans* (1973); R. Oliver, ed., *The Cambridge History of Africa*, vol. 3, ca. 1050–1600 (1977).

2. "Comparing African and European Kingdoms." What institutions did the African kingdoms of the period have in common with their counterparts in Europe of the later Middle Ages and in early modern Europe? Sources: D. Gamble, *The Wolof of Senegambia* (1976); A. F. C. Ryder, *Benin and the Europeans, 1485–1897* (1969); R. Coulborn, *Feudalism in History* (1956).

USING PRIMARY SOURCES

Have students compare the kingdom of Kanem-Bornu with the Hausa city-state of Kano by using primary sources from the period: for Kanem-Bornu, students should read selections from A. Ibn Fartura (ed. T. Hodgkin, London, 1966); for Kano, students should read selections from *The Kano Chronicle* (ed. Hodgkin, pp. 89–90). Students should write short papers comparing the two African states.

ACTIVITIES FOR DISCOVERING THE PAST

I. Classroom Discussion Suggestions

1. Did color prejudice become a factor in African slavery after the intrusion of the Europeans?
2. How did the Swahili city-states achieve such a high standard of living?
3. How did Muhammad Toure create such a powerful kingdom of Songhay?

II. Doing History

1. Have students read primary accounts of the transatlantic slave trade to learn what fostered it and how contemporaries viewed it. Sources: R. E. Conrad, *Children of God's Fire: A Documentary History of Black Slavery in Brazil* (1983); P. E. Lovejoy, *Transformations in Slavery: A History of Slavery in Africa* (1983).
2. Students usually conclude that Africa was greatly influenced by the European intrusion. Africa also influenced Europe, and, if so, in what ways. Sources: G. J. Bender, *Angola Under the Portuguese: The Myth and the Reality* (1978); E. Isichei, *The Ibo People and the Europeans* (1973).

III. Cooperative Learning Activities

1. Organize the class into six groups. Assign each group the task of researching and reporting on the following African states: (1) Senegambia, (2) Songhay, (3) Hausaland, (4) Ethiopia, (5) Swahili City-States, and (6) Benin. Groups should focus their reading and research on the following areas: (1) political/social organization, (2) religion, (3) the economy, (4) recreation/art, and (5) technology.
2. Allow representatives from the six groups mentioned above to meet with representatives from the other five groups to discuss their respective research areas (political/social organization, religion, economy, recreation/art, and technology). Afterward, have all groups reform so that comparative information about the other five groups can be disseminated.
3. Based on the research and discussion in activities A and B (above), each group should make presentations to the class.

MAP ACTIVITY

Using the map on page 25 of the *Historical Atlas of the World,* have students list the following on an outline map of Africa (IRM page 185):
1. Red Sea
2. Gulf of Aden
3. Somalia
4. Mogadishu
5. Mombasa
6. Madagascar
7. Kalahari Desert
8. Nigeria
9. Congo River
10. Sahara Desert
11. Alexandria
12. Tripoli
13. Atlas Mountains
14. Gulf of Guinea
15. Lake Chad

Audiovisual Bibliography

1. *City-States of East Africa.* (30 min. B/W. Holt, Rinehart, and Winston.)
2. *Roots, Episodes 2–4.* (47 min each. Color. Films, Inc.)
3. *Islam: The Prophet and the People.* (34 min. Color. Texture Films.)
4. *The Lost World of the Kalahari.* (Videodisc. 7 Discs. Each disc 28–31 mins. Color. Films for the Humanities and Sciences.)
5. *The Glories of Ancient Benin.* (Videodisc. Films for the Humanities and Sciences.)
6. *The Ashanti Kingdom.* (Videodisc. Films for the Humanities and Sciences.)
7. *Black Sugar: Slavery from the African Perspective.* (Videodisc. Films for the Humanities and Sciences.)
8. *Trading in Africans: The Dutch Outposts in West Africa.* (Videodisc. 50 mins. Films for the Humanities and Sciences.)

CHAPTER 21

THE MIDDLE EAST AND INDIA, CA 1450–1800

Instructional Objectives

After reading and analyzing this chapter, students should be able to distinguish between the Ottomans and the Safavids. Students should also be able to explain how the Ottoman and Safavid empires were governed. Finally, students should also be able to discuss how Islam affected the Hindu population of India.

CHAPTER OUTLINE

I. The Ottoman State
   A. The Ottoman Empire grew out of the expansionist policies of Osman, a Turkish ruler (1299–1326).
      1. The Ottoman state expanded out of western Anatolia.
      2. The Ottoman state was led by the Ghazis, fighters in the Holy War.
      3. Mehmed II conquered Constantinople in 1453.
      4. They threatened Italy and conquered much of the territory surrounding the Mediterranean, including the Italian port of Otranto.
      5. Selim the Grim added Syria, Palestine, and Egypt to the empire.
      6. Suleiman extended the empire further, adding Greece and the Balkans, and attacking Vienna.
      7. Cyprus was conquered in 1570.
      8. Military organization and goals dominated Ottoman life.
   B. Ottoman Social Organization
      1. The ruling class was Muslim and loyal to the sultan.
      2. All property belonged to the sultan.
      3. The system of devshirme placed boys in the sultan's service.
      4. Slaves were acquired through purchase, capture in battle, and through devshirme.
      5. Pashas were the sultan's highest servants; there were also generals, governors, police officers, and others.
   C. Suleiman I's reign was one of extraordinary artistic flowering.
      1. Suleiman's legal code prescribed penalities for most crimes.
      2. Suleiman's decrees, or Kanuns, became imperial law.
      3. His expenditures surpassed any monarch in Europe.
      4. He adorned Constantinople with palaces and mosques.
      5. Poetry was the main literary expression.
      6. Great achievements were made in poetry, painting, history, mathematics, geographical literature, astronomy, and medicine.

       7.   Ottoman rulers used historical writing to justify their power and position.

    D.   Grave political, social, and economic difficulties afflicted the Ottoman state in the seventeenth and eighteenth centuries.

       1.   Administrative training for the imperial heirs was abandoned following Suleiman's reign.

       2.   Factionalism replaced a strong centralized state.

       3.   Defeat at Vienna in 1683 led to decline.

       4.   By 1800 the Ottoman state was known as the "sick man of Europe."

II.   The Persian State

    A.   All of Persia was united by Shah Ismail, the founder of the Safavid Dynasty.

       1.   Safavid power rested on the loyalty of the Qizilbash tribesmen.

       2.   Safavid power was also supported by the skills of urban bureaucrats.

       3.   The Shi'ite faith became the official religion of Persia, making the state a theocracy.

    B.   Safavid power reached its height under Shah Abbas the Great.

       1.   He built a national army and adopted English military skills.

       2.   He captured Baghdad, Mosul, and Diarbakr.

       3.   The most important city was Isfahan, the center of Persian arts.

       4.   In the eighteenth century Persia was divided among the Turks, Afghans, and Russians.

III. India: From Mughal domination to British dominion (ca. 1498–1805)

    A.   The Mughal period of Indian history began in 1525.

       1.   Mughal rule in India began with Babur's conquests of northern India.

       2.   Babur's grandson, Akbar, gave the Mughal state its form.

       3.   Akbar carried out an expansionist policy, adding Mala, Gondwana, Gujarat, and Bengal to the empire.

       4.   He used mansabdars to administer imperial policy.

       5.   Akbar sought universal religious tolerance.

       6.   He worked for the mutual assimilation of Hindus and Muslims.

       7.   He abolished taxes (jizya) on non-Muslims, married Hindu women, and employed Hindus in his government.

    B.   Akbar was succeeded by his son Jahangir, and his grandson, Shah Jahan.

       1.   Shah Jahan moved the court to Delhi and built the Peacock Throne and the Taj Mahal.

       2.   Aurangzeb's puritanical rule undid many of the reforms of Akbar and his successors.

       3.   Europeans competed for Indian trade.

    C.   Europeans used different ways of exploiting Indian trade.

       1.   The Portuguese used piracy and terrorism to push the Muslims from the Indian and Arabian oceans.

       2.   The British and Dutch formed trading companies.

       3.   The Europeans introduced the "factory," a trade settlement.

       4.   To deal with local disorder, companies from Europe got increasingly involved in local politics.

    D.   The British East India Company

       1.   India became a battleground in the French-British struggle.

       2.   Colbert's French East India Company established factories in India in the 1670s.

       3.   British seapower and Clive's victory at Plassey (1757) led to British control of India.

4.   Hastings put forward the parliamentary legislation that transferred power from the East India Company to a governor.

5.   He laid the foundations for the civil service, instituted reforms, and blocked Indian coalition.

6.   At the beginning of the nineteenth century, Britain controlled India through the support of the Indian princes, a large army of sepoys, and the civil service.

Lecture Suggestions

1.   "What Made Akbar Great?" In which areas of life did Akbar have the greatest influence? What were some of his reforms? Sources: P. M. Holt et al., eds., *The Cambridge History of Islam*, 2 vols. (1970); M. Mujeeb, *The Indian Muslims* (1967).

2.   "Agricultural Progress in Mughal India." What farming techniques did farmers employ in Mughal India? How did these techniques compare with those of Europeans in the early modern period? Source: I. Habib, *The Agrarian System of Mughal India, 1556–1707* (1963).

USING PRIMARY SOURCES

Have students read about the Turkish siege of Constantinople in 1453 in the Muslim historian Oruc's description (passage contained in B. Lewis, *The Muslim Discovery of Europe*, New York, 1982). After reading the passage, engage the students in a discussion of how the fall of Constantinople was a significant watershed in the history of world societies.

ACTIVITIES FOR DISCOVERING THE PAST

I.   Classroom Discussion Suggestions

1.   How successful was Akbar's policy of sulahkul (universal religious tolerance)?
2.   How did the Persian invasion of India factor into the European imperialist ventures into India?
3.   What kind of impact might the Ottomans have made on the West had they not been halted at the Battle of Vienna in 1683?

II.   Doing History

1.   What does a historical figure have to do to be dubbed "the Great"? Have students read biographies of rulers who have been called "the Great." What similarities exist among these individuals? Sources: M. L. Roychowdoui, *The State and Religion in Mughal India* (1951); J. R. Hamilton, *Alexander the Great* (1973).

2.   Show slides of the Taj Mahal and of Buckingham Palace (or some other Western royal residence). Ask students to compare architectural styles. In addition, have them list significant royal symbols that they observe on the palaces and discuss these symbols in class.

III.   Cooperative Learning Activities

1.   Organize the class into three groups. Have each group research and report on one of the following: (1) Ottomans, (2) Safavids, and (3) Mughals. The groups should focus on the following aspects of these societies: (1) political/social organization, (2) religion, (3) the economy, (4) recreation/art, and (5) technology.

2. After collecting their research, representatives from each group should meet with representatives from the other two groups. This meeting should stimulate discussion of a comparative nature.

3. After the groups have reformed and discussions of what the representatives learned from the other groups have been completed, each group should then make an oral presentation to the class.

MAP ACTIVITY

Using the map on page 36 of the *Historical Atlas of the World*, have students list the following on an outline map of Asia (IRM page 186):

1. Bay of Bengal
2. Arabian Sea
3. Ceylon
4. Nepal
5. Bengal
6. Mysore
7. Maratha Empire
8. Mughal Empire
9. Afghan Empire
10. Madras
11. Bombay
12. Panipat
13. Kabul
14. Calcutta
15. Delhi

Audiovisual Bibliography

1. *Ahmedabad—Life of a City in India.* (30 min. Color. Center for South African Studies, University of Wisconsin.)
2. *An Indian Pilgrimage: Ramdevra.* (26 min. Color. Center for South Asian Studies, University of Wisconsin.)
3. *Islam: The Prophet and the People.* (34 min. Color. Texture Films.)
4. *Israel: Land of Destiny.* (Videodisc. 29 min. Color. Films for the Humanities and Sciences.)
5. *From Moghuls to Independence.* (Videodisc. 42 min. Color. Films for the Humanities and Sciences.)
6. *The Dutch in India.* (Videodisc. 50 min. Color. Films for the Humanities and Sciences.)
7. *The Paths of Colonialism.* (Videodisc. 17 min. B&W/Color. Films for the Humanities and Sciences.)
8. *The Taj Mahal: A Royal Geographic Society Electronic Guide.* (CD-ROM. National School Products.)
9. *World Factbook.* (CD-ROM. National School Products.)

CHAPTER 22

CHINA AND JAPAN, CA 1400–1800

Instructional Objectives

After reading and analyzing this chapter, students should be able to discuss the governmental features of the Ming and Qing dynasties in China and the Tokugawa Shogunate in Japan. Then, students should be able to explain how Chinese and Japanese societies were affected by agricultural and commercial developments. Finally, students should be able to discuss how Chinese intellectuals explained the transition from the Ming to the Qing.

Chapter Outline

   I. China: From the Ming Dynasty to the mid-Manchu Dynasty (ca. 1368–1795)
       A. Hong Wu drove the Mongols out of China.
           1. He was the founder of the Ming Dynasty.
       B. Agricultural and Commercial Revolutions
           1. The Ming innovations were a recovery of the chaos of the Mongol Period.
           2. Rice improvements were affected during the Ming Period.
           3. Irrigation also increased the food supply.
           4. Land reclamation and reforestation also led to growth.
       C. Hong Wu's Government
           1. He instituted a number of reforms.
           2. He centralized his rule by giving land to the peasants.
           3. He was supported by land taxes.
           4. Hong Wu instituted a rigorous examination for the civil service.
           5. He strengthened and extended the Great Wall.
       D. There was maritime expansion under the Ming.
           1. Yong Luo's reign is highlighted by naval accomplishments.
           2. New trade, tribute, and Chinese immigration into Asia resulted from the naval improvements.
       E. Decline of the Ming Dynasty
           1. Yong Luo's extravagances hurt China's economy.
           2. Yong Luo's successors had trouble in foreign affairs.
           3. Japan stepped up its raids on China's coasts.
           4. Nevertheless, by the sixteenth century, China was developing into an urban mercantile society.
           5. However, China did not undergo an industrial revolution like the West.
           6. Under Nurhachi, the Manchus conquered China.
       F. Manchu Rule
           1. The Manchus established the Qing Dynasty in 1644.

2. Manchu rule was based on traditional Chinese methods.
3. The central bureaucracy managed the state.
4. Under Emperor Kang-xi, the emperorship was revitalized and the Mongolian threat was eliminated.

G. Daily Life in Ming and Manchu China
1. The family exercised great social influence.
2. The family guided the education of children, marriage, religious life, and welfare services.
3. Power in both nuclear and extended families rested with the father.
4. Marriages were arranged between parents.
5. Divorce was open only to men.
6. Age was respected.
7. Village schools for boys stressed preparation for civil service.
8. Girls received training that prepared them to be wives and mothers.
9. Scholars held the highest rank in the social order.

II. Japan (ca. 1400–1800)
A. The Ashikaga Shogunate was a period of civil war and feudalism.
1. Feudalism in Japan resulted from the native warrior and Chinese Confucian ethics.
2. The shoen, or land, was one of two key elements of Japanese feudalism.
3. The other was the warrior class.
4. By 1500, the samurai warriors lived by the code of Bushido which stressed honor, loyalty, and hardship.
5. The mounted samurai was made obsolete by cannon and musket.

B. Nobunaga and national unification
1. The samurai Nobunaga extended his power and emerged as ruler of central Japan by 1568.
2. 1568–1600 is the period of national unification.
3. Nobunaga subdued most of Japan by force.
4. He proved to be an able ruler.
5. Nobunaga's successor Hideyoshi reduced the threat of the daimyos (lords).
6. He extended his control over agriculture and the peasantry.

C. The Tokugawa Regime
1. Ieyasu completed the work begun by Nobunaga and Hideyoshi.
2. The daimyos became his hostages at the capital at Edo.
3. Taxes were imposed on villages, not individuals.
4. Sakoku, or the closed country policy, was instituted by Ieyasu's descendants.
5. The Japanese were not allowed to leave.
6. Foreigners were excluded.

D. The Life of the People
1. Japanese life changed dramatically in the seventeenth and eighteenth centuries.
2. The powerless nobility pursued pleasure.
3. Women were subordinate to men.
4. The kabuki theater, with its crude and bawdy skits, was a favorite pastime of the nobility.
5. Homosexuality, long accepted in Japan, was practiced by the warrior class.
6. Peasant village life was regulated by the state.
7. Low rice prices, overpopulation, and famines led to discontent among the peasantry.

Lecture Suggestions

1. "The Impact of Christianity on Tokugawa Japan." Source: C. R. Boxer, *The Christian Century in Japan, 1549–1650* (1967).
2. "Chinese Government Through the Eyes of an Insider." How did the Chinese bureaucracy work? What were its strengths and weaknesses? Source: J. D. Spence, *Ts'Ao Yin and the K'Ang–Hsi Emperor: Bondservant and Master* (1966).

Using Primary Sources

Students should read the seventeenth-century description of peasants that is quoted in G.B. Sansom, *A History of Japan, 1615–1867*, Vol. 3 (Stanford, Calif., 1978), and compare with the twelfth-century European writer Andreas Capellanus's comments about peasants in his work *The Art of Courtly Love*. Then, students should write short papers comparing the image and status of peasants in both Japanese and European societies.

ACTIVITIES FOR DISCOVERING THE PAST

I. Classroom Discussion Suggestions

1. What kind of schooling did boys and girls receive in China during this period?
2. What was the role of women in China and Japan from around 1400 to 1800?
3. In what ways was the crisis of the samurai similar to the crisis of the nobility in early modern Europe?
4. What were some of the factors in the transition from feudalism to centralized government in China and Japan?

II. Doing History

1. Show students pictures or slides (or both) of samurai warriors and European knights (ca. 1300–1500) and have them list things that impress them. Use these lists for class discussions. When the samurai and the knight were not at war, how did they spend their time? Source: R. Coulborn, *Feudalism in History* (1956).
2. Have students pretend to be Christian missionaries living in either China or Japan in the sixteenth century. Ask them to write a letter home describing what they have observed.

III. Cooperative Learning Activities

1. Organize the class into five groups. Charge each group with the task of reading and discussing early European perceptions of Japan by using M. Cooper, ed., *They Came to Japan: An Anthology of European Reports on Japan, 1543–1640* (1981). Have each group present summaries of the reports. Follow the reports with a class discussion on how European views of Japan reflected reality.
2. Cooperative Learning Examination
   At this point in the term, instructors may wish to administer an examination covering material studied since the last exam. Before or after giving an individual exam to the class, instructors may wish to test the effectiveness of their cooperative learning activities by giving an exam to cooperative learning groups. Individual and group exam grades might be averaged together.

Map Activity

Using the map on page 37 of the *Historical Atlas of the World,* have students list the following places and features on an outline map of China and Japan (IRM page 179):
1. China Sea
2. Pacific Ocean
3. Formosa
4. Peking
5. Nagasaki
6. Hangchow
7. Yangtze River
8. Manchuria
9. Korea
10. Hsi River
11. Kyoto
12. Osaka
13. Kwangchow
14. Outer Mongolia
15. Macao

Audiovisual Bibliography

1. *China: A Portrait of a Land.* (18 min. Color. Britannia Films.)
2. *China: The Coming of the West.* (20 min. Color. Indiana University AV Center.)
3. *Japan: The Bamboo Bends, But Does Not Break.* Part I. (26 min. Color. Australian News and Information Bureau, New York.)
4. *Astonishing Asia.* (CD-ROM. National School Products.)
5. *Exotic Japan: A Guide to Japanese Culture and Language.* (CD-ROM. National School Products.)
6. *Barbarians in Chinese Waters.* (Videodisc. 50 min. Color. Films for the Humanities and Sciences.)
7. *The Coming of the Barbarians.* (Videodisc. 50 min. Color. Films for the Humanities and Sciences.)
8. *The Age of the Shoguns.* (Videodisc. 50 min. Color. Films for the Humanities and Sciences.)

CHAPTER 23

THE REVOLUTION IN WESTERN POLITICS, 1775–1815

Instructional Objectives

After reading and studying this chapter, students should be able to distinguish between the causes of the American and French revolutions. Students should also be able to explain the effect of these revolutions on the people. Finally, students should be able to discuss the impact of the French Revolution on the status of women.

Chapter Outline

I. The American and French revolutions dominated the West in this period.
   A. Revolutions came in the wake of Enlightenment ideas.
      1. The Judeo-Christian tradition of individualism supported the liberalism of the Enlightenment.
      2. Liberalism was attractive to both the aristocracy and the middle class.
   B. Fundamental to both was the popular demand for liberty and equality.
      1. Liberty meant human rights and freedoms and the sovereignty of the people.
      2. Equality meant equal rights and equality of opportunity.

II. The American Revolution freed the thirteen British colonies from the power of Britain.
   A. Conflict between British government and American colonies escalated after the mid-eighteenth century.
      1. The American colonists believed they had the right to make their own laws.
   B. The conflict over increased taxation increased the growing discontent of the colonists.
      1. The British wanted the Americans to pay their share of imperial expenses.
      2. Americans actually paid very low taxes.
      3. Parliament passed the Stamp Act to raise revenue.
   C. Conflict broadened to include questions about control over colonial legislatures, representation, and the right to legislate.
      1. The British refused to compromise and lost the support of many colonists.

III. Revolutionary fervor moved the crisis from debate to open hostilities.
   A. Armed conflict erupted in April 1775.
      1. The Declaration of Independence further encouraged the colonists to seek independence.
      2. European assistance, especially from France, contributed to the eventual American victory.
      3. After eight years of fighting, Britain recognized the independence of the thirteen colonies.

B. The United States was formed and defined by its Constitution.
   1. A federal system was given important powers such as the right to tax and to regulate trade.
   2. Representative self-government reflected the colonists' antagonism to British authority.
   3. A system of checks and balances was designed to balance governmental powers.

IV. The French Revolution became a Europeanwide struggle in the last decades of the eighteenth century.
   A. The French Revolution was partly precipitated by the American Revolution and the ultimate breakdown of the old order.
      1. Many French soldiers served in America during the American Revolution.
      2. By the 1780s, the French government was nearly bankrupt.
      3. The second estate, the nobility, taxed the peasantry for its own profit.
   B. Some modern historians have challenged the traditional view of the origins of the French Revolution.
      1. Some argue that key sections of the nobility were liberal.
      2. Others point out that the nobility and the bourgeoisie were not necessarily economic rivals.
   C. A plethora of problems paved the way for revolution in 1789.
      1. Louis XVI called for a meeting of the Estates General when his plan to tax landed property was opposed.
      2. The Third Estate constituted the real strength of France in 1789.
      3. Rising bread prices in 1788–89 pushed the people into action.
      4. The people took the Bastille.
      5. A limited monarchy was established by the bourgeoisie.
      6. The National Assembly grasped all lawmaking power.
      7. The nobility was abolished.

Lecture Suggestions

1. "What Kind of Revolution Was the American Revolution?" Did the American Revolution start from the bottom up? How does it compare with the causes and effects of the French Revolution? Sources: P. Higonnet, *Sister Republics: The Origins of French and American Republicanism* (1988); C. Brinton, *Anatomy of Revolution* (1965).
2. "The Social History of the French Revolution." What was life like for the Parisian poor in 1789? How did their lot compare with that of the peasants in the provinces? Sources: N. Hampson, *A Social History of the French Revolution* (1963); S. Schama, *Citizens: A Chronicle of the French Revolution* (1989); G. Rudé, *The Crowd in the French Revolution* (1959).
3. "The American Revolutionaries and Their Allies." Who aided America in the struggle for independence? What role did the French play in the American Revolution? Sources: B. Bailyn, *The Ideological Origins of the American Revolution* (1967); P. Higonnet, *Sister Republics: The Origins of French and American Republicanism* (1988).

Using Primary Sources

Compare the French "Declaration of the Rights of Man" in the "Primary Sources" section of this manual to the excerpts from the Magna Carta in the same section. What evidence of the Enlightenment thinking is noticeable in the "Declaration of the Rights of Man"?

Activities for Discovering the Past

I.   Classroom Discussion Suggestions

1.   What kind of man was George Washington?
2.   Was Britain merely fighting a rearguard action against the American colonists? Had the British marshaled their total military resources against the Americans, could they have suppressed the Americans?
3.   What role did blacks play in the American Revolution?
4.   How did Napoleon rise to power?
5.   What role did fear play in the outbreak of the French Revolution?

II.   Doing History

1.   Distribute outline maps of Europe and have students label the sites of the following Napoleonic battles: Austerlitz, Jena, Borodino, Waterloo. Sources: D. Chandler, *The Campaigns of Napoleon* (1973); R. Quimby, *The Background of Napoleonic Warfare* (1957).
2.   What kind of man was Napoleon? How did he achieve such monumental success at such an early age? Why did he ultimately fail? Sources: P. Geyl, *Napoleon: For and Against* (1949); R. R. Jones, *Napoleon: Man and Myth* (1977); V. Cronin, *Napoleon Bonaparte* (1972).
3.   Have students read Charles Dickens's classic *A Tale of Two Cities.* Afterward, show the film in class (*A Tale of Two Cities*, 117 min., B/W, Films for the Humanities and Sciences). Is the film true to Dickens's story? Has the film taken liberties with the novel? Have students write short papers in which they analyze the filmmaker's interpretation of the novel.

III.   Cooperative Learning Activities

1.   Charge student teams with learning about the military history of the American Revolution. Five teams should learn about significant battles: (1) Lexington/Concord, (2) Trenton, (3) Saratoga, (4) Guilford Courthouse, (5) Yorktown. Each team should develop a report focused on the following questions: (1) commanders for both sides, (2) terrain of the battlefield, (3) tactics and strategy employed, (4) outcome of battle, (5) implication for the future course of the war. Presentations should be made in class.
2.   Organize the class into teams of four each. Have each team investigate the commonalities of the following so-called revolutions: (1) Protestant Reformation; (2) American Revolution; (3) French Revolution; (4) Russian Revolution. Students should read Crane Brinton's *Anatomy of a Revolution* to discuss the underlying factors for their respective revolutions. Research completed, each group presents its findings to the class. Then discuss similarities and differences in the revolutions. Finally, how does Brinton's thesis stand up under the weight of your students' investigations?

Map Activity

1.   Using Map 23.1 in the text, have students shade in French territory, Napoleonic allies, and Napoleonic enemies in 1810 on an outline map of Europe (IRM page 183).
2.   Using the map on page 20 of the *Historical Atlas of the World*, have students list the battles of the American Revolutionary War on a blank outline map of North America.

Audiovisual Bibliography

1. *French Revolution: Death of the Old Regime.* (18 min. Color. Encyclopaedia Britannica Films.)
2. *French Revolution: Birth of a New France.* (21 min. Color. Encyclopaedia Britannica Films.)
3. *Prelude to Revolution.* (12 min. Color. Encyclopaedia Britannica Films.)
4. *A More Perfect Union.* (40 min. Color. Encyclopaedia Britannica Films.)
5. *Thomas Jefferson.* (13 min. Color. Encyclopaedia Britannica Films.)
6. *Benjamin Franklin.* (15 min. Color. Encyclopaedia Britannica Films.)
7. *Napoleon Bonaparte.* (Videodisc. 12 min. Color. Films for the Humanities and Sciences.)
8. *The Battle of Austerlitz: 1805.* (Videodisc. 30 min. Color. Films for the Humanities and Sciences.)
9. *The Battle of Yorktown: 1781.* (Videodisc. 30 min. Color. Films for the Humanities and Sciences.)
10. *Let's Visit France.* (CD-ROM. Learning Services.)
11. *The American Revolution.* (CD-ROM. Learning Services.)

CHAPTER 24

THE INDUSTRIAL REVOLUTION IN EUROPE

Instructional Objectives

After reading and studying this chapter, students should be able to discuss the factors that led to the revolution in energy and industry. Students should also be able to explain the effects of the Industrial Revolution on people's lives. Finally, students should be able to analyze the positive and negative outcomes of the Industrial Revolution.

Chapter Outline

I. The industrial transformation of Western society culminated in the so-called Industrial Revolution.
    A. England "takes off" first in the age of the Industrial Revolution.
        1. The influence of Calvinism was an important factor in England's early lead.
        2. Social and economic factors influenced England's take off.
        3. A stable government also fostered industrial growth in England.
        4. A growing demand for textiles led to the creation of the world's first large factories.
        5. The putting-out system could not keep up with the demand.
    B. The harnessing of steam power helped to transform Europe industrially.
        1. This was one of the hallmarks of the Industrial Revolution.
        2. Part of the general revolution was the transformation from wood-burning to coal-burning.
        3. Transportation and manufacturing were revolutionized by steam power.
        4. The early steam engines of Savery and Newcomen were converters of coal into energy.
        5. James Watt increased the efficiency of the steam engine.
        6. Steam power was used in many industries.

II. After Britain, other European nations began to industrialize.
    A. There were several variations on the industrialization theme.
        1. Belgium followed Britain's lead.
        2. France only showed gradual growth in the early nineteenth century.
        3. By 1913 Germany and the United States were closing in on Britain.
    B. The Napoleonic wars retarded the industrial growth of continental European nations.
        1. However, most continental countries had a tradition of a successful putting-out system.
        2. The other countries could simply follow Britain's lead.

III. There were many social implications of the Industrial Revolution.
   A. The growth of a middle class altered European society.
      1. A new class of factory owners emerged in this period.
   B. Factory workers emerged as a new group in society.
      1. Many writers portrayed the harsh working conditions for factory workers.
      2. Engels lashed out at the middle classes in his *The Condition of the Working Class in England* (1844).
   C. The issues of working conditions, wages, and quality of life led to struggles between labor and capital.
      1. Ure and Chadwick argued that industrialization had improved the quality of life for people.
   D. Conditions of work changed in the newly emerging capitalist age.
      1. Factory work meant more discipline and lost personal freedom.
      2. Child labor was increased.
      3. Children and parents worked long hours.
      4. Parliament sought to limit child labor.

IV. A historical debate on the Industrial Revolution continues to the present day.
   A. Capitalists view it as a positive step toward fulfilling human wants and needs.
   B. Socialists and communists view it as the further exploitation of the have-nots by the haves.

Lecture Suggestions

1. "The Final Movement Toward Industrial Capitalism." What transformed European society in the eighteenth century? What factors contributed to the making of an urban working class? Sources: E. P. Thompson, *The Making of the English Working Class* (1963); D. Bythell, *The Handloom Weavers* (1969).
2. "The Evils of the Industrial Revolution." What were the negative results of the Industrial Revolution? How did the Industrial Revolution affect the lives of the working class? Sources: B. Harrison, *Drink and the Victorians* (1971); F. Engels, *The Condition of the Working Class in England* (1844).

Using Primary Sources

Reread the excerpt from Robert Owen in this chapter. Write a brief essay in which you paraphrase Owen's reasons for not employing children under ten.

Activities for Discovering the Past

I. Classroom Discussion Suggestions

1. What impact did the Industrial Revolution have on working-class women?
2. What role did children of the working class play in late eighteenth- and nineteenth-century England?
3. To what extent were writers like Dickens sensitive to the plight of the urban proletariat?
4. According to Engels, what was the condition of the working class in England?

II. Doing History

1. Have students read selections from the following sources and discuss their findings. The discussion might lead to the writing of a short historiographical paper on the Industrial Revolution. Sources: R. H. Hilton et al., *The Transition from Feudalism to Capitalism* (1976); W. A. Hayek, ed., *Capitalism and the Historians* (1954).
2. If slides are available, give a slide presentation of some of the works of William Hogarth, Gustave Doré, and Honoré Daumier. Have students discuss the emphasis of these works. Were these painters sensitive to the plight of the urban proletariat, or did they merely observe and record their impressions of an artistic subject?
3. Have students read selections from the following sources and write short papers on how these works reflect the times. Sources: C. Dickens, *Hard Times, Oliver Twist, A Christmas Carol;* A. Ure, *The Philosophy of Manufacturers* (1835); E. Gaskell, *Mary Barton* and *North and South;* E. Zola, *Germinal.*

III. Cooperative Learning Activities

1. Charge six student teams with creating murals of their impressions of the Industrial Revolution. After the murals are completed, have teams share them with the class, explaining why they included certain features and images. Instructors may wish to display murals on classroom walls.
2. Using the murals created in Activity 1 above, have each team write an essay describing the various elements in their murals. Have a representative from each team read the team essay to the class.

Map Activity

1. Using Map 24.1 in the text, have students identify the locations of British cottage industries and discuss the transportation network among them.
2. Using the map on page 30 of the *Historical Atlas of the World,* have students list the major languages of western Europe on a blank outline map of Europe (IRM page 183).

Audiovisual Bibliography

1. *The Industrial Revolution in England.* (26 min. Color. Encyclopaedia Britannica Films.)
2. *The Industrial Revolution: Beginnings in the U.S.* (23 min. Color. Encyclopaedia Britannica Films.)
3. *Great Rivers of the World.* (Videodisc. 5 discs, 40–50 min. ea. Films for the Humanities and Sciences.):
    a. The Danube
    b. The Loire
    c. The Rhine
    d. The Thames
    e. The Volga
4. *City of the Big Shoulders.* (Videodisc. 52 min. Color. Films for the Humanities and Sciences.)

CHAPTER 25

IDEOLOGIES AND UPHEAVALS, 1815–1871

Instructional Objectives

After reading and studying this chapter, students should be able to discuss the factors in the romantic revolt against the age of classicism and the French Revolution. Students should also be able to explain the implications of this revolt for politics, the arts, and society. Finally, students should be able to analyze the lingering remnants of the French Revolution and explain how they exerted influence on political development in the first half of the nineteenth century.

Chapter Outline

I. The reaction against the French Revolution took creative forms in the nineteenth century.
   A. Although liberalism and nationalism flourished, these tendencies were checked by the conservative reaction of the Great Powers.
      1. Conservative monarchial states wanted to prevent revolutions in their own states.
   B. Klemens von Metternich is viewed as the symbol of the age of reaction against the ideas of the French Revolution.
      1. Metternich presided over the Congress of Vienna and towered over European politics in the first third of the nineteenth century.

II. The Congress of Vienna attempted to restore the old order upset by the French Revolution.
   A. It sought to restore conservatism and absolute monarchies.
   B. It established a balance of power among European nations.
      1. A Holy Alliance was formed to check future liberal and revolutionary activity.
   C. The Congress of Vienna also initiated the "congress system" to settle international crises.
      1. It was believed that an international equilibrium of power would preserve peace in Europe.

III. Liberalism was reflected in economic thinking.
   A. The principle of *laissez-faire* formulated by Adam Smith.
      1. Smith was critical of mercantilism and argued that a free economy would bring wealth for all, including workers.
      2. The laissez-faire-ists believed that the economy should be left unregulated.
   B. Thomas Malthus was an influential economic writer of the period.
      1. Malthus believed that marrying late was the best method of birth control.
   C. David Ricardo's ideas gained credence in this period as well.
      1. Ricardo argued that because of the pressure of population, wages would always be low.

IV. Nationalism was another radical idea in the years after 1815.
    A. Nationalism helped engender feelings of cultural unity.
        1. Nationalists sought to turn cultural unity into political reality.
        2. Modern nationalism had its roots in the French Revolution.
    B. Nationalism created the desire to match state boundaries with cultural boundaries.
        1. Nationalists believed that common language and traditions would bring about unity and common loyalties.
        2. Nationalism also encouraged ideas of racial and cultural superiority.

V. Socialism gained force during the nineteenth century.
    A. Socialism was a desire to reorganize society to establish cooperation and a new sense of community.
        1. The early French socialists proposed a system of greater economic equality planned by the government.
        2. Saint-Simon and Fourier proposed a planned economy and socialist communities.
    B. Karl Marx created an additional form of socialism.
        1. Marx believed that class warfare was an integral part of historical evolution.
        2. Class struggle for economic hegemony formed a chief principle of Marxism.
        3. Violent revolution was advocated to achieve socialist ends.
        4. A proletarian victory over the capitalists would bring about the perfect society.

VI. Political and romantic revolutions colored the map of Europe.
    A. National revolts in Greece, France, and the Netherlands achieved some of their aims.
        1. Greek nationalists fought for freedom from Turkey.
        2. Greece became independent in 1830.
    B. Political and social reform swept Great Britain.
        1. The British aristocracy feared liberalism.
        2. The Corn Law (1815) is a good example of how the British aristocracy protected itself from liberal ideas.
        3. The growth of the middle class and its desire for reform led to the Reform Bill of 1832.
        4. The Chartist movement for universal male suffrage failed.
        5. The Corn Laws were repealed in 1846.
    C. The Austrian Empire faced uprisings from Hungarian and Czech nationalists.
    D. Liberals, artisans, and factory workers struggled against monarchy in Prussia.

Lecture Suggestions

1. "Metternich's Europe." How thoroughly did Metternich's politics control Europe between 1815 and 1848? What precipitated Metternich's desire for the return of the old order? Sources: H. Nicolson, *The Congress of Vienna* (1946); A. J. May, *The Age of Metternich, 1814–1848* (1963).
2. "The Growth of Nationalism." What inroads did nationalism make in the nineteenth century? How did European monarchs deal with this phenomenon? Sources: E. Kedourie, *Nationalism* (1960); L. Snyder, *Roots of German Nationalism* (1978).
3. "Women and Nationalism." What impact did growing nationalism have on the status of women? What effect did liberalism have on the status of women? Sources: B. Taylor, *Eve and the New Jerusalem: Socialism and Feminism in the Nineteenth Century* (1983); J. Bowditch and C. Ramsland, *Voices of the Industrial Revolution* (1961).

Using Primary Sources

Read Wordsworth's poem "Daffodils" in this chapter. What lines underscore Wordsworth's strong belief in the instructive power of nature? In essence, which lines illustrate Wordsworth's romanticism? How was he a romantic?

Activities for Discovering the Past

I.   **Classroom Discussion Suggestions**

1.   How widely read was Goethe's *Sorrows of Young Werther?*
2.   Why is Beethoven seen as a transitional figure between classical and romantic music?
3.   Discuss Coleridge's idea of the clerisy.
4.   What features characterize a work of literature, art, or music as romantic?

II. **Doing History**

1.   Play selections from Bach and Beethoven for students. Ask them to make notes on the differences in the music. Engage them in a discussion of classical versus romantic music.
2.   Read Coleridge's poem "Kublai Khan" to students. Use the poem to help students understand the nature of romantic poetry.
3.   Have students read pertinent selections from Edmund Burke's *Reflections on the Revolution in France* as the basis of a discussion about the conservative reaction to the French Revolution.

III. **Cooperative Learning Activities**

1.   Using the following list of romantic figures, have six teams make class reports on six of the romantic figures. After the reports, discuss the romantic qualities of each figure.
     William Wordsworth
     Walter Scott
     George Sand
     Victor Hugo
     Eugene Delacroix
     Ludwig van Beethoven
2.   As a follow-up to Activity 1 above, have the teams create posters of the six romantics. Each poster should include a title, a picture (or pictures) of the artist, lyrics or lines illustrating a work (or works). You may wish to display posters on classroom walls.

Map Activity

1.   Using the objectives exercise in Chapter 25 of the *Study Guide,* Vol. II, have students pinpoint on an outline map of Europe (IRM page 183) the seven revolutionary areas on the objectives chart.
2.   Using the map on page 25 of the *Historical Atlas of the World*, have students identify the political entities of Europe after the Treaty of Vienna. Have them demonstrate their knowledge of the changes to the map of Europe resulting from the Napoleonic Wars.

Audiovisual Bibliography

1. *William Wordsworth: William and Dorothy.* (52 min. Color. Films for the Humanities.)
2. *Coleridge: The Fountain and the Cave.* (57 min. Color. Pyramid Films and Video.)
3. *Beethoven: Ordeal and Triumph.* (52 min. Color. ABC-CRM McGraw-Hill.)
4. *Socialism.* (25 min. Color. National Geographic.)
5. *Communism.* (27 min. Color. National Geographic.)
6. *Capitalism.* (24 min. Color. National Geographic.)
7. Poe's Tales of Terror. (CD-ROM. Learning Services.)
8. Favorite Fairy Tales. (CD-ROM. Learning Services.)
9. *The Younger Romantics.* (Videodisc. 28 min. Color. Films for the Humanities and Sciences.)
10. *Romantic Pioneers.* (Videodisc. 28 min. Color. Films for the Humanities and Sciences.)

CHAPTER 26

EUROPEAN LIFE IN THE AGE OF NATIONALISM

Instructional Objectives

After reading and studying this chapter, students should be able to explain how views concerning urbanization differed and the impact that urbanization had on people in Western society in the nineteenth century. Students should also be able to discuss the public health movement and Louis Pasteur's contributions to public health.

Chapter Outline

I. Life in Europe in the nineteenth century reflected considerable changes.
   A. Social classes became more distinct.
      1. Higher wages improved the standard of living for many workers.
      2. The gap between rich and poor widened.
      3. There developed a coalition between the upper middle class and the aristocracy.
      4. Skill specialization and diverse lifestyles resulted in little unity among the members of the working class.
   B. Industrialization and increased urbanization influenced ideas about family matters.
      1. Both premarital sex and illegitimacy increased.
      2. Marriage was now the result of romantic love, not economic necessity.
      3. Family life was strengthened.

II. The status of women changed during the nineteenth century.
   A. The division of labor became more defined by gender.
   B. Economic inferiority led some women to organize for equality and women's rights.
   C. Inspired by Marxist and socialist ideas, some women equated women's rights with the proletarian revolution.
      1. Socialist women called for the liberation of working-class women through revolution.
      2. Women's control and influence in the home increased.

III. Attitudes toward children also changed during this period.
   A. Emotional ties between mothers and infants deepened.
      1. There was more breast-feeding and less swaddling and abandonment of babies.
      2. The birthrate declined, so each child became more important.
   B. Families became more intimate and protective.
      1. Many children suffered the effects of excessive parental concern.

IV. Advances in scientific thought and technology were significant during this period.
   A. The triumph of science improved the lives of many people.
      1. Theoretical discoveries resulted in practical benefits, as in chemistry and electricity.
      2. Scientific achievements gave science considerable prestige.
   B. New social sciences were used to gather data and scientifically test theories.
      1. Darwin believed that all life had evolved gradually from a common origin.
      2. Social Darwinists such as Spencer applied Darwin's ideas to human affairs.

V. The realist movement in literature reflected the ethos of European society.
   A. This was an expression of writers who sought to depict life as it really was.
      1. Realism stressed the hereditary and environmental determinants of human behavior.
   B. Realist writers focused on middle class and working class lives.
      1. The realists believed that human actions were caused by unalterable natural laws.

Lecture Suggestions

1. "Improvements in Public Health." How did public health and sanitation improve in the nineteenth century? Sources: E. Gauldie, *Cruel Habitations: A History of Working Class Housing, 1780–1918* (1974); E. Chadwick, *Report on the Sanitary Condition of the Labouring Population of Great Britain*, ed. M. W. Flinn (1965).
2. "Building New Cities." What architectural developments emerged during this period? What architects created the new modern cities? Sources: D. Pinckney, *Napoleon III and the Rebuilding of Paris* (1972); D. Grew, *Town in the Ruhr: A Social History of Bochum, 1860–1914* (1979).
3. "Sexual Attitudes in the Nineteenth Century." How widespread were prostitution and pornography in the nineteenth century? What were people's attitudes toward sexuality? Sources: E. Trudgill, *Madonnas and Magdalenas: The Origin and Development of Victorian Sexual Attitudes* (1976); A. McLaren, *Sexuality and Social Order: Birth Control in Nineteenth Century France* (1982).

Activities for Discovering the Past

I. Classroom Discussion Suggestions

1. How sanitary were houses of the British lower orders?
2. How did women's status change during the nineteenth century?
3. Discuss the philosophy of Auguste Comte.
4. How was transportation transformed in the nineteenth century?

II. Doing History

1. Have students read selections from Darwin's *The Origin of Species* as a basis for discussing his ideas.
2. Ask students to find illustrations of realism in the following novels: T. Dreiser, *Sister Carrie*; S. Crane, *Maggie: A Girl of the Streets*; I. Turgenev, *Fathers and Sons*.

III. **Cooperative Learning Activities**

1. Organize the class into twelve teams. Each team should be assigned one of the rooms in the picture of the apartment building shown in the text. Each team should write a creative essay chronicling the life of the people in the apartments. Each team should read its essay in class.
2. Six teams should decide on a nineteenth-century painting that best expresses urban living. After deciding on a particular painting, teams should show the painting in class, explaining it and telling how it reflects urban living.

Map Activity

1. Using Map 26.1 in the text, students should dot in cities of 100,000 or more inhabitants in 1900 on an outline map of Europe (IRM page 183).
2. Using the map on page 28 of the *Historical Atlas of the World*, have students list the major ethnic groups in Russia.

Audiovisual Bibliography

1. *Daumier's France.* (60 min. Color. Films for the Humanities and Sciences.)
2. *Charles Darwin.* (24 min. Color. University of California Extension Media Center.)
3. *Louis Pasteur.* (24 min. Color. University of California Extension Media Center.)
4. *Dickens: Oliver Twist.* (Videodisc. 116 min. Color. Films for the Humanities and Sciences.)
5. *Dublin Suite.* (Videodisc. 25 min. Color. Films for the Humanities and Sciences.)
6. *National Gallery of Art.* (Laserdisc. Learning Services.)

CHAPTER 27

THE WORLD AND THE WEST

Instructional Objectives

After reading and studying this chapter, students should be able to define imperialism and explain its impact on European and non-Western societies. Students should also be able to compare and analyze nineteenth-century imperialism with imperialism in other historical periods.

Chapter Outline

I. The European race for overseas empires resulted in Europe's domination of non-European areas of the world.
    A. The race was stimulated by industrial, commercial, and transportation revolutions.
        1. Europe sought markets in Africa and Asia.
    B. World trade increased considerably because of transportation innovations.
        1. The railroad, the steamship and other technological innovations revolutionized trade patterns.

II. The "New Imperialism" emerged in the European race for overseas markets.
    A. Economic concerns played a subordinate role to political ones.
    B. Nationalist and Social Darwinist impulses motivated Westerners.
        1. Europeans saw themselves as protectors and educators of the people of color in Asia and Africa.
        2. They believed the "white man's burden" should be shouldered by the white Christian community of Europe.

III. Critics of imperialism portrayed the bleak side of the European incursion into non-European areas of the world.
    A. They argued that overseas colonies benefited only the well-to-do.
        1. The English critic Hobson influenced Marxist and socialist thinkers with his diatribes against imperialism.
        2. The subject peoples responded in a variety of ways: resistance, violence, resignation, or acceptance.

IV. Western imperialism made its way into Africa and Asia in the nineteenth century.
    A. Between 1880 and 1914, European nations scrambled for political as well as economic control over foreign nations.
        1. This scramble led to new tensions among the competing European powers.
        2. The Berlin Conference of 1884–85 laid the ground rules for imperialism.

B. A multiplicity of causes motivated the European nations and the United States in their quest for foreign dominions.
    1. Economic motives were important but limited.
    2. Colonies were believed to be crucial for national security.
    3. Nationalism, racism, and Social Darwinism contributed to imperialism.
    4. The writer Kipling set forth the notion of the "white man's burden."
    5. Missionaries brought Christianity and education but also racism.

Lecture Suggestions

1. "The Impact of Social Darwinism." How did the application of Darwin's ideas to society help to stimulate the race for overseas colonies? How did social Darwinism help to shape the attitude of the "white man's burden"? Sources: C. Darwin, *The Origin of Species* (1859); R. R. Hofstadter, *Social Darwinism in American Thought* (1955); W. Baumgart, *Imperialism: The Idea and Reality of British and French Colonial Expansion* (1982).
2. "Drugs and Diplomacy: The Opening of Japan." How did the opium trade contribute to the opening of Japan? Sources: A. Waley, *The Opium War Through Chinese Eyes* (1958); J. W. Hall, *Japan, From Prehistory to Modern Times* (1970); E. Reischauer, *Japan: The Story of a Nation* (1981).

Using Primary Sources

Read the passage from Kipling's poem in this chapter. How has the poem been interpreted by the critics of imperialism over the past century? In light of developments in the twentieth century, what other interpretations of the poem are possible, justifiable? Write a short essay in which you attempt to answer these questions.

Activities for Discovering the Past

I. Classroom Discussion Suggestions

1. Discuss how European ventures in Africa and Asia during the nineteenth century nearly led to war.
2. Discuss U.S. imperialism from 1880 to 1914. How did it compare with that of European states?
3. Discuss British policy in the Middle East during this period.
4. Why was India so important to Britain?

II. Doing History

1. What are the many views of nineteenth-century imperialism? How have historical interpretations changed over time? How does the Marxist view differ from other interpretations? Sources: J. A. Hobson, *Imperialism* (1902); V. G. Kiernan, *Marxism and Imperialism* (1975); H. Wright, ed., *The "New Imperialism"* (1975).
2. What can we gain from poetry and novels that helps us to understand the motives of the imperialists and the feelings of the victims? Have students read one or more of the following novels. Ask them to make notes on the motivations of imperialists and the responses of the colonists in these works. These notes can then be used to form the basis of a longer-term project. H. R. Haggard, *King Solomon's Mines*; R. Kipling, *Kim* and *Soldiers Three*; J. Conrad, *Heart*

of Darkness; A. Gide, *The Immoralist.* Selections from Rudyard Kipling's poetry can be found in *The Norton Anthology of English Literature.*

III. Cooperative Learning Activities

1. Charge five teams with learning about imperialism in Africa, India, Egypt, China, and Japan. Have each team make a report to the class on the nature of imperialism in each area. Launch a discussion at the end of the reports.
2. Team-teach the last six chapters. Explain to the student teams that they are responsible for covering the material in the last six chapters of the text. Enable them to use whatever materials and methods they choose.

Map Activity

1. Using Map 27.1 in the text, have students shade in the territories possessed by European states on an outline map of Africa (IRM page 185).
2. Using the map on page 35 of the *Historical Atlas of the World*, have students shade in British possessions in Asia in about 1900 on a blank outline map of Asia (IRM page 186).

Audiovisual Bibliography

1. *The Scramble for Africa.* (37 min. Color. Encyclopaedia Britannica Films.)
2. *China: Agonies of Nationalism 1800–1927.* (29 min. B/W. Films, Inc.)
3. *India's History: British Rule to Independence.* (11 min. Color. Coronet Films.)
4. *Masters in the Colonies.* (Videodisc. 30 min. Color. Films for the Humanities and Sciences.)
5. *The Dawn of Tomorrow.* (Videodisc. 30 min. Color. Films for the Humanities and Sciences.)
6. *The Paths of Colonialism.* (Videodisc. 17 min. Color. Films for the Humanities and Sciences.)

CHAPTER 28

NATION BUILDING IN THE WESTERN HEMISPHERE AND IN AUSTRALIA

Instructional Objectives

After reading and analyzing this chapter, students should be able to explain how the Spanish colonies of Latin America were able to win their independence from Europe. Students should also be able to explain how the concept of "manifest destiny" played an active role in the development of the United States. Students should also be able to discuss how the Americas and Australia assimilated new peoples. Finally, students should be able to delineate the geographical, economic, and political factors that aided in the development of Canada and Australia.

Chapter Outline

I. Latin America (ca. 1800–1929)
   A. The Spanish Empire in the West went through a series of civil wars or revolutions.
      1. Creoles, peninsulares, mestizos, and mulattos fought the Spanish and one another.
      2. After 1850, another flood of immigrants came to Latin America.
   B. The Origins of the Revolutions
      1. The Spanish colonies had achieved much economic diversity and independence by the late seventeenth century.
      2. The mercantilist imperialism of Spain had declined.
      3. Colonial manufacture and agriculture were highly taxed.
      4. Economic development was frustrated.
      5. Tax reforms fueled colonial discontent.
   C. Race Relations
      1. Creoles did not extend the idea of "rights of man" to nonwhites.
      2. The lack of women led to mixed marriages of Indians, Spaniards, and Africans.
      3. Dark skin was linked with servile manual labor.
      4. The Spanish controlled the economy.
      5. However, manumission was more frequent than in North America.
      6. Many black slaves fled to the jungles or mountains.
   D. The Comunero Revolution
      1. Amaru led an Indian uprising in Peru in 1779.
      2. The revolt was crushed by the Spanish; some reforms were granted.
      3. In Socorro, where a large mestizo population lived, increased taxes and a new alcabala led to the Comunero Revolution.
      4. Creole captains led an Indian army on Bogota.
      5. The government agreed to the rebels' demands.

E. Independence
    1. The removal of the Spanish king by Napoleon led to revolt in Latin America.
    2. The wealthy Creoles seized power for themselves.
    3. Each separate area went its own way.
    4. Bolívar's dream of a continental union did not materialize.
    5. Only Brazil won its independence without violent upheaval.
F. The Consequences of Independence
    1. The expulsion of the Spanish left a power vacuum.
    2. The dictator Rosas ruled in Argentina while other dictators ruled in Venezuela.
    3. Continual revolutions occurred in Bolivia and Venezuela.
    4. Economic prosperity was lost as warfare disrupted the economy.
    5. Slavery was abolished except in Brazil and Cuba.
    6. Blacks in Latin America enjoyed greater economic and social mobility than in North America.
    7. A tripartite social order existed: white, colored, and black.
    8. The advent of stable dictatorship led to economic growth.
    9. Political stability encouraged foreign investment.
    10. By 1900, foreigners controlled Latin American economies.

II. The United States (ca. 1789–1929)
    A. Manifest Destiny
        1. Many agreed with O'Sullivan that God had foreordained the United States to cover the entire continent.
        2. The purchase of Louisiana from France, that of Florida from Spain, and the settlement of 1814 with Britain, extended the United States south, southwest, northwest, and to the Gulf Plains.
        3. The Mexican War led to the U.S. acquisition of California and New Mexico.
        4. Trickery was used to gain Indian land.
        5. Indians were removed to reservations.
    B. Black slavery in the South
        1. The liberal and democratic beliefs of Americans conflicted with their dependence on black slavery.
        2. Economic historians suggest that economic gain was the main force behind slavery.
        3. The conflict between religious beliefs and slaveholding produced deep psychological stresses for the slave-owning class.
    C. The American Civil War (1861–1865)
        1. The growth of the cotton industry raised the question of the further expansion of slavery.
        2. Lincoln's election caused South Carolina (and then other states) to secede from the Union in 1860.
        3. Lincoln became a spokesman for the antislavery movement.
        4. The American Civil War had important political consequences in Europe.
        5. Some historians refer to the American Civil War as the first modern war.
    D. The Black Family
        1. In spite of slavery, blacks established strong family units.
        2. Slaveowners encouraged slave marriage and large families.
        3. Until the 1920s, most black households were headed by two parents.
    E. Following the American Civil War, the U.S. underwent an industrial boom.
        1. The entry of millions of new immigrants met the labor needs of growing industry.
        2. Cheap farmland in the West encouraged cultivation by pioneers.
        3. Immigration led to rapid urbanization.
        4. Urbanization brought serious problems.

5. Anti-immigrant prejudices, largely against non–Anglo-Saxons, Catholics, and Asians, arose among Americans born here.
6. Racist immigration laws established quotas on some groups.

III. Canada
   A. Champlain established a trading post in 1608 on the site of present-day Quebec.
      1. The British challenged the French for control of Canada.
      2. The British defeated the French in 1759; France ceded Canada to Great Britain by the Treaty of Paris in 1763.
      3. The Quebec Act of 1774 placed power in the hands of an appointed governor and council.
      4. Civil discontent led to the Constitution Act of 1791, which divided Canada into Lower and Upper Canada.
   B. Confederation, Expansion, and Development (1840–1905)
      1. The Union Act of 1840 united Lower and Upper Canada under one government composed of a governor, an appointed legislative council, and an elective assembly.
      2. The Dominion of Canada was established by the British North America Act of 1867.
      3. John A. Macdonald became the Dominion's first prime minister.
      4. The Canadian Pacific Railroad opened in 1885.
      5. Between 1897 and 1912, a wave of immigrants arrived in Canada.
      6. Canadians supported the Allied cause in World War One.

IV. Australia
   A. Australia was claimed for the British king by James Cook in 1770.
      1. It is the world's smallest continent.
      2. It has three topographical zones:
         a. western desert and semidesert
         b. a central eastern lowlands
         c. an eastern highlands
      3. After the American Revolution, the British needed new places to send convicts.
      4. Crowded English prisons led to the establishment of a penal colony at Botany Bay, although the first governor moved the colony to Port Jackson (Sydney).
      5. The convicts knew little about agriculture and the colony nearly failed.
   B. Economic Development
      1. After 1815, a steady stream of people moved to Australia.
      2. Sealing and wool production were two important enterprises.
      3. Wheat farming became an important part of the economy by 1900.
      4. The gold rush of 1851–1861 greatly affected life and the economy.
      5. Great population growth occurred.
      6. The Commonwealth Immigration Restriction Act of 1901 closed immigration to Asians.
      7. The Commonwealth of Australia was formed in 1901.
      8. It tooks its parliamentary system from Britain and its concept of decentralized government from the United States.

Lecture Suggestions

1. "The Real Simón Bolívar." Who was Simón Bolívar and what was he really like? Sources: G. Masur, *Simón Bolívar*, 2nd ed. (1969); J. J. Johnson and D. M. Ladd, *Simón Bolívar and Spanish American Independence, 1783–1830* (1968).
2. "Brazil's Independence." How did Brazil win independence without bloodshed? Sources: K. R. Maxwell, *Conflicts and Conspiracies: Brazil and Portugal, 1750–1808* (1973); A. J. R. Russell-Wood, ed., *From Colony to Nation: Essays on the Independence of Brazil* (1975).

Using Primary Sources

Contemporary Responses to Slavery in the United States.
Have students read selections from Mary B. Chesnut's diary (*Mary Chesnut's Civil War*, ed. C. V. Woodward, New Haven, CT, 1981) and George Fitzhugh's *Treatise on Sociology* to get a contemporary flavor of differing views about slavery from the American South.

Activities for Discovering the Past

I. Classroom Discussion Suggestions

1. How did racial prejudice in Latin America differ from that in North America?
2. What were some of the problems of the postindependence period in Latin America?
3. Why was the Emancipation Proclamation a "tiger without teeth" when it went into effect on January 1, 1863?
4. What was the role of the slave mother in the United States?
5. What impact did immigration have on urbanization in the United States?

II. Doing History

1. Have students read Mary Chesnut's *A Diary from Dixie* to obtain a contemporary view of how women responded to the challenges of the war. Have them list observations drawn from Chesnut's diary as a starting point for a discussion about women and the home front in the American Civil War.
2. Show parts of the classic film *Gone With the Wind*. Have students list the customs and mannerisms they observe in the film and discuss whether the film accurately portrays the South of the period.

III. Cooperative Learning Activities

1. Organize the class into five groups and charge them with researching and reporting on nation building in the following areas: (1) Brazil, (2) Peru, (3) Canada, (4) Mexico, and (5) Australia. Each group should research and write a short history of the road to nationhood for each of the areas mentioned above. Groups should present their findings to the class. Groups should be encouraged to make timelines on poster board for use in their presentations.
2. The Art of Independence
   As a follow-up to the above activity, students should create collages of people, events, and symbols of independence in each of the nations reported on. They might use magazines, books (photocopies of pictures), and other materials to create their collages of independence.

Map Activity

Using the map on page 43 of the *Historical Atlas of the World*, have students list the following on an outline map of South America (IRM page 187):

1. Caracas
2. Caribbean Sea
3. Gulf of Maracaibo
4. Bogota
5. Quito
6. Lima
7. Santiago
8. Tierra Del Fuego
9. Montevideo
10. Falkland Islands
11. Buenos Aires
12. Asuncion
13. Rio de Janeiro
14. French Guiana
15. Dutch Guiana

Audiovisual Bibliography

1. *The Civil War.* (30 min. Color. Finely-Holiday Inn Film Corp.)
2. *Civil War: The Background Issues.* (16 min. Color. Coronet Films.)
3. *Civil War (1863–1865).* (16 min. Color. Coronet Films.)
4. *The Red Badge of Courage.* (69 min. B/W. MGM/UA.)
5. *An Occurrence at Owl Creek Bridge.* (27 min. B/W. Festival Films.)
6. *Latin America: Neighbors to the South.* (17 min. Color. Universal Educational and Visual Arts.)
7. *Bolivar: South American Liberator.* (11 min. Color. Coronet Films.)
8. *The Immigrant Experience.* 28 min. Color. Learning Corporation of America.)
9. *The African American Experience: A History.* (CD-ROM. National School Products.)
10. *Black American History: Slavery to Civil Rights.* (CD-ROM. National School Products.)
11. *Australia Down Under.* (Videodisc. 3 Discs. Each disc 48 mins. Color. Films for the Humanities and Sciences.)

CHAPTER 29

THE GREAT BREAK: WAR AND REVOLUTION

Instructional Objectives

After reading and studying this chapter, students should be able to list the causes of World War One. Students should also be able to discuss the impact of World War One, describing some of the major results and discussing how the war affected the common people of the West.

Chapter Outline

I.   World War I was a turning point in Western civilization.
   A.   Europe was changed dramatically.
   B.   The Austro-Hungarian Empire, the German Empire, and Ottoman Empire were defeated.
   C.   Growing nationalism exerted an even greater influence on the political makeup of Europe.

II.   There was a multiplicity of causes of the Great War.
   A.   Forces unleashed during the nineteenth century had a great impact.
       1.   Imperialism fueled competition among European states for foreign dominions.
       2.   Social Darwinism encouraged feelings of European superiority.
   B.   Military and industrial buildup created a war-footing in Europe.
       1.   Militarism led to a belief in the inevitability of a European war.
       2.   Industrialism provided modern weaponry for mass destruction.

III.   The participants succumbed to the belief that war was inevitable.
   A.   The Triple Entente was composed of Britain, France, and Russia.
       1.   The integrity of Belgium was at stake.
       2.   The Entente encircled Germany and her allies.
   B.   The Triple Alliance included Germany, Austria, and Italy.
       1.   Germany expressed a feeling of encirclement.

IV.   The war had a tremendous impact on Europe and left many unsolved problems.
   A.   German defeat led to the development of radical political movements that exerted pressure on German politics.
       1.   Communist factions attempted to transform Germany.
       2.   Right-wing groups such as the Nazis propagandized that Germany had been betrayed.
   B.   Germany was kept out of the international community.
   C.   Wilson's League of Nations was a failure.
       1.   Wilson's own Congress opposed his ideas.

V. The downfall of tsarist Russia followed in the wake of World War One.
   A. Deteriorating conditions and agitating political groups combined to bring down the tsar.
      1. War losses and mistakes pointed to the weak leadership of the tsar.
      2. Food shortages led to revolution in March 1917.
      3. A provisional government was proclaimed by the Duma.
      4. The tsar abdicated.
   B. Vladimir Lenin led the Bolshevik Revolution.
      1. Lenin believed that revolution was necessary to destroy capitalism.
      2. Lenin led an attack against the provisional government in July 1917.
      3. Trotsky led a Soviet overthrow of the provisional government (November 1917).
      4. The Bolsheviks came to power because they were the answer to anarchy.
      5. The Bolshevik victory in the Russian Civil War led to the establishment of a Soviet dictatorship.

Using Primary Sources

Film as a Primary Source.
Show students the film *The Guns of August*. Ask them to take notes while watching the film. Then ask them to use the film as a stimulus for a paper entitled "World War I: Who Was Responsible?" What viewpoint is the film taking? What axe do the filmmakers have to grind? After reading and discovering papers in class, have students read several passages in D. Lee, *The Outbreak of the First World War* (1970). Then, have another discussion about the film and its intent.

Activities for Discovering the Past

I. Classroom Discussion Suggestions

1. What prompted the United States to enter World War One?
2. Why did a communist revolution take place in Russia rather than in Britain or France?
3. What demands did World War One place on the home fronts of the major powers?
4. How were Wilson's "Fourteen Points" accepted by the leaders of the other allied powers?
5. Was leaving Germany out of the League of Nations a strategic blunder?

II. Doing History

1. Historians continue to debate who was responsible for World War One. Involve students in the debate by having them read selections from the following sources in preparation for a class discussion and/or a short historiographical paper. Sources: L. Lafore, *The Long Fuse* (1971);   J. Remak, *The Origins of World War I* (1967); L. C. F. Turner, *The Origins of World War I* (1970).
2. How did the Bolsheviks see themselves and their revolution? What insights can we gain about the personal lives of these leaders and the period in which they live by reading primary sources? Sources: L. Trotsky, *History of the Russian Revolution* (1932); J. Reed, *Ten Days That Shook the World* (1919).
3. What was battle like for the common soldier? What were the people like who filled the trenches and cared for the wounded and sustained the war effort back home? Sources: J. Keegan, *The Face of Battle* (1983) (students should read the third part of the book, on the Battle of the Somme); A. Horne, *The Price of Glory: Verdun, 1916* (1979); J. Ellis, *Eye-Deep in Hell* (1976); V. Brittain, *Testament of Youth* (1933; reprinted in 1980).

4. How is the war reflected in literature? What can we gain by reading some of the period's masterpieces? Sources: E. M. Remarque, *All Quiet on the Western Front* (1929); H. Barbusse, *Under Fire* (1917); J. Romains, *Verdun* (1939); E. Hemingway, *A Farewell to Arms* (1929).

III. Cooperative Learning Activities

1. Organize the class into five teams. Have each team read selections in one of the following works about the origins of World War One: A. J. P. Taylor, *From Sarajevo to Potsdam*; L. Lafore, *The Long Fuse*; F. Fischer, *German War Aims in the First World War*; B. Tuchman, *The Guns of August*; G. Ritter, *The Schlieffen Plan*. After students have read and discussed material, have each group present the author's explanation of the origins of World War One.

2. Assign five student teams the task of discovering a poem that best illustrates the horrors of World War One. Allow time in class for discussion. When teams have decided on poems, have a member from each team read the poem in class. Discuss all five poems. Students might then be asked to write short poems on World War One.

Map Activity

1. Using a blank outline map of Europe (IRM page 183), have students shade in the countries that constitute the Triple Entente and the Triple Alliance.

2. Using the map on page 33 of the *Historical Atlas of the World*, have students list the various states in the Balkans in about 1914 on a blank outline map of Europe. How has the map of Eastern Europe changed today?

Audiovisual Bibliography

1. *World War I: A Documentary on the Role of the USA.* (28 min. B/W. Encyclopaedia Britannica Films.)
2. *The Outbreak of the First World War.* (29 min. Color. Encyclopaedia Britannica Films.)
3. *1917: Revolution in Russia.* (28 min. Color. National Geographic Films.)
4. *Lenin.* (39 min. B/W. Learning Corporation of America.)
5. *Versailles: The Lost Peace.* (26 min. Color. Films, Inc.)
6. *World War I: The War That Failed to End Wars.* (Videodisc. 14 min. Color. Films for the Humanities and Sciences.)
7. *The Battle of Verdun.* (Videodisc. 26 min. B/W. Films for the Humanities and Sciences.)
8. *American Journey, 1896–1945.* (CD-ROM. Learning Services.)
9. *Multimedia World Factbook.* (CD-ROM. Learning Services.)

CHAPTER 30

NATIONALISM IN ASIA, 1914–1939

Instructional Objectives

After reading and analyzing this chapter, students should be able to explain how modern nationalism developed in Asia between the two world wars. Students should also be able to discuss how national movements arose in different countries and how some of those parallel movements came into conflict.

Chapter Outline

I. The First World War and Western Imperialism
    A. The First World War greatly altered relations between Asia and Europe.
        1. The Chinese and Japanese saw the war as a family quarrel that divided Europe and made it vulnerable.
        2. In India and Indochina the enthusiasm for war was limited but the war's impact was greater.
    B. The British and the French needed the aid and the resources of their colonial peoples.
        1. Many Asians served in the French and British armies.
        2. The British and French, in turn, made promises of postwar reform and self-rule.
    C. Soviet communism denounced imperialism and encouraged national independence movements.
        1. The domination of the world economy by the West created hostility toward Europe and the United States.

II. The Middle East
    A. Beginning with the revolution of 1908, the Young Turks strengthened the Ottoman state at the expense of the Arabs, largely Syria and Iraq.
        1. After defeat in Europe, they concentrated on control of their Asian possessions.
        2. Instead of liberal reform, they implemented a narrow Turkish nationalism.
        3. The Turks joined forces with Germany and Austria-Hungary in 1914, hoping to regain influence in Europe.
    B. The Arabs sided with Britain and successfully revolted against the Turks in 1916.
        1. Hussein Ibn Ali led the Arab revolt, joined by T. E. Lawrence.
        2. The British Balfour Declaration of 1917 promised the Jews a national home in Palestine.
        3. Mustafa Kemal led the Turkish national liberation movement.
        4. Kemal's forces won a great victory over the foreigners.
        5. Kemal was a secularist and a modernizer.
        6. He deposed the sultan and established a republic with himself as president.

    C.   Iran and Afghanistan
        1.   Iran was not as successful as Turkey in building a modern state.
        2.   The Iranian revolution of 1906 ended with Russian and British occupation of Iran.
        3.   By 1919, all of Iran was under British control.
        4.   Afghanistan won independence but found modernization difficult.
    D.   The Arab states and Palestine
        1.   The Arab states gradually gained independence, although the West remained a strong presence.
        2.   Faisal won independence for Iraq in 1939 by agreeing to a long-term military alliance with Great Britain.
        3.   The British proclaimed Egypt independent in 1932 but maintained a strong military presence.
        4.   Relations between Arabs and the West were complicated by Palestine.
        5.   The key issue was Jewish migration from Europe to Palestine.
        6.   Arab resentment over Jewish settlement, combined with cultural and economic friction, caused anti-Jewish violence and undeclared civil war.

III. Toward Self-Rule in India
    A.   India gave significant support to the British cause during the First World War.
        1.   The Lucknow Pact brought the Muslim minority and the Hindu majority together under the banner of self-government.
        2.   The Government of India Act of 1919 permitted Indians to participate in government.
    B.   Hindu Society and Mahatma Gandhi
        1.   He came from a wealthy Indian family of merchants.
        2.   Gandhi studied law in England and eventually became a lawyer in British South Africa.
        3.   Gandhi undertook the legal defense of Indians who had finished their terms as indentured laborers.
        4.   Gandhi called his spiritual theory of social action "Satyagraha," meaning "Soul Force."
        5.   Its tactic of nonviolent resistance owed a good deal to the teachings of Christ.
        6.   Gandhi's movement brought tax and immigration reforms and recognition of non-Christian marriages for the nonwhites of South Africa.
        7.   By 1929, Indian desire for a speedier path to self-rule led to Gandhi's famous march to the sea.
        8.   In 1931, Gandhi and the British negotiated a new constitution that strengthened India's parliament and paved the way to self-rule.

IV. Turmoil in East Asia
    A.   The Chinese movement toward independence from the West and toward modernism was undermined by internal conflict and war with Japan.
        1.   Yuan Shikai, the leader of the revolution against the Manchus, dissolved the parliament and ruled as dictator.
        2.   Foreign imperialism, the power of local lords, and other factors led to an alliance between Sun Yat-sen's Nationalists and the Chinese Communists.
        3.   Sun placed nationalism above all else, including communism.
        4.   Between 1926 and 1928, the Nationalists under Chiang Kai-shek unified China under a new government at Nanking.
    B.   China's intellectual revolution
        1.   Nationalism was only one part of the New Culture Movement.
        2.   Marxism was attractive because it was a single, all-encompassing creed.

3. Mao Zedong believed that peasant revolution would free China.
C. From Liberalism to Ultranationalism in Japan
1. The First World War accelerated economic expansion and imperial growth in Japan.
2. Serious problems accompanied Japan's rise.
3. Japan's population grew while natural resources and food remained scarce.
4. The most serious problem was ultranationalism.
5. The ultranationalists wanted to restore traditional Japanese practices and reject Western institutions.
6. Japanese army officers in Manchuria turned to ultranationalism as a solution to Japan's problems.
7. Manchuria was taken from China in 1931–32 by the Japanese army.
8. By late 1938, sizable portions of coastal China were under Japanese control.
D. Southeast Asia
1. Events elsewhere in Asia inspired nationalism in French Indochina and the Dutch East Indies.
2. French imperialism in Vietnam stimulated the growth of a Communist-led nationalist movement.
3. In Indonesia, Dutch determination to keep their colonies led to the rule of a successful nationalist movement.
4. The Philippine nationalist movement succeeded.

Lecture Suggestions

1. "Japanese Expansion." What impact did Japan's mainland forays have on China and other Asian states? Source: R. Myers and M. Peattie, *The Japanese Colonial Expansion, 1895–1945* (1984).
2. "China's Move Toward Communism." How did Chinese communists during the new Culture Movement adapt Marxian socialism to suit their needs? Sources: J. Spence, *The Gate of Heavenly Peace: The Chinese and Their Revolution, 1895–1980* (1981); J. Sheridan, *China in Disintegration: The Republican Era in Chinese History* (1975).

Using Primary Sources

Have students read selections from W. Laqueur, *A History of Zionism* (1972) and A. Eban, *My People*, especially the parts on the Balfour Declaration of 1917. Then, discuss the problems for both Jews and Arabs that were inherent in this significant action of Western geopolitics.

ACTIVITIES FOR DISCOVERING THE PAST

I. Classroom Discussion Suggestions

1. How were women's rights improved by Kemal Atatürk?
2. What role did Mao Zedong play in the Chinese Nationalist movement?
3. What factors influenced the Balfour Declaration?
4. How did Gandhi's experiences in South Africa help in his work in India?
5. How did the Great Depression affect U.S. imperialist ventures in Asia?

II. **Doing History**

1. Have students find passages in the New Testament that may have influenced Gandhi's development of a philosophy of passive resistance and militant nonviolence. Have students write short essays analyzing the concepts of Gandhi and Christ.

2. Give students two outline maps of Asia. On one, have them fill in the major political entities before the First World War. On the other, have them list the places where nationalism held sway after 1918.

III. **Cooperative Learning Activities**

1. Organize the class into six groups. Charge each group with the task of researching and reporting on nationalist movements in: (1) Egypt, (2) Turkey, (3) Iran, (4) Afghanistan, (5) India, and (6) China. Each group should develop a historical sketch of rising nationalism in each area between the end of World War One and the beginning of World War Two. Each group should also construct a timeline of important developments to be used in the group's presentation.

1. World Societies *Jeopardy*
   To bring fun to an exam review, allow teams/groups to compete in a World Societies version of the popular television show *Jeopardy*. Create a *Jeopardy* game board on the chalkboard or give students photocopied sheets with the game categories. The game board should include categories that relate to the material covered since the last exam. This game format can be used anytime throughout the term and always seems to spark great interest and enthusiasm among students.

Map Activity

Using the map on pages 64–65 of the *Historical Atlas of the World*, have students list the following on an outline map of Asia (IRM page 186):
1. Philippine Islands
2. Sea of Japan
3. Tokyo
4. Manchuria
5. Korea
6. Seoul
7. Peking
8. Shanghai
9. Hong Kong
10. Taiwan
11. Laos
12. Siam
13. Borneo
14. South China Sea
15. Sumatra

Audiovisual Bibliography

1. *The Sand Pebbles.* (195 min. Color. CBS/Fox Video.)
2. *China: A Century of Revolution. Part I: 1800–1927.* (24 min. B/W. Films, Inc.)
3. *China: A Century of Revolution. Part II: 1927–1944.* (26 min. B/W. Films, Inc.)

4. *Japan: East Is West.* (22 min. Color. NCB, Inc.)
5. *Japan: A Century of Imperialism (1850–1945).* (30 min. B/W. Films, Inc.)
6. *Being Muslim in India.* (40 min. Color. Center for South Asian Studies, University of Wisconsin.)
7. *Gandhi.* (188 min. Color. RCA/Columbia Pictures Home Video.)
8. *Arab Identity: Who Are the Arabs?* (26 min. Color. Learning Corporation of America.)
9. *The Rocky Road to Chinese Revolution.* (Videodisc. Films for the Humanities and Sciences.)
10. *Mao by Mao.* (Videodisc. 28 min. Color. Films for the Humanities and Sciences.)
11. *Chinese Prison Labor: Inside China's Gulag.* (Videodisc. 52 min. Color. Films for the Humanities and Sciences.)
12. *Hirohito: Japan in the Twentieth Century.* (Videodisc. 58 min. Color. Films for the Humanities and Sciences.)
13. *Who's Who in China.* (CD-ROM. National School Products.)

CHAPTER 31

THE AGE OF ANXIETY IN THE WEST

Instructional Objectives

After reading and studying the chapter, students should be able to discuss the impact of the "Lost Peace" of 1919. Students should also be able to explain the political climate in Germany during the 1920s. Finally, students should be able to discuss why people were alienated after World War One and how the postwar alienation was reflected in the arts, psychology, philosophy, and literature.

Chapter Outline

I. World War One spelled the death of the old order.
    A. World War One dealt a staggering blow to Western civilization.
    B. A new world began to take shape in the ashes of the old.
    C. The building process created an age of anxiety in Western society.

II. The critics of the pre-war world anticipated many of the postwar ideas.
    A. Nietzsche believed that only the creativity of a few supermen could restructure the maligned world.
    B. Logical empiricists maintained that only experience was worth analyzing.
        1. Abstract concepts like God were sheer folly.
    C. Existentialists viewed a world where the individual has to find his own meaning.
        1. Sartre and Camus are representatives of this group.
    D. Christian existentialists like Kierkegaard believed that Christian faith could anchor the individual caught in the tempestuous sea of modernity.
    E. The above views gained greater acceptance after the Great War's destruction.

III. The horrors of war brought about Christianity's revival.
    A. T. S. Eliot created his work within a perceived traditional Christian framework.
        1. Eliot advocated literary allegiance to tradition.
    B. Graham Greene turned to religion for hope and meaning.

IV. The postwar world witnessed many developments in physics and psychology.
    A. Einstein's theory about the relativity of time and space challenged traditional ideas of Newtonian physics.
        1. The Newtonian system that had dominated society since the seventeenth and eighteenth centuries began to give way.
    B. Freudian psychology seemed to reflect the spirit of the age, with its emphasis on men and women as greedy, grasping, irrational creatures.
        1. Freud believed that human behavior is irrational.

    2.   He believed that the key to understanding human behavior is the irrational unconscious (the id).

V. Postwar literature and the arts witnessed a minor renaissance.
    A.   Literary figures such as Proust, Eliot, and Joyce experimented with language in an attempt to reflect the dynamics of society.
        1.   The postwar moods of pessimism, relativism, and alienation influenced novelists and poets.
    B.   The music of Stravinsky, Berg, and Schoenberg challenged traditional standards of musical theory.
        1.   The concept of expressionism affected music.
        2.   Schoenberg and other composers abandoned traditional harmony and tonality.
    C.   Architecture tended toward functionalism.
        1.   The Bauhaus Movement appeared at first to be a sinister, inhuman reflection of the anxiety of the age.
    D.   Artists like Cezanne, Picasso, and Dali revolutionized art by turning to increasingly nonrepresentational expressions.
        1.   Cubism concentrated on zigzagging lines and overlapping planes.
        2.   Nonrepresentational art focused on mood, not objects.

Lecture Suggestions

1.   "Political Blunders by the Western Democracies." What political mistakes helped to increase tensions during the Age of Anxiety? Was there a leadership crisis in the postwar period? Sources: J. Sontag, *A Broken World, 1919–1939* (1971); A. Bullock, *The Twentieth Century* (1971).

2.   "Changing Social Strata." How did World War One affect the social structure of Europe? Was there more social mobility after the war? Why? Sources: C. Maier, *Recasting Bourgeois Europe* (1975); M. Childs, *Sweden: The Middle Way* (1961); J. Ortega y Gasset, *The Revolt of the Masses* (1932).

3.   "The Impact of Sigmund Freud." How did Freud's theories of psychoanalysis contribute to the Age of Anxiety? How did these ideas reach the masses? Sources: A. Starr, *Freud* (1989); M. White, ed., *The Age of Analysis* (1955); P. Rieff, *Freud* (1956).

4.   "The Impact of Mass Leisure." How did the development of more leisure time affect the postwar world? How was mass leisure organized? What sports and pastimes were engaged in by the masses in the 1920s? Sources: M. Marrus, ed., *Emergence of Leisure* (1974); W. Baker, *Sports in Western Society* (1983).

Using Primary Sources

Read aloud in class "The Love Song of J. Alfred Prufrock" by T. S. Eliot. Then have students read the poem again to themselves. Discuss passages that illustrate the anxiety Eliot expressed about life in the modern world. Then have students write an essay on Prufrock as the prototypical alienated person in the Age of Anxiety.

Activities for Discovering the Past

I. Classroom Discussion Suggestions

1. What impact did Nietzsche's ideas have on supporters of totalitarianism?
2. Why did the League of Nations fail?
3. How was the radio successfully exploited by political leaders of the 1920s and 1930s?
4. Discuss the development of the film industry. What effect did it have on leisure time?
5. Discuss the status of women in Weimar Germany.
6. What impact did service in World War One have on American blacks?

II. Doing History

1. Give students an outline map of Europe and ask them to label the new nations and boundaries of Europe after World War One.
2. If slides are available, show students slides depicting the work of Cézanne, Picasso, Matisse, Dali, and other artists discussed in the chapter. Discuss how the artist and artwork reflect their historical context. Students should be directed to read selections from the following sources: A. H. Barr, *What Is Modern Painting?* (1966); J. Rewald, *The History of Impressionism* (1956); H. Gardner, *Art Through the Ages* (1961).
3. How could there have been such a resurgence of arts and letters during the politically corrupt Weimar Republic? Are there parallels in the history of Western civilization where artistic and literary renaissances occur during periods of political dysfunction? Sources: P. Gay, *Weimar Culture* (1970); T. Wolfe, *From Bauhaus to My House* (1981); P. Fritzsche, *Rehearsals for Fascism: Populism and Political Mobilization in Weimar Germany* (1990).
4. Have students read selections from one or more of the following works and write short analytical papers on the social themes presented in them: E. Hemingway, *The Sun Also Rises* (1926); W. Holtby, *South Riding* (1936); W. Greenwood, *Love on the Dole* (1933); H. Fallada, *Little Man, What Now?* (1932); A. Gide, *The Counterfeiters*; A. Camus, *The Plague* (1942), and *The Stranger* (1942).

III. Cooperative Learning Activities

1. Have six student teams read selections from the following modern philosophers and present the philosophers' ideas to the class:
   Nietzsche
   Bergson
   Wittgenstein
   Sartre
   Heidegger
   Kierkegaard
2. Have five student teams decide on paintings that best express modern characteristics and anxieties. Have them show reproductions of the paintings in class and explain why they feel these particular paintings best represent the modern ethos.

Map Activity

1. On an outline map of North and South America (IRM page 187), have students pinpoint the birthplaces of the following significant artists and writers of the Age of Anxiety:
    Virginia Woolf
    Marcel Proust
    James Joyce
    William Faulkner
    Thomas Wolfe
    T. S. Eliot
    Ezra Pound
    Ernest Hemingway
    Gertrude Stein
    Salvador Dali
    Pablo Picasso
    Paul Cézanne
    George Grosz
    Gustav Klimt
    Edvard Munch
2. Using the map on page 36 of the *Historical Atlas of the World,* have students shade in the principal status quo powers and the principal revisionist powers on a blank outline map of Europe (IRM page 183).

Audiovisual Bibliography

1. *1929–1941: The Great Depression.* (25 min. B/W. National Geographic Films.)
2. *Vienna: Stripping the Facade.* (25 min. Color. Media Guild Films.)
3. *Picasso: Artist of the Century.* Parts I and II. (30 min. each. Color. Films, Inc.)
4. *League of Nations: The Hope of Mankind.* Parts I and II. (26 min. each. Color. Time-Life Films.)
5. *Cabaret.* (134 min. Color. Films, Inc.)
6. *The Blue Angel.* (91 min. B/W. Films, Inc.)
7. *James Joyce.* (Vidcodisc. 80 min. Color. Films for the Humanities and Sciences.)
8. *Ezra Pound: Poet's Poet.* (Videodisc. 28 min. Color. Films for the Humanities and Sciences.)
9. *Gertrude Stein and a Companion.* (Videodisc. 87 min. Color. Films for the Humanities and Sciences.)
10. *Ernest Hemingway: Grace Under Pressure.* (Videodisc. 55 min. Color. Films for the Humanities and Sciences.)

CHAPTER 32

DICTATORSHIPS AND THE SECOND WORLD WAR

Instructional Objectives

After reading and studying this chapter, students should be able to explain how unsolved problems that lingered after World War One helped ignite another worldwide conflict. Students should also be able to distinguish between Nazi totalitarianism and Soviet totalitarianism. Finally, students should be able to discuss how the Allies were able to defeat Nazi Germany and the Axis powers in World War Two.

Chapter Outline

I. The lingering effects of World War One contributed significantly to the outbreak of World War Two.
   A. International economic collapse plagued Europe and the U.S.
      1. Inflation in Germany devastated the economy.
      2. Economic collapse in the U.S. came in October of 1929.
   B. Political ineptitude by major political leaders of world powers helped advance the cause of dictatorships.
      1. The League of Nations was unable to solve international crises.
      2. Germany was kept out of the League.

II. Italy and Mussolini fashioned a fascist government after World War One.
   A. Mussolini's fascists used street politics, nationalist sentiment, and romanticism to create a conservative authoritarian state.
      1. By the early 1920s, most Italians were opposed to liberal, parliamentary government.
      2. The Catholic church supported Mussolini because he did not try to absorb it into the fascist government.
   B. Mussolini's was not the ideal totalitarian state.
      1. Mussolini did not establish a fully totalitarian state.

III. Germany and Hitler established the model totalitarian state.
   A. Adolf Hitler became an ardent nationalist in Vienna.
      1. He used his oratorical gifts and keen perception of German society to turn Germany into a Nazi empire.
   B. The Nazis appealed to nationalistic sentiment, a romantic yearning for the "glorious" German past, and anti-Semitic tendencies.
      1. In *Mein Kampf*, Hitler outlined his desire to achieve German racial superiority.

C. The promises of "work and bread" had a tremendous appeal to Germans who suffered from post–World War One inflation and unemployment.

D. The Enabling Act of 1933 gave Hitler absolute dictatorial powers.
   1. Hitler was able to achieve a measure of economic recovery.
   2. He reduced traditional class distinctions.
   3. He appealed to the nationalistic urges of many Germans.

IV. Russia and Stalin devised another kind of totalitarian state.
   A. Political purges helped Stalin remove the major political threats to his power.
   B. Failed economic programs of the past gave way to spectacular growth of heavy industry.
      1. Russia succeeded with the aid of government control.
      2. Foreign technological experts also played a key role in Russia's success.

V. World War Two became an effort by the Western democracies to stamp out fascism.
   A. It reflected the growing technological might of the great powers.
   B. It demonstrated organizing abilities of Churchill, Roosevelt, and Hitler.
      1. The key to Hitler's military success was speed and force (the blitzkrieg).
      2. Churchill and Britain withstood heavy bombing by the Germans.
      3. Roosevelt got the U.S. on a quick war footing.
   C. It brought into sharp contrast the brutality of the Nazis against Jews, Slavs, and other peoples Nazis considered subhuman.
      1. Hitler attempted to build a new order based on race.
      2. The Slavs, for example, were treated as *untermenschen* ("subhumans").
      3. Jews, Gypsies, Jehovah's witnesses, and communists were condemned to death.

VI. The Allied victory came first in Europe, then in Japan.
   A. The Allied forces finally encircled the Nazi state.
      1. They adopted a principle of "unconditional surrender."
      2. American aid to the British and the Soviets contributed to the eventual victory.
      3. German defeat at Stalingrad in 1942 signaled the beginning of the end for the Nazi state.
      4. The British defeat of Rommel in North Africa paved the way for the eventual encirclement of the Nazi state.
      5. The allied invasion of German-held France in 1944 began the final chapter of the war in Europe.
      6. The U.S. dropped two atomic bombs on Japan in August 1945, forcing the Japanese to surrender.
   B. Hitler gave the world a glimpse of the modern totalitarian state.
      1. The Nazis gave an illustration of how a nation's people can be manipulated under the appropriate economic and social consequences.

Lecture Suggestions

1. "European Fascism—Its Many Faces." What are the forms of fascism? What countries developed fascist movements in addition to Germany and Italy? Why were those fascist groups unsuccessful? Sources: E. Weber, *Varieties of Fascism* (1964); F. L. Carsten, *The Rise of Fascism* (1982).

2. "Soviet Communism and Fascism—Similarities and Differences." How are communism and Nazism alike? How are they different? Sources: H. Arendt, *The Origins of Totalitarianism* (1951); E. Halévy, *The Era of Tyrannies* (1965).

3. "The Tide Turning in World War Two." What led to the Allied victory over the Nazis? How were the Allies able to encircle Germany? Sources: G. Wright, *The Ordeal of Total War, 1939–1945* (1968); B. H. Liddell Hart, *The History of the Second World War* (1971).

Using Primary Sources

Visual Arts as Propaganda.
Have students view the short version of *Triumph of the Will* (80 min. B/W. Films, Ltd.). After viewing the film, they should write an interpretive essay on what the director was trying to express about Nazism. Have some students read their papers in class as the basis for a class discussion.

Activities for Discovering the Past

I. Classroom Discussion Suggestions

1. How did Stalin defeat Trotsky?
2. Why did France and Britain choose a policy of appeasement?
3. Why did the Nazis implement policies that resulted in the Holocaust?
4. What was the status of women under Stalinist rule?
5. How did women fare in Mussolini's fascist state?

II. Doing History

1. What motivated Hitler? How can psychohistory help us to understand his psychological make-up? Sources: A. Bullock, *Hitler* (1953); J. Fest, *Hitler* (1974); A. Hitler, *Mein Kampf* (1924); A. Hitler, *Hitler's Secret Conversations, 1941–44* (1953).
2. What did the postwar world think of Neville Chamberlain? How has his image changed over the years? Sources: K. D. Bracher, *The German Dictatorship* (1970); A. L. Rowse, *Appeasement* (1961).
3. What about Hitler appealed to lower-middle-class Germans who accepted his leadership? Sources: M. Mayer, *The Germans: They Thought They Were Free* (1955); A. Speer, *Inside the Third Reich* (1970).

III. Cooperative Learning Activities

1. Leaders of World War Two. Have six teams do research and make reports on six significant leaders of World War Two: Hitler, Mussolini, Stalin, Churchill, Roosevelt, and de Gaulle. After the presentations, have the class write short papers analyzing the leadership characteristics of the six leaders.
2. Have five student teams create propaganda pieces related to World War Two. The teams decide whether or not they are pro-fascist or pro-Allies. Each team should use a different medium: (1) poster, (2) song, (3) film script, (4) radio address, (5) T-shirt (or any others students may come up with).

Map Activity

1. Why Do We Call It a World War? On an outline map of the world (IRM page 181), have students identify all the places where military action took place in World War II.
2. Using the map on page 37 of the *Historical Atlas of the World*, have students shade in the Axis and Allied Powers on a blank outline map of Europe (IRM page 183).

Audiovisual Bibliography

1. *Triumph of the Will.* (80 min. B/W. Films, Ltd.)
2. *The Rise of Dictatorship, 1920–1939.* (58 min. B/W. Films for the Humanities and Sciences.)
3. *Il Duce.* (20 min. B/W. Films for the Humanities and Sciences.)
4. *The Life of Anne Frank.* (25 min. Color. Films for the Humanities and Sciences.)
5. *Hiroshima: The Legacy.* (30 min. Color. Films for the Humanities and Sciences.)
6. *U.S.A. Wars: WW II.* (CD-ROM. Learning Services.)
7. *Hitler's Assault on Europe.* (Videodisc. 17 min. Color. Films for the Humanities and Sciences.)
8. *Holocaust: Liberation of Auschwitz.* (Videodisc. 18 min. Color. Films for the Humanities and Sciences.)

CHAPTER 33

RECOVERY AND CRISIS IN EUROPE AND THE AMERICAS

Instructional Objectives

After reading and studying this chapter, students should be able to explain what led Russia and the United States into the Cold War. Students should also be able to explain how Stalin, Roosevelt, and Churchill realigned Europe. Then, students should be able to discuss how the Marshall Plan rejuvenated a devastated Europe. Finally, students should be able to elaborate on the success of the Common Market in revitalizing European economies and on the Arab world's asserting itself after World War Two.

Chapter Outline

I. The aftermath of World War Two witnessed the recovery of Europe and the Americas and the beginning of the Cold War.
   A. Europe was nearly destroyed by World War Two.
   B. The price of victory was substantial.

II. The Cold War giants, the U.S. and the U.S.S.R. loomed over the face of the globe.
   A. The U.S. and U.S.S.R. stood like two giants over the shattered continent of Europe.
      1. The U.S. became the undeclared champion of democratic countries.
      2. The U.S.S.R. became the leader of the communist and totalitarian states.
   B. The U.S. wanted the nations of eastern Europe to hold free elections.
   C. Conferences at Teheran, Yalta, and Potsdam resulted in communist-dominated eastern European governments.
      1. Stalin, Churchill, Roosevelt, and Truman virtually divided the world.
   D. By 1949, Europe was divided into two camps: the Western democracies and the Soviet-backed Eastern bloc.
      1. 1949 also witnessed the appearance of a communist regime in China.
      2. Eastern Europe became a kind of transition zone between democracy and communist totalitarianism.

III. U.S. policy toward the U.S.S.R. was verbally aggressive during the early post–World War Two era.
   A. Truman, Eisenhower, and Kennedy exercised a "get tough" policy with Stalin and his successors.
      1. Several tense moments could have led to all-out global war.
   B. Stalin and his successors exported Soviet communism to countries all over the world.
      1. Castro's Cuba became a major Soviet satellite in the western hemisphere.
   C. Khrushchev began a "de-Stalinization" period in 1956.

IV. The Marshall Plan
    A. Provided funds to rebuild the devastated European economy.
    B. The European Economic Community also played a major role in revitalizing postwar Europe.

V. Changes in Asia and Africa came rapidly after the end of World War Two.
    A. China was divided into two armed camps in 1949.
        1. Soviet-backed Chinese Communist army of Mao Zedong drove the Chinese Nationalists onto the island of Taiwan.
    B. African independence movements went much more smoothly during the 1950s and 1960s than did those in the Middle East and Asia.
        1. Nationalism brought forth demands for self-determination in colonial areas after the First World War.
        2. The Second World War reduced European power.
        3. Arab nationalism challenged imperial power and the new Jewish nation of Israel.

VI. The postwar U.S. witnessed a period of almost untold prosperity.
    A. An improved economy and renewed prosperity highlighted the 1950s and 1960s.
    B. It was a time of stability for many Americans.
    C. The black community continued to seek equal rights.
        1. Leaders like M. L. King, Jr., gave the civil rights movement a new impetus.
        2. *Brown v. Board of Education* (1954) was a turning point in the struggle for civil rights.
        3. During Lyndon Johnson's presidency, tremendous advances were made by African Americans.

VII. Mexico and Brazil provided models of national economic development and social reform for much of Latin America.
    A. Mexico made an effort to become an industrial state.
        1. The Mexican state successfully promoted industrialization from the early 1940s to the 1960s.
    B. Brazil also made significant social and economic advances.
        1. Under Vargas, Brazil also accepted economic nationalism and moderate social reform.
        2. Fidel Castro led a successful revolution in 1958 and established a communist dictatorship.

Lecture Suggestions

1. "The Road to Recovery: From the Inside and the Outside." How did foreign aid help to rejuvenate Europe after 1945? What reforms did Europeans themselves make? Sources: T. White, *Fire in the Ashes* (1953); G. Ambrosius and W. Hubbard, *A Social and Economic History of Twentieth-Century Europe* (1989).
2. "The Changing Face of Eastern Europe." What did the United States want for Eastern European governments after 1945? How did U.S. goals run counter to Soviet expectations? How were the conflicts resolved? Sources: H. Seton-Watson, *The East European Revolution* (1965); S. Fisher-Galati, ed., *Eastern Europe in the Sixties* (1963); P. Zinner, *National Communism and Popular Revolt in Eastern Europe* (1956).
3. "The Changing Face of Britain Since 1945." What have been the major changes in British society since 1945? How has Britain recovered from wartime destruction? Sources: A. Marwick, *British Society Since 1945* (1982); A. Sampson, *The Changing Anatomy of Britain* (1983).

Using Primary Sources

Have students read the *Life* magazine article by W. Bullitt, "How We Won the War and Lost the Peace" (*Life*, August 30, 1948, p. 94). What are the author's main points? What does the author mean when he says that "we lost the peace"?

Activities for Discovering the Past

I. **Classroom Discussion Suggestions**

1. How did Khrushchev hope to de-Stalinize the Soviet Union?
2. How did Brezhnev re-Stalinize the country?
3. What was the impact of the Berlin Wall?
4. What has been Cuba's role in Western politics since Castro came to power?
5. What obstacles have African Americans overcome in the United States?

II. **Doing History**

1. Have students read selections from the following novels as the basis for a discussion about Soviet purges, the police-state mentality, and life in a concentration camp. Sources: A. Solzhenitsyn, *One Day in the Life of Ivan Denisovich* (1984), and *The Gulag Archipelago* (1975); A. Koestler, *Darkness at Noon* (1940).
2. Give students an outline map of Europe and have them label the postwar communist bloc nations and the nations of the North Atlantic Treaty Organization. Then have students indicate how the alliance systems were changed as a result of revolution in Eastern Europe during 1989.
3. How did Franklin Delano Roosevelt's image continue to influence American politics throughout the second half of the twentieth century? How has this image been interpreted differently by different historians? Sources: I. and D. Unger, *Postwar America: The United States Since 1945* (1990); W. Leuchtenberg, *In the Shadow of FDR: From Harry Truman to Ronald Reagan* (1989).

III. **Cooperative Learning Activities**

1. Putting the World Back Together.
    Have five student teams analyze and discuss the geopolitical outcomes of Teheran, Yalta, and Potsdam. Have each group present an alternative to the actual historical outcome. How would students' alternative solutions have been different and better?
2. Teams—Teaching the Chapter
    Since Chapter 33 surveys a broad world perspective, have student groups present summaries of the world in 1945. Teams may choose to present broad surveys on continents: (1) North America, (2) Europe, (3) Africa, (4) Asia, (5) South America, (6) Australia.

Map Activity

1. Have students compare Map 33.3 of Africa with Map 27.1. What changes did World War Two create in Africa? Have students list the new countries and compare them with the old ones.
2. Using the map on page 39 of the *Historical Atlas of the World*, have students shade in the major economic alliances on a blank outline map of the world (IRM page 181).

Audiovisual Bibliography

1. *Exodus.* (52 min. Color. Films for the Humanities and Sciences.)
2. *Budapest 1956.* (52 min. Color. Films for the Humanities and Sciences.)
3. *The Suez Crisis: 1956.* (20 min. B/W. Films for the Humanities and Sciences.)
4. *The Berlin Wall: 1961.* (20 min. B/W. Films for the Humanities and Sciences.)
5. *The Cuban Missile Crisis: 1962.* (20 min. B/W. Films for the Humanities and Sciences.)
6. *Mao by Mao.* (28 min. Color. Films for the Humanities and Sciences.)
7. *Soweto: Class of '76.* (20 min. B/W. Films for the Humanities and Sciences.)
8. *Great Cities of the World.* (CD-ROM. Society for Visual Education, Inc.)
9. *Countries of the World.* (CD-ROM. Society for Visual Education, Inc.)
10. *Languages of the World.* (CD-ROM. Society for Visual Education, Inc.)
11. *Seven Days in August.* (CD-ROM. Learning Services.)
12. *Let's Visit South America.* (CD-ROM. Learning Services.)

CHAPTER 34

ASIA AND AFRICA IN THE CONTEMPORARY WORLD

Instructional Objectives

After reading and analyzing this chapter, students should be able to discuss how Asian and African countries reasserted or established their independence in the postwar era. Then, students should be able to explain how leading states faced up to growing challenges in the postindependence world.

Chapter Outline

I. The Communist Victory in China
   A. The triumph of communism was the result of two forces.
      1. The first was Mao's strong communist guerrilla movement, based on peasant interests.
      2. The second was war with Japan, which weakened the Nationalists and resulted in three million dead or wounded.
      3. After Japan surrendered, civil war between the Nationalists and the Communists resumed.
      4. Chiang Kai-shek and one million Chinese fled to the island of Taiwan in 1949.
      5. The Communists transformed China.
      6. Land was redistributed to the poor peasants as collective farms.
      7. They liquidated many "class enemies."
      8. At first, China followed the Soviet model and allied itself with Stalin's Soviet Union.
      9. In 1958, Mao led China in an independent Great Leap Forward.
      10. The Great Leap Forward ended in economic disaster and hostility between Russia and China.
      11. Mao then launched the Great Proletarian Cultural Revolution.
      12. His goal was to eliminate bureaucrats and recapture the fervor of the revolution.
      13. Led by Deng Xiaoping, the "second revolution" opened the door to reconciliation between China and the United States (1971).
      14. Major reforms were initiated, the most important being a move from communal to a free-market peasant family agriculture.
      15. Communist party control over politics and family size led to university student protest demonstrations in 1986.
      16. New demonstrations in 1989 led to the massacre of students in Tiananmen Square and a victory for authoritarian rule.
   B. Japan's American Revolution
      1. After the war, power in Japan resided in the hands of American occupiers.
      2. General Douglas MacArthur and his advisers exercised almost absolute control.

3.   MacArthur wisely allowed the emperor to remain as figurehead.
4.   A powerful Japanese bureaucracy pushed reforms through the Diet.
5.   American-style antitrust laws broke the old zaibatsu firms.
6.   Slow economic recovery turned into a great economic burst between 1950 and 1970.
7.   By 1986, per capita income in Japan exceeded the United States.
8.   Government and big business shared the leading roles in bringing about economic growth.
9.   Government supported and encouraged big business.

II.   New Nations in South Asia and the Muslim World
   A.   The Second World War accelerated India's desire for independence and worsened Indian-British relations.
      1.   The British promise of independence led to clashes between Hindu and Muslim.
      2.   After 1947 India was ruled by Jawaharlal Nehru.
      3.   Nehru and the Congress party initiated major social reforms.
      4.   Indira Gandhi took on the task of population control.
   B.   Southeast Asia
      1.   Sri Lanka (Ceylon) gained independence quickly and smoothly.
      2.   A federated Malaysia was formed.
      3.   Philippine independence was granted in 1946.
      4.   The Netherlands East Indies became the independent Indonesia.
      5.   France's attempt to re-impose its rule in Vietnam led to an independence movement led by the nationalist Ho Chi Minh.
      6.   Despite American help, the French were defeated in 1954.
      7.   Civil war between communists and anticommunists led, eventually, to a communist victory and a defeat for the U.S.
   C.   The Muslim World
      1.   Arab nationalism had two faces.
         a.   the practical side has concentrated on nation building.
         b.   the idealistic side has concentrated on Arab unification.
      2.   After the Second World War, conflict over Jewish immigration led to conflict between Jews and the Palestinian Arabs and the Arab League states.
      3.   In 1947, the United Nations proposed that Palestine be divided into Jewish and Arab states.
      4.   The Palestine Liberation Organization was formed after the war to continue the opposition to Israel.
      5.   The Arab humiliation triggered a nationalist revolution, led by Nasser.
      6.   Nasser drove out the pro-Western king Farouk in 1952.
      7.   Arab-Israeli conflicts in the 1960s and 1970s point to the volatile nature of the Middle East in the last quarter of the twentieth century.
      8.   Turkey followed Ataturk's vision of a modern, secularized, and Europeanized state.
      9.   After an Islamic revolution led by Ayatollah Khomeini in 1979, the shah fled and U.S. diplomats were seized in Iran.

III.   Imperialism and Nationalism in Black Africa
   A.   All but two areas of black Africa—Portugal's territory and South Africa—won political independence after the Second World War.
      1.   By 1900, most of black Africa had been taken by the Europeans.
      2.   Imperialism shattered the existing black society.
   B.   Ghana and Kenya illustrate the variations of the impact of imperialism.

1. Precolonial Ghana was the powerful and economically vigorous kingdom of Ashanti.
2. The British made Ashanti into a crown colony.
3. British-controlled Kenya experience a harsher colonial rule.

C. The Growth of African Nationalism
   1. Western imperialism caused the rise of African nationalism.
   2. The impetus for black nationalism came from the United States and the British West Indies.
   3. With the Great Depression, African nationalism became more radical.

D. Independence
   1. The Second World War speeded up the nationalist movement.
   2. New leaders like Nkrumah, Azikiwe, and Touré succeeded in bringing independence to Africa.
   3. Ghana showed the way to African independence.
   4. Under Nkrumah, Ghana became the first independent African state.
   5. Nkrumah's independence movement followed the Second World War.
   6. French West Africa and French Equatorial Africa were formed into a federation and participated in French government.

IV. Black Africa Since 1960
   A. In the years since independence, democracy has given way to one-party rule or military dictatorship.
      1. Imperialism has been thrown off.
      2. Imperialism affected Africa in several positive ways.
      3. About forty states were created.
      4. Disruption of traditional life caused suffering and unfulfilled expectations.
      5. Western-style democracy and political systems have not worked well.
      6. Military takeovers have been common in Africa.
   B. Nigeria, Africa's giant, illustrates the difficulties of nation building.
      1. Nigeria contains many religious, regional, and tribal groups.
      2. The key issue in preindependence years was the relationship between the central government and the regions.
      3. Ethnic rivalry in 1964 led to violence, a military coup, and civil war.
      4. A new Nigeria federal government was formed, with nineteen states.
   C. The Struggle in Southern Africa
      1. Black nationalist guerrillas moved Portugal and the white population out of Angola and Mozambique.
      2. The roots of racial conflict in the Republic of South Africa are complex.
      3. The Afrikaner racist-totalitarian system is the efficient and well-organized system of apartheid (meaning "separation" or "segregation").
      4. Black nationalist protest has a long history.
      5. Peaceful civil disobedience has existed since the 1950s but has not worked.
      6. The United States and the Common Market imposed economic sanctions on South Africa.
      7. A major step forward came in 1990 when black nationalist leader Nelson Mandela was freed and the African National Congress was legalized.

Lecture Suggestions

1. "The effect of Communism on the Chinese Family." To what extent and in what ways has the advance of communism changed the traditional Chinese family? Sources: C. K. Yang, *The*

Chinese Family in the Communist Revolution (1959); M. Mersner, *Mao's China: A History of the People's Republic* (1977).

2. "Made in Japan." How influential is Japan's industrial and technological know–how? What are Japan's economic weaknesses? Sources: F. Gibney, Japan, *The Fragile Superpower* (1977); E. Vogel, *Japan as Number One: Lessons for America* (1979).

Using Primary Sources

Have students compare Marx and Engels's *Communist Manifesto* of 1848 with the revolutionary ideas of Mao (see P. B. Elvey, ed., *Chinese Civilization and Society: A Source Book,* New York, 1981). What are the similarities? How does Mao differ from Marx? Use students' investigations as the focal point for a discussion on Chinese communism.

Activities for Discovering the Past

I.   Classroom Discussion Suggestions

1. What changes occurred in Mao's relationship with the Soviet Union?
2. Why did the United States establish relations with communist China?
3. What role did Nehru play in Indian independence?
4. What vestiges of imperialism remain in contemporary Africa?
5. What is the status of apartheid today?

II.   Doing History

1. Show students excerpts from the following movies: *The World of Suzie Wong, The Sand Pebbles,* and *The Bridge on the River Kwai.* Have them list what they see as stereotypical images of Asians in these movies and discuss how these images have shaped American thinking about Asians.
2. Have students interview a number of Vietnam-era veterans. The students should bring their written interviews to class for discussion. The class interviews might be compiled into an oral history of the Vietnam War.

III.   Cooperative Learning Activities

1. Organize class into six "research" groups with the task of writing group papers on leaders of modern Africa and Asia: (1) Mao Zedong, (2) Gandhi, (3) Sukarno, (4) Ho Chi Minh, (5) Shah Muhammad Reza Pahlavi, (6) Kwame Nkrumah. The groups' initial tasks should be to conduct a fairly exhaustive research of materials in the college or university library on the Asian and African leaders. After an adequate amount of time, groups should present an alphabetized bibliography to the instructor and make oral presentations on what they consider to be the most significant sources on their respective research topics.
2. During the next stage of the group paper projects, each group should present their theses to the class.
3. The next stage is the reading of first drafts of papers to the class. Each group should select a member to read the group paper to the class. Time should be allotted for class response to the papers.
4. Groups should exchange papers. Papers should be read by students of at least two other groups. Students reading papers should write out responses and give them to the authors of the papers they read.

5. Final papers should be turned in and each group should present an overview of their findings in an oral presentation to the class.

Map Activity

Using the map on pages 70–71 in the *Historical Atlas of the World*, have students list the following on an outline map of the Middle East (IRM page 184):
1. Gulf of Oman
2. Arabian Sea
3. Persian Gulf
4. Kabul
5. Teheran
6. Caspian Sea
7. Oman
8. Yemen
9. Muscat
10. Red Sea
11. Dahlak Archipelago
12. Mecca
13. Khartoum
14. Cairo
15. Hebron
16. Jerusalem
17. Beirut
18. Istanbul
19. Ankara
20. Tel Aviv

Audiovisual Bibliography

1. *Changing Ghana.* (19 min. Color. International Film Bureau.)
2. *East African Crisis—Idi Amin.* (25 min. Color. Journal Video.)
3. *Libya.* (28 min. Color. Marilyn Perry TV Productions.)
4. *Life in the Sahara.* (15 min. Color. Britannia Films.)
5. *An Indian Pilgrimage: Kashi.* (30 min. Color. Center for South Asian Studies, University of Wisconsin.)
6. *Zanboko Homeland.* (194 min. Color. Library of African Cinema.)
7. *China Communes.* (25 min. Color. Westinghouse Broadcasting Corporation.)
8. *Mao: The Long March to Power.* (24 min. Color. Learning Corporation of America.)
9. *Who's Who in China.* (CD-ROM. National School Products.)
10. *Middle East Diary.* (CD-ROM. National School Products.)
11. *Desert Storm.* (CD-ROM. National School Products.)
12. *The Wildebeest Migration.* (CD-ROM. National School Products.)
13. *Mount Everest.* (CD-ROM. National School Products.)
14. *Hiroshima: The Legacy.* (Videodisc. 30 min. Color. Films for the Humanities and Sciences.)
15. *Ho Chi Minh.* (Videodisc. 14 min. Color. Films for the Humanities and Sciences.)
16. *Vietnam: A Television History.* (Videodisc. 13 Discs. Each disc 60 min. Color. Films for the Humanities and Sciences.)

CHAPTER 35

THE CHANGING LIVES OF THIRD WORLD PEOPLE

Instructional Objectives

After reading and analyzing this chapter, students should be able to explain how emerging nations of the Third World sought to escape from poverty and what has resulted from their efforts. Then, students should be able to discuss the prodigious growth of Third World cities and what such growth has meant for the cities' inhabitants. Finally, students should be able to discuss how Third World thinkers and artists have interpreted the modern world and the experiences of their peoples before, during, and after foreign domination.

Chapter Outline

I. The Third World
   A. Despite some limitations, the concept of a "Third World" is valid.
      1. All Third World countries have experienced foreign domination and a struggle for independence and have a common consciousness.
      2. Third World countries are united by an awareness of their poverty.
   B. Third World peoples and leaders hoped that, with independence, they could fulfill the promises of a brighter future.
      1. At first it was thought that the answer to rural poverty was rapid industrialization and "modernization."
      2. By the late 1960s, the Third World became less unified and more complex.

II. The Medical Revolution and the Population Explosion
   A. An ongoing medical revolution came with the independence most Third World nations achieved after the Second World War.
      1. Modern methods of immunology and public health were adopted.
      2. This revolution lowered the death rate and lengthened life expectancy.

III. The Race to Industrialize (1950–1970)
   A. Most Third World countries adopted the theory that European-style industrialization was the answer to their development.
      1. Much reliance was placed on state action and enterprise.
      2. The result for most was a "mixed economy," part socialist, part capitalist.
      3. South Korea and Taiwan changed from typically underdeveloped nations into economic powers.
      4. "Capitalist" land reform drew farmers into a market economy.
   B. Agriculture and Village Life

1. Since the late 1960s, the limitations of industrialization have forced attention toward rural development and rural life.
2. Some consider agriculture a mark of colonial servitude.
3. Following the Indian food crisis of 1966–67, however, fears of famine caused a shift of interest to Third World agriculture.
4. The Green Revolution works best in countries where peasants own land.
5. The Green Revolution has not been successful in Africa or Latin America.

IV. The Growth of Cities
    A. Runaway urban growth is a feature of the Third World.
        1. Cities have grown rapidly, and the proportion of the total population living in the city has increased.
        2. Inadequate social services have made urban life difficult.
        3. Overcrowding, as in Singapore, has reached staggering proportions.
        4. The gap between rich and poor is monumental.
        5. The gap is greatest in urban areas.
        6. A "modern" (Western) lifestyle is the byword of the urban elite.
        7. Education distinguishes the wealthy from the masses and is the road to governmental positions.
        8. In Asia and Africa the great majority of migrants to the city are young men.
        9. In Latin America, permanent migration of whole families is more typical.

V. Mass Culture and Contemporary Thought in the Third World
    A. Third World leaders and people view education as the avenue to jobs and economic development.
        1. The number of young people in school has increased.
        2. Mass communication propagates modern lifestyles and challenges traditional values.
        3. Intellectuals and writers have responded differently to the search for meaning.
        4. Some have merely followed a Western-style Marxist or capitalist line.
        5. Others have broken with Western thought and values.

Lecture Suggestions

1. "Third World Agriculture." Is there a solution for Third World agricultural problems? Sources: L. R. Brown, *Seeds of Change: The Green Revolution and Development in the 1970s; In the Human Interest: A Strategy to Stabilize World Population* (1974).
2. "Third World Women." Have women in the Third World found it possible to voice their concerns? Have they been agents for change, and, if so, in what ways? Sources: P. Hudson, *Third World Women Speak Out: Interviews in Six Countries on Change, Development, and Basic Needs* (1979); L. Iglitzen and R. Ross, *Women in the World: A Comparative Study* (1976); A. de Sonza, *Women in Contemporary India and South Asia* (1980).

Using Primary Sources

Have students read selections from the following modern studies on life in postcolonial Africa: R. Austen, *African Economic History* (1987); K. Patterson, *History and Disease in Africa* (1978); J. Iliffe, *The African Poor: A History* (1987). Use students' discoveries as the basis for a class discussion on postcolonization and independence problems and promises.

Activities for Discovering the Past

I.   Classroom Discussion Suggestions

1.   What have capitalism and communism done to aid the Third World? Are there alternatives to these two economic systems?
2.   How have Third World countries helped themselves?
3.   Which diseases have been especially devastating in Africa?
4.   How has urbanization contributed to the growing list of problems in Africa and Asia?

II.   Doing History

1.   What can we learn about life in the Third World from reading its literature? Students might be asked to read selections from the following books and write short papers on their impressions about life as described in these literary works. Sources: F. Fanon, *The Wretched of the Earth* (1968); C. Achebe, *Things Fall Apart* (1959), *A Man of the People* (1966); G. Moore and U. Beier, eds., *Modern Poetry from Africa* (1963); V. S. Naipaul, *The Mimic Men* (1967); L. Heng and J. Shapiro, *Son of the Revolution* (1983).
2.   Give students outline maps of Asia, Africa, and Oceania. Have them list the newest nations since 1970.

III.   Cooperative Learning Activities

1.   Organize the class into five groups and have them read modern novels and poetry written by Third World authors: (1) C. Achebe, *Things Fall Apart*; (2) C. Achebe, *A Man of the People*; (3) G. Moore and U. Beier, eds., *Modern Poetry from Africa*; (4) V. S. Naipaul, *A Bend in the River*; (5) L. Heng and J. Shapiro, *Son of the Revolution*. After groups have read and discussed the writings, have each group share some of the work with the whole class.
2.   Third World Women
     Organize the class into five groups and assign them both written and oral book reviews on the following: (1) P. Hudson, *Third World Women Speak Out* (1979); L. Iglitzen and R. Ross, *Women in the World* (1976); (2) A. de Sonza, *Women in Contemporary India and South Asia* (1980); (3) N. J. Hafkin and E. Bay, eds., *Women in Africa* (1977); (4) J. Ginat, *Women in Muslim Rural Society* (1982). Have each group submit a group book review (instructors should suggest that students follow the book review formats of scholarly journals such as the *American Historical Review*, *The Journal of Modern History*, *The Journal of Middle Eastern Studies*, or others). Groups should also present an oral version of their book reviews. After oral reviews are presented, engage the class in a discussion of the problems faced by contemporary Third World women.

Map Activity

Using the map on pages 74–75 of the *Historical Atlas of the World*, have students display the statistical data on world population in either a vertical line graph or a pie graph. Allow each student the opportunity to show his/her work to the class as a whole. Instructors may wish to display the student work on classroom walls or a bulletin board.

Audiovisual Bibliography

1. *Mapantsula.* (104 min. Color. Library of African Cinema.)
2. *Tilai.* (81 min. Color. Library of African Cinema.)
3. *Skyscrapers and Slums.* (20 min. Color. Films, Inc.)
4. *Atatürk: Father of the Turks.* (46 min. Color. Time-Life Films.)
5. *Saudi Arabia, The Oil Revolution.* (17 min. Color. Learning Corporation of America.)
6. *Village Man, City Man.* (38 min. Color. Center for South Asian Studies, University of Wisconsin.)
7. *Voices of the People: The Elections in India 1977.* (30 min. Color. Center for South Asian Studies, University of Wisconsin.)
8. *Imperialism.* (CD-ROM. National School Products.)
9. *Cambodia: Year Ten.* (CD-ROM. National School Products.)
10. *Old Peoples, New Consciousness.* (Videodisc. 30 min. Color. Films for the Humanities and Sciences.)

CHAPTER 36

ONE SMALL PLANET

Instructional Objectives

After reading and analyzing this chapter, students should be able to discuss how planet Earth has organized itself politically and to speculate on the future of the nation-state as a dominant political state structure. Students should also be able to discuss how humans have used their resources to meet their material needs. Finally, students should be able to explain key ideas that have guided human behavior as our planet has moved toward an uncertain future.

Chapter Outline

I. World Politics
   A. The human race has not matched its technological achievements with an effective global political organization.
      1. Sovereign states still reign supreme.
      2. Many Europeans and Americans have expressed disillusionment with the nation-state system.
      3. The United Nations was founded in 1945 to maintain international peace and security.
      4. The U.N. also exists to solve international problems and promote human rights.
      5. Through the 1980s, cold war politics deadlocked the Security Council of the U.N.
      6. The U.N. took almost unprecedented action in 1990 when it imposed sanctions on Iraq and passed resolutions against Saddam Hussein that were enforced by the U.S. and its allies.
   B. Complexity and Violence
      1. The old East-West cold war still raged in the 1980s.
      2. A "third force" of nonaligned nations was formed in 1955, leading to Latin American, African, and Asian nations working together at the U.N.
      3. Many countries are developing nuclear weapons capability.
      4. Popular concern over nuclear fallout led to test ban and nonproliferation treaties.

II. Global Interdependence
   A. Although political and military competition between nations continues, nations find themselves increasingly dependent on one another in economic affairs, a fact that should promote peaceful cooperation.
      1. Predictions of a shortage of resources have led to doubts about unlimited growth.
      2. The greatest pressure on world resources comes from population growth.
      3. However, birthrates have begun to fall in many Third World countries.

4. Many in the Third World (the "South") argue that the present international system is exploitive and needs to be reformed.
5. The "theory of dependency" argument claims that Third World "underdevelopment" is deliberate and permanent.
6. The international debt crisis illustrates North-South dependency.

B. The multinational corporations
1. Multinationals are huge business firms that operate on a global, not national, basis.
2. The multinationals emerged with the postwar economic revival.
3. The social consequences of the multinationals are great.
4. Third World governments have learned how to control and manipulate the multinationals.

III. Patterns of Thought
A. Secular Ideologies
1. Most secular ideologies, such as liberalism and nationalism, evolved out of the Enlightenment and nineteenth-century Europe.
2. Since 1945, Marxist ideology has been revised and criticized.
B. Religious Beliefs
1. Pope John II exemplifies the surge of popular Christianity.
2. He preaches a liberal social gospel along with conservative religious doctrines.
3. Islam has also experienced a powerful resurgence.
4. Recently, the trend to modernize has swung back to a strict fundamentalism.
5. Meditation, mysticism, and a turn to the supernatural have become popular in industrialized societies.
6. More people today are receptive to mysticism.

Lecture Suggestions

1. "Technology and Food." How can the technological superpowers help the millions of starving people? What role will the Third World play in resolving the problem of starvation? Sources: R. Barnet, *The Lean Years: The Politics of the Age of Scarcity* (1980); F. M. Lappe and J. Collins, *Food First: Beyond the Myth of Scarcity* (1977).
2. "Nuclear Weapons as a Deterrent." Have nuclear weapons been a deterrent to world war in the late twentieth century? Sources: W. Epstein, *The Last Chance: Nuclear Proliferation and Arms Control* (1976); L. Freedman, *The Evolution of Nuclear Strategy* (1982).

Using Primary Sources

Have students read selections from (or all of) the following as the basis for a discussion on the problems and promises of the future: (1) W. Epstein, *The Last Chance: Nuclear Proliferation and Arms Control* (1976); (2) E. F. Schumacher, *Small Is Beautiful* (1973); (3) L. Stavrianos, *The Promise of the Coming Dark Age* (1976); (4) F. Fukuyama, *The End of History and the Last Man* (1992). After students have had the opportunity to read some of the above selections, use their discoveries as the basis for a class discussion on the uncertainties of the future. Instructors may wish to have students write short papers on their speculations about the future.

Activities for Discovering the Past

I. Classroom Discussion Suggestions

1. Why have so many Westerners turned to Eastern religions and cults for guidance in these perplexing times?
2. How should the United Nations be reorganized to secure a more successful world order?
3. How has Muslim fundamentalism changed the international community?
4. How has the feminist movement affected the Western world in the late twentieth century?

II. Doing History

1. What role have MTV and other video music channels played in international politics? Have students observe MTV and report about videos that have a clear political message.
2. Have students read Jeremy Rifkin's *Entropy* as the basis for discussing the shortcomings of computers, recycling, and other modern trends.

III. Cooperative Learning Activities

1. Organize the class into five groups, each group with the task of hypothesizing how world political organization will be by the mid-twenty-first century. Groups should make an oral presentation to the class on their hypotheses.
2. Cooperative Learning Final Examination
   Instructors may wish to give a Cooperative Learning examination to parallel the individual final exam that is given at the end of the term. Instructors may wish to average the Cooperative Learning examination with the individual final exam grade to get a composite score.

Map Activity

Using the world map on pages 74–75 of the *Historical Atlas of the World,* have students hypothesize how the political map of the world will look in the mid-21st century. Have them draw their hypotheses on an outline map of the world (IRM page 181), showing their hypothetical political divisions. Allow time for students to compare their maps in class.

Audiovisual Bibliography

1. *The Food Revolution.* (17 min. Color. McGraw-Hill Films.)
2. *Energy: The Nuclear Alternative.* (23 min. Color. Film Fair Communications.)
3. *World Within a World.* (52 min. Color. Time-Life Films.)
4. *Altered States.* (102 min. Color. Warner Bros.)
5. *2001: A Space Odyssey.* (143 min. Color. MGM/UA.)
6. *Soylent Green.* (98 min. Color. MGM/UA.)
7. *Rollerball.* (123 min. Color. MGM/UA.)
8. *Logan's Run.* (118 min. Color. MGM/UA.)
9. *Computers in Society.* (17 min. Color. Britannia Films.)
10. *The Impact of Television.* (20 min. Color. Britannia Films.)
11. *Women and Power in the Nuclear Age.* (30 min. Color. High Hopes; Media—Women in Focus.)
12. *A Hard Day's Night.* (90 min. Color. MPI Home Video.)

13. *U2: Rattle and Hum.* (99 min. Color. Paramount Pictures.)
14. *Paul Simon, Graceland.* (Audiocassette.)
15. *The Rolling Stones, Steel Wheels.* (Audiocassette.)
16. *George Harrison et al., The Concert for Bangladesh.* (Video and/or audiocassette.)
17. *On Earth As It Is in Heaven.* (Videodisc. 60 min. Color. Films for the Humanities and Sciences.)
18. *Future Talk.* (Videodisc. 60 min. Color. Films for the Humanities and Sciences.)
19. *The Biology of Death.* (Videodisc. 29 min. Color. Films for the Humanities and Sciences.)
20. *Countries of the World Encyclopedia.* (CD-ROM. National School Products.)
21. *Material World: A Global Family Portrait.* (CD-ROM. National School Products.)

THE FLOOD STORIES OF THE ANCIENT NEAR EAST

The Old Testament story of Noah's Ark is one of the best known stories of the Judeo-Christian tradition. What are the origins of this famous story? Of the four flood stories below, the first three are from ancient Mesopotamia. The first to have appeared is the *Sumerian King List* in about 2000 B.C., but it is probably based on an earlier version; the second flood story is the account from the *Myth of Atrahasis III*, which was written on a tablet in about 1600 B.C., and the third is from the "Standard Version" of the famous *Epic of Gilgamesh* written about 1300 B.C. The *Genesis* story most certainly came last, but there is no way of knowing exactly when this version was first composed and written down. The book of *Genesis* was a part of the Hebrew Torah, which was essentially complete and recognized as authoritative at least as early as the fourth century B.C.

Why did this story appear and acquire significance in several of the Near Eastern cultures? Do these references to a great flood represent some commonly believed myth, or do they reflect an actual event? When reading, consider the point of each story and its significance to the larger story being told. What do all of these stories have in common? In what ways do the narratives differ? How do the stories add to or complement when we know about the ways these societies functioned and in what they believed?

The Flood Story from the *Sumerian King List*[1]

When kingship was lowered from heaven, kingship was (first) in Eridu. (In) Eridu, A-lulim (became) king and ruled 28,800 years. Alalgar ruled 36,000 years. Two kings (thus) ruled it for 64,800 years.

I drop (the topic) Eridu (because) its kingship was brought to Bad-tibira. (In) Bad-tibira, En-men-lu-Anna ruled 28,800 years; the god Dumu-zi, a shepherd, ruled 36,000 years. Three kings (thus) ruled it for 108,000 years.

I drop (the topic) Bad-tibira (because) its kingship was brought to Larak. (In) Larak, En-sipa-zi-Anna ruled 28,800 years. One king (thus) ruled it for 28,800 years.

I drop (the topic) Larak (because) its kingship was brought to Sippar. (In) Sippar, En-men-dur-Anna became king and ruled 21,000 years. One king (thus) ruled it for 21,000 years.

I drop (the topic) Sippar (because) its kingship was brought to Shuruppak. (In) Shuruppak, Ubar-Tutu became king and ruled 18,600 years. One king (thus) ruled it for 18,600 years.

These are five cities, eight kings ruled them for 241,000 years. (Then) the Flood swept over (the earth).

---

[1] Sumerian King List Flood Story—From "The Sumerian King List," translated by Thorkild Jacobsen from *Ancient Near Eastern Texts Relative to the Old Testament*, edited by James B. Pritchard. Copyright © 1969 by Princeton University Press. Reprinted by permission of Princeton University Press.

After the Flood had swept over (the earth) (and) when kingship was lowered (again) from heaven, kingship was (first) in Kish. In Kish, Ga[...]ur became king and ruled 1,200 years—(original) destroyed! legible (only) to heavenly Nidaba (the goddess of writing)—ruled 960 years. [Pala-kinatim ruled 900 years; Nangish-lishma ruled ... year]; Bah[i]na ruled ... years; BU.AN. [..] . [um] ruled [8]40 ye[ars]; Kalibum ruled 960 years; Qalumum ruled 840 years; Zuqaqip ruled 900 years; Atab ruled 600 years; [Mashda, son] of Atab ruled 840 years; Arwi'um, son of Mashda, ruled 720 years; Etana, a shepherd, he who ascended to heaven (and) who consolidated all countries, became king and ruled 1,560 (var.: 1,500) years; Balih, son of Etana, ruled 400 (var.: 410) years; En-me-nunna ruled 660 years; Melam-Kishi, son of En-me-nunna ruled 900 years; Bar-sal-nunna, son of En-me-nunna, ruled 1,200 years; Samug, son of Bar-sal-nunna, ruled 140 years; Tizkar, son of Samug, ruled 305 years; Ilku' ruled 900 years; Ilta-sadum ruled 1,200 years; En-men-barage-si, he who carried away as spoil the "weapon" of Elam, became king and ruled 900 years; Aka, son of En-men-barage-si, ruled 629 years. Twenty-three kings (thus) ruled it for 24,510 years, 3 months, and 3 1/2 days.

The Flood Story from the *Myth of Atrahasis III*[2]

Atrahasis made his voice heard
And spoke to his master,
    'Indicate to me the meaning of the dream,
    [   ] let me find out its portent(?)'
Enki made his voice heard
And spoke to his servant,
    'You say, "I should find out in bed(?)".
    Make sure you attend to the message I shall tell you!
    Wall, listen constantly to me!
    Reed hut, make sure you attend to all my words!
    Dismantle the house, build a boat,
    Reject possessions, and save living things.
    The boat that you build
    [   ]
    [   ]
    Roof it like the Apsu
    So that the Sun cannot see inside it!
    Make upper decks and lower decks.
    The tackle must be very strong,
    The bitumen strong, to give strength.
    I shall make rain fall on you here,
    A wealth of birds, a hamper (?) of fish.'
He opened the sand clock and filled it,
He told him the san (needed) for the Flood was
Seven nights' worth.
Atrahasis received the message.
He gathered the elders at his door.
Atrahasis made his voice heard
And spoke to the elders,
    'My god is out of favour with your god.
    Enki and [Ellil (?)] have become angry with each other.

---

[2] Myth of Atrahasis III Flood Story—Reprinted from *Myths From Mesopotamia*, translated by Stephanie Dalley (1989) by permission of Oxford University Press. Copyright © S. M. Dalley 1989.

They have driven me out of [my house].
Since I always stand in awe of Enki,
He told (me) of this matter.
I can no longer stay in [   ]
I cannot set my foot on Ellil's territory (again).
[I must go down to the Apsu and stay] with (my) god (?).
This is what he told me.'

(gap of 4 or 5 lines to end of column)

(gap of about 9 lines)

The elders [   ]
The carpenter [brought his axe,]
The reed worker [brought his stone,]
[A child brought] bitumen.
The poor [fetched what was needed.]

(9 lines very damaged)

Everything there was [   ]
Everything there was [   ]
Pure ones [   ]
Fat ones [   ]
He selected [and put on board.]
[The birds] that fly in the sky,
Cattle [of Shak]kan,
Wild animals (?) [   ] of open country,
[he] put on board
[   ] ...
He invited his people [   ]
[   ] to a feast.
[   ] he put his family on board.
They were eating, they were drinking.
But he went in and out,
Could not stay still or rest on his haunches,
His heart was breaking and he was vomiting bile.
The face of the weather changed.
Adad bellowed from the clouds.
When (?) he (Atrahasis) heard his noise,
Bitumen was brought and he sealed his door.
While he was closing up his door
Adad kept bellowing from the clouds.
The winds were raging even as he went up
(And) cut through the rope, he released the boat.

(6 lines missing at beginning of column)

Anzu was tearing at the sky with his talons,
[   ] the land,
He broke [   ]
[   ] the Flood [came out (?)].

The *kasusu*-weapon went against the people like an army.
No one could see anyone else,
They could not be recognized in the catastrophe.
The Flood roared like a bull,
Like a wild ass screaming the winds [howled]
The darkness was total, there was no sun.
[   ] like white sheep.
[   ] of the Flood.
[   ]
[   ]
[   ] the noise of the Flood.
[   ]
[Anu (?)] went berserk,
[The gods (?)] ... his sons ... before him
As for Nintu the Great Mistress,
Her lips became encrusted with rime.
The great gods, the Anunna,
Stayed parched and famished.
The goddess watched and wept,
Midwife of the gods, wise Mami:
    'Let daylight (?) ...
    Let it return and ...!
    However could I, in the assembly of gods,
    Have ordered such destruction with them?
    Ellil was strong enough (?) to give a wicked order.
    Like Tiruru he ought to have cancelled that wicked order!
    I heard their cry levelled at me,
    Against myself, against my person.
    Beyond my control (?) my offspring have become like white sheep.
    As for me, how am I to live (?) in a house of bereavement?
    My noise has turned to silence.
    Could I go away, up to the sky
    And live as in a cloister (?)?
    What was Anu's intention as decision-maker?
    It was his command that the gods his sons obeyed,
    He who did not deliberate, but sent the Flood,
    He who gathered the people to catastrophe
    [   ]

      (3 lines missing at beginning of column)
Nintu was wailing [   ]
    'Would a true father (?) have given birth to the [rolling (?)] sea
    (So that) they could clog the river like dragonflies?
    They are washed up (?) like a raft on [a bank (?)],
    They are washed up like a raft on a bank in open country!
    I have seen, and wept over them!
    Shall I (ever) finish weeping for them?'
She wept, she gave vent to her feelings,
Nintu wept and fueled her passions.
The gods wept with her for the country.
She was sated with grief, she longed for beer (in vain).
Where she sat weeping, (there the great gods) sat too,

But, like sheep, could only fill their windpipes (with bleating).
Thirsty as they were, their lips
Discharged only the rime of famine.
For seven days and seven nights
The torrent, storm and flood came on.

(*gap of about 58 lines*)

He put down [   ],
Provided food [   ]
[   ]
The gods smelt the fragrance,
Gathered like flies over the offering.
When they had eaten the offering,
Nintu got up and blamed them all,
     'Whatever came over Anu who makes the decisions?
     Did Ellil (dare to) come for the smoke offering?
     (Those two) who did not deliberate, but sent the Flood,
     Gathered the people to catastrophe—
     You agreed the destruction.
     (Now) their bright faces are dark (forever).'
Then she went up to the big flies
Which Anu had made, and (declared) before the gods,
     'His grief is mine! My density goes with his!
     He must deliver me from evil, and appease me!
     Let me go out in the morning (?) [   ]
     [   ]
     Let these flies be the lapis lazuli of my necklace
     By which I may remember it (?) daily (?) [forever (?)].'
The warrior Ellil spotted the boat
And was furious with the Igigi.
     'We, the great Anunna, all of us,
     Agreed together on an oath!
     No form of life should have escaped!
     How did any man survive the catastrophe?'
Anu made his voice heard
And spoke to the warrior Ellil
     'Who but Enki would do this?
     He made sure that the [reed hut] disclosed the order.'
Enki made his voice heard
And spoke to the great gods,
     'I did it, in defiance of you!
     I made sure life was preserved [   ]

(*5 lines missing*)

     Exact your punishment from the sinner.
     And whoever contradicts your order

(*12 lines missing*)

I have given vent to my feelings!'
Ellil made his voice heard
And spoke to far-sighted Enki,
  'Come, summon Nintu the womb-goddess!
  Confer with each other in the assembly.'
Enki made his voice heard
And spoke to the womb-goddess Nintu,
'You are the womb-goddess who decrees destinies.
    [   ] to the people.
[Let one-third of them be   ]
   [   ]
[Let another third of them be]
In addition let there be one-third of the people,
Among the people the woman who gives birth yet does
Not give birth (successfully);
Let there be the *pasittu*-demon among the people,
To snatch the baby from its mother's lap.
Establish *ugbabtu, entu, egisitu*-women:
They shall be taboo, and thus control childbirth.'

    (26 lines missing to end of column)
    (8 lines missing at beginning of column)

How we sent the Flood.
But a man survived the catastrophe.
You are the counsellor of the gods;
On your orders I created conflict.
Let the Igigi listen to this song
In order to praise you,
And let them record (?) your greatness.
I shall sing of the Flood to all people:
Listen!
 (Colophon)
The End.
Third tablet,
'When the gods instead of man'
390 lines,
Total 1245
For the three tablets.
Hand of Nur-Aya, junior scribe.
Month Ayyar [x day],
Year Ammi-saduqa was king.
A statue of himself [ ]
[   ]

The Flood Story from the *Epic of Gilgamesh*[3]

This document begins as a discussion is under way between Gilgamesh and Utanapishtim, a human who attained eternal life. This section begins as the god Ea gives instructions to Utanapishtim.

> O man of Shuruppak, son of Ubartutu:
> Tear down the house and build a boat!
> Abandon wealth and seek living beings!
> Spurn possessions and keep alive living beings!
> Make all living beings go up into the boat.
> The boat which you are to build,
> its dimensions must measure equal to each other:
> its length must correspond to its width.
> Roof it over like the Apsu.'

I [Utanapishtim] understood and spoke to my lord, Ea:

> 'My lord, thus is the command which you have uttered
> I will heed and will do it.
> But what shall I answer the city,[4] the populace, and the Elders?

Ea spoke, commanding me, his servant:

> 'You, well then, this is what you must say to them:
>> "It appears that Enlil[5] is rejecting me
>> so I cannot reside in your *city* (?),
>> nor set foot on Enlil's earth.
>> I will go down to the Apsu to live with my lord, Ea,
>> and upon you he will rain down abundance,
>> a profusion of fowl, myriad(?) fishes.
>> He will bring to you a harvest of wealth,
>> in the morning he will let loaves of bread shower down
>> and in the evening a rain of wheat!"

Just as dawn began to glow
the land assembled *around me*—
the carpenter carried his hatchet,
the reed worker carried his (flattening) stone,
... the men ...
...
The child carried the pitch,
the weak brought whatever else was needed.
On the fifth day I laid out her exterior.
It was a field in area,
its walls were each 10 times 12 cubits in height,
the sides of its top were of equal length, 10 times 12 cubits each.
I laid out its (interior) structure and drew a picture of it (?).
I provided it with six decks,
thus dividing it into seven (levels).

---

[3] *Source:* Reprinted from *The Epic of Gilgamesh*, translated, with an Introduction and Notes by Maureen Gallery Kovacs with the permission of the publishers, Stanford University Press. Copyright © 1985, 1989 by the Board of Trustees of the Leland Stanford Junior University.

[4] The city of Shuruppak, on the Euphrates River.

[5] The adviser to the Greek Gods of Shuruppak.

The inside of it I divided into nine (compartments).
I drove plugs (to keep out) water in its middle part.
I saw to the punting poles and laid in what was necessary.
Three times 3,600 (units) of raw bitumen I poured into the bitumen kiln,
three times 3,600 (units of) pitch ... into it,
there were three times 3,600 porters of casks who carried (vegetable) oil,
apart from the 3,600 (units of) oil which they consumed (?)
and two times 3,600 (units of) oil which the boatman stored away.
I butchered oxen for *the meat*(?),
and day upon day I slaughtered sheep.
I gave the workmen(?) ale, beer, oil, and wine, as if it were river water,
so they could make a party like the New Year's Festival.
... and I set my hand to the oiling(?).
The boat was finished by sunset.
The launching was very difficult.
They had to keep carrying a runway of poles front to back,
until two-thirds of it had gone into the water(?).
Whatever I had I loaded on it:
whatever silver I had I loaded on it,
whatever gold I had I loaded on it.
All the living beings that I had I loaded on it,
    I had all my kith and kin go up into the boat,
    all the beasts and animals of the field and the craftsmen I had go up.
    Shamash had set a stated time:
      'In the morning I will let loaves of bread shower down,
      and in the evening a rain of wheat!
      Go inside the boat, seal the entry!'
That stated time had arrived.
In the morning he let loaves of bread shower down,
and in the evening a rain of wheat.
I watched the appearance of the weather—
the weather was frightful to behold!
I went into the boat and sealed the entry.
For the caulking of the boat, to Puzuramurri, the boatman,
I gave the palace together with its contents.
Just as dawn began to glow
there arose from the horizon a black cloud.
Adad rumbled inside of it,
before him went Shullat and Hanish,
heralds going over mountain and land.
Erragal pulled out the mooring poles,
forth went Ninurta and made the dikes overflow.
The Anunnaki lifted up the torches,
setting the land ablaze with their flare.
Stunned shock over Adad's deeds overtook the heavens,
and turned to blackness all that had been light.
The ... land shattered like a ... pot.
All day long the South Wind blew ...,
blowing fast, *submerging the* mountain *in water*,
overwhelming *the people* like an attack.
No one could see his fellow,
they could not recognize each other in the torrent.

The gods were frightened by the Flood,
and retreated, ascending to the heaven of Anu.
The gods were cowering like dogs, crouching by the outer wall.
Ishtar shrieked like a woman in childbirth,
the sweet-voiced Mistress of the Gods wailed:
'The olden days have alas turned to clay,
because I said evil things in the Assembly of the Gods!
How could I say evil things in the Assembly of the Gods,
ordering a catastrophe to destroy my people?!
No sooner have I given birth to my dear people
than they fill the sea like so many fish!'
The gods—those of the Anunnaki—were weeping with her,
the gods humbly sat weeping, sobbing with grief(?),
their lips burning, parched with thirst.
Six days and seven nights
came the wind and flood, the storm flattening the land.
When the seventh day arrived, the storm was pounding,
the flood was a war—struggling with itself like a woman writhing (in labor).
The sea calmed, fell still, the whirlwind (and) flood stopped up.
I looked around all day long—quiet had set in
and all the human beings had turned to clay!
The terrain was as flat as a roof.
I opened a vent and fresh air (daylight?) fell upon the side of my nose.
I fell to my knees and sat weeping,
tears streaming down the side of my nose.
I looked around for coastlines in the expanse of the sea,
and at twelve leagues there emerged a region (of land).
On Mt. Nimush the boat lodged firm,
Mt. Nimush held the boat, allowing no sway.
One day and a second Mt. Nimush held the boat, allowing no sway.
A third day, a fourth, Mt. Nimush held the boat, allowing no sway.
A fifth day, a sixth, Mt. Nimush held the boat, allowing no sway.
When a seventh day arrived
I sent forth a dove and released it.
The dove went off, but came back to me;
no perch was visible so it circled back to me.
I sent forth a swallow and released it.
The swallow went off, but came back to me;
no perch was visible so it circled back to me.
I sent forth a raven and released it.
The raven went off, and saw the waters slither back.
It eats, it scratches, it bobs, but does not circle back to me.
Then I sent out everything in all directions and sacrificed (a sheep).
I offered incense in front of the mountain-ziggurat.
Seven and seven cult vessels I put in place,
and (into the fire) underneath (or: into their bowls) I poured reeds, cedar, and myrtle.
The gods smelled the savor,
the gods smelled the sweet savor,
and collected like flies over a (sheep) sacrifice.
Just then Beletili arrived.

She lifted up the large flies (beads[6]) which Anu had made for his enjoyment(?):

'You gods, as surely as I shall not forget this lapis lazuli around my neck,
may I be mindful of these days, and never forget them!
The gods may come to the incense offering,
but Enlil may not come to the incense offering,
because without considering he brought about the Flood
and consigned my people to annihilation.'

Just then Enlil arrived.
He saw the boat and became furious,
he was filled with rage at the Igigi gods:

'Where did a living being escape?
No man was to survive the annihilation!'

Ninurta spoke to Valiant Enlil, saying:

'Who else but Ea could devise such a thing?
It is Ea who knows every machination!'

Ea spoke to Valiant Enlil, saying:

'It is *you*, O Valiant One, who is the Sage of the Gods.
How, how could *you* bring about a Flood without consideration?
Charge the violation to the violator,
charge the offense to the offender.
but be compassionate lest (mankind) be cut off,
be patient lest *they be killed*.
Instead of your bringing on the Flood,
would that a lion had appeared to diminish the people!
Instead of your bringing on the Flood,
would that a wolf had appeared to diminish the people!
Instead of your bringing on the Flood,
would that famine had occurred to slay the land!
Instead of your bringing on the Flood,
would that (Pestilent) Erra had appeared to ravage the land!
It was not I who revealed the secret of the Great Gods,
I (only) made a dream appear to Atrahasis, and (thus) he heard the secret of the gods.
Now them! The deliberation should be about him!'

Enlil went up inside the boat
and, grasping my hand, made me go up.
He had my wife go up and kneel by my side.
He touched our forehead and, standing between us, he blessed us:

'Previously Utanapishtim was a human being.
But now let Utanapishtim and his wife become like us, the gods!
Let Utanapishtim reside far away, at the Mouth of the Rivers.'

They took us far away and settled us at the Mouth of the Rivers."

---

[6] A necklace with carved lapis lazuli fly beads, representing the dead offspring of the mother goddess Beletili/Aruru.

The Flood Story from the *Book of Genesis*[7]

Wild animals of every kind, cattle of every kind, reptiles of every kind that move upon the ground, and birds of every kind—all came to Noah in the ark, two by two of all creatures that had life in them. Those which came were one male and one female of all living things; they came in as God had commanded Noah, and the LORD closed the door on him. The flood continued upon the earth for forty days, and the waters swelled and lifted up the ark so that it rose high above the ground. They swelled and increased over the earth, and the ark floated on the surface of the waters. More and more the waters increased over the earth until they covered all the high mountains everywhere under heaven. The waters increased and the mountains were covered to a depth of fifteen cubits. Every living creature that moves on earth perished, birds, cattle, wild animals, all reptiles, and all mankind. Everything died that had the breath of life in its nostrils, everything on dry land. God wiped out every living thing that existed on earth, man and beast, reptile and bird; they were all wiped out over the whole earth, and only Noah and his company in the ark survived.

[....]

After forty days Noah opened the trap-door that he had made in the ark, and released a raven to see whether the water had subsided, but the bird continued flying to and fro until the water on the earth had dried up. Noah waited for seven days, and then he released a dove from the ark to see whether the water on the earth had subsided further. But the dove found no place where she could settle, and so she came back to him in the ark, because there was water over the whole surface of the earth. Noah stretched out his hand, caught her and took her into the ark. He waited another seven days and again released the dove from the ark. She came back to him towards evening with a newly plucked olive branch in her beak. Then Noah knew for certain that the water on the earth had subsided still further. He waited yet another seven days and released the dove, but she never came back. And so it came about that, on the first day of the first month of his six hundred and first year, the water had dried up on the earth, and Noah removed the hatch and looked out of the ark. The surface of the ground was dry.

By the twenty-seventh day of the second month the whole earth was dry. And God said to Noah, 'Come out of the ark, you and your wife, your sons and their wives. Bring out every living creature that is with you, live things of every kind, bird and beast and every reptile that moves on the ground, and let them swarm over the earth and be fruitful and increase there.' So Noah came out with his sons, his wife, and his sons' wives. Every wild animal, all cattle, every bird, and every reptile that moves on the ground, came out of the ark by families. Then Noah built an altar to the LORD. He took ritually clean beasts and birds of every kind, and offered whole-offerings on the altar. When the LORD smelt the smoothing odor, he said within himself, 'Never again will I curse the ground because of man, however evil his inclinations may be from his youth upwards. I will never again kill every living creature, as I have just done.

> While the earth lasts
> seedtime and harvest, cold and heat,
> summer and winter, day and night,
> shall never cease.'

God blessed Noah and his sons and said to them, 'Be fruitful and increase, and fill the earth. The fear and dread of you shall fall upon all wild animals on earth, on all birds of heaven, on

---

[7] *Source:* From *The New English Bible.* Copyright © the Delegates of Oxford University Press and the Syndics of the Cambridge University Press, 1961, 1970. Reprinted by permission.

everything that moves upon the ground and all fish in the sea; they are given into your hands. Every creature that lives and moves shall be food for you; I give you them all, as once I gave you all green plants. But you must not eat the flesh with the life, which is the blood, still in it. And further, for your life-blood I will demand satisfaction; from every animal I will require it, and from a man also I will require satisfaction for the death of his fellow-man.

> He that sheds the blood of a man,
> for that man his blood shall be shed;
> for in the image of God
> has God made man.

But you must be fruitful and increase, swarm throughout the earth and rule over it.'

God spoke to Noah and to his sons with him: 'I now make my covenant with you and with your descendants after you, and with every living creature that is with you, all birds and cattle, all the wild animals with you on earth, all that have come out of the ark. I will make my covenant with you: never again shall all living creatures be destroyed by the waters of the flood, never again shall there be a flood to lay waste the earth.'

God said, 'This is the sign of the covenant which I establish between myself and you and every living creature with you, to endless generations:

> My bow I set in the cloud,
> sign of the covenant
> between myself and earth.
> When I cloud the sky over the earth,
> the bow shall be seen in the cloud.

Then will I remember the covenant which I have made between myself and you and living things of every kind. Never again shall the waters become a flood to destroy all living creatures.

MAGNA CARTA, 1215[8]

Although its initial purpose was to protect the interests of the barons under King John of England (1199–1216), the Magna Carta eventually came to protect the interests of other social classes as well. As a result, the document was regarded as a guarantee of certain rights. Sections 6, 7, 8, included below, were interpreted to allow women some powers. What were these? Sections 13, 20, and 35 afforded merchants of the towns a greater degree of freedom. What were these? Sections 39 and 40 contain the germ of the modern legal idea of due process of law for all people. On the other hand, Articles 10 and 11 reflect anti-Semitic attitudes deep in medieval society. In what ways do they indicate discrimination?

6. Heirs shall be married with disparagement; yet so that, before the marriage is contracted, it shall be announced to the blood-relatives of the said heir.

7. A widow shall have her marriage portion and inheritance immediately after the death of her husband and without difficulty; nor shall she give anything for her dowry or for her marriage portion or for her inheritance—which inheritance she and her husband were holding on the day of that husband's death. And after his death she shall remain in the house of her husband for forty days, within which her dowry shall be assigned to her.

8. No widow shall be forced to marry so long as she wishes to live without a husband; yet so that she shall give security against marrying without our consent if she holds of us, or without the consent of her lord if she holds of another.

10. If any one has taken anything, whether much or little, by way of loan from Jews, and if he dies before that debt is paid, the debt shall not carry usury so long as the heir is under age, from whomsoever he may hold. And if that debt falls into our hands, we will take only the principal contained in the note.

11. And if any one dies owing a debt to Jews, his wife shall have her dowry and shall pay nothing on that debt. And if the said deceased is survived by children who are under age, necessities shall be provided for them in proportion to the tenement that belonged to the deceased; and the debt shall be paid from the remained, saving the service of the lords. In the same way let action be taken with regard to debts owed to others besides Jews.

---

[8] *Source:* Carl Stephenson and Frederick G. Morcham, *Sources of English Constitutional History* (New York: Harper & Brothers, 1937).

13. And the city of London shall have all its ancient liberties and free customs, both by land and by water. Besides we will and grant that all the other cities, boroughs, towns, and ports shall have all their liberties and free customs.

20. A freeman shall be amerced [punished] for a small offence only according to the degree of the offence; and for a grave offence he shall be amerced according to the gravity of the offence, saving his contentment. And a merchant shall be amerced in the same way, saving his merchandise; and a villein in the same way, saving his wainage [agricultural implements]— should they fall into our mercy. And none of the aforesaid amercements shall be imposed except by the oaths of good men from the neighbourhood.

35. There shall be one measure of wine throughout our entire kingdom, and one measure of ale; also one measure of grain, namely the quarter of London; and one width of dyed cloth, russet [cloth], and hauberk [cloth], namely, two yards between the borders. With weights, moreover, it shall be as with measures.

39. No freeman shall be captured or imprisoned or disseised [unlawfully removed] or outlawed or exiled or in any way destroyed, nor will we go against him or send against him, except by the lawful judgement of his peers or by the law of the land.

40. To no one will we sell, to no one will we deny or delay right or justice.

THE RULE OF SAINT FRANCIS, 1223[9]

The medicants, or orders of begging friars, were founded as a response to the spiritual needs of a growing urban society. Chief among these orders was the order of friars founded by Saint Francis of Assisi. Can you tell what the goals and practices of the Franciscans were? How did they differ from the older monastic orders like the Benedictines and Cistercians? What in these rules indicates that the Franciscans are involved in an urban as opposed to a monastic society?

This is the rule and life of the Minor Brothers, namely, to observe the holy gospel of our Lord Jesus Christ by living in obedience, in poverty, and in chastity. Brother Francis promises obedience and reverence to Pope Honorius and to his successors who shall be canonically elected, and to the Roman Church. The other brothers are bound to obey brother Francis, and his successors . . .

I counsel, warn, and exhort my brothers in the Lord Jesus Christ that when they go out into the world they shall not be quarrelsome or contentious, nor judge others. But they shall be gentle, peaceable, and kind, mild and humble, and virtuous in speech, as is becoming to all. They shall not ride on horseback unless compelled in manifest necessity or infirmity to do so. When they enter a house they shall say, "Peace be to this house." According to the holy gospel, they may eat of whatever food is set before them.

I strictly forbid all the brothers to accept money or property either in person or through another. Nevertheless, for the needs of the sick, and for clothing the other brothers, the ministers and guardians may, as they see that necessity requires, provide through spiritual friends, according to the locality, season, and the degree of cold which may be expected in the region where they live. But, as has been said, they shall never receive money or property.

Those brothers to whom the Lord has given the ability to work shall work faithfully and devotedly, so that idleness, which is the enemy of the soul, may be excluded and not extinguish the spirit of prayer and devotion to which all temporal things should be subservient. As the price of their labors they may receive things that are necessary for themselves and the brothers, but not money or property. And they shall humbly receive what is given them, as is becoming to the servants of God and to those who practise the most holy poverty.

The brothers shall have nothing of their own, neither house, nor land, nor anything, but as pilgrims and strangers in this world, serving the Lord in poverty and humility, let them confidently go asking alms. Nor let them be ashamed of this, for the Lord made himself poor for us in this world. This is that highest pitch of poverty which has made you, my dearest brothers, heirs and kings of the kingdom of heaven, which has made you poor in goods, and exalted you in virtues. . . .

---

[9] *Source:* Oliver J. Thatcher and Edgar H. McNeal, eds. and trans., *A Source Book for Medieval History* (New York: Scribner's, 1905), 499–507.

I strictly forbid all the brothers to have any association or conversation with women that may cause suspicion. And let them not enter nunneries, except those which the pope has given them special permission to enter. Let them not be intimate friends of men or women, lest on this account scandal arise among the brothers or about brothers.

THE RIGHTS OF MAN AND OF WOMAN

Drawing upon the ideas of the Enlightenment, particularly those of John Locke and Jean-Jacques Rousseau, the bourgeois-dominated French National Assembly issued on August 26, 1789, *The Declaration of the Rights of Man and of the Citizen*. Thousands of copies of this document circulated in France, and it became the ideological manifesto of the Revolution. Its influence on the rest of Europe and the world was equally noteworthy. In 1792 an Englishwoman, Mary Wollstonecraft, wrote *A Vindication of the Rights of Woman*, which was a reply to Edmund Burke's attack on the French Revolution and the starting point for the debate over whether the natural rights of man should apply, in full, to women.

Declaration of the Rights of Man and of the Citizen, 1789

The representatives of the French people, organized as a National Assembly, believing that the ignorance, neglect, or contempt of the rights of man are the sole cause of public calamities and of the corruption of governments, have determined to set forth in a solemn declaration the natural, unalienable, and sacred rights of man, in order that this declaration, being constantly before all the members of the Social body, shall remind them continually of their rights and duties; in order that the acts of the legislative power, as well as those of the executive power, may be compared at any moment with the objects and purposes of all political institutions and may thus be more respected, and, lastly, in order that the grievances of the citizens, based here-after upon simple and incontestable principles, shall tend to the maintenance of the constitution and redound to the happiness of all. Therefore the National Assembly recognizes and proclaims, in the presence and under the auspices of the Supreme Being, the following rights of man and of the citizen:

Article

1. Men are born and remain free and equal in rights. Social distinctions may be founded only upon the general good.

2. The aim of all political association is the preservation of the natural and imprescriptible rights of man. These rights are liberty, property, security, and resistance to oppression.

3. The principle of all sovereignty resides essentially in the nation. No body nor individual may exercise any authority which does not proceed directly from the nation.

4. Liberty consists in the freedom to do everything which injures no one else; hence the exercise of the natural rights of each man has no limits except those which assure to the other

members of the society the enjoyment of the same rights. These limits can only be determined by law.

5. Law can only prohibit such actions as are hurtful to society. Nothing may be prevented which is not forbidden by law, and no one may be forced to do anything not provided for by law.

6. Law is the expression of the general will. Every citizen has a right to participate personally, or through his representative, in its foundation. It must be the same for all, whether it protects or punishes. All citizens, being equal in the eyes of the law, are equally eligible to all dignities and to all public positions and occupations, according to their abilities, and without distinction except that of their virtues and talents.

7. No person shall be accused, arrested, or imprisoned except in the cases and according to the forms prescribed by law. Any one soliciting, transmitting, executing, or causing to be executed, any arbitrary order, shall be punished. But any citizen summoned or arrested in virtue of the law shall submit without delay, as resistance constitutes an offense.

8. The law shall provide for such punishments only as are strictly and obviously necessary, and no one shall suffer punishment except it be legally inflicted in virtue of a law passed and promulgated before the commission of the offense.

9. As all persons are held innocent until they shall have been declared guilty, if arrest shall be deemed indispensable, all harshness not essential to the securing of the prisoner's person shall be severely repressed by law.

10. No one shall be disquieted on account of his opinions, including his religious views, provided their manifestation does not disturb the public order established by law.

11. The free communication of ideas and opinions is one of the most precious of the rights of man. Every citizen may, accordingly, speak, write, and print with freedom, but shall be responsible for such abuses of this freedom as shall be defined by law.

12. The security of the rights of man and of the citizen requires public military forces. These forces are, therefore, established for the good of all and not the personal advantage of those to whom they shall be entrusted.

13. A common contribution is essential for the maintenance of the public forces and for the cost of administration. This should be equitably distributed among all the citizens in proportion to their means.

14. All the citizens have a right to decide, either personally or by their representatives, as to the necessity of the public contribution; to grant this freely; to know to what uses it is put; and to fix the proportion, the mode of assessment and of collection and the duration of the taxes.

15. Society has the right to require of every public agent an account of his administration.

16. A society in which the observance of the law is not assured, nor the separation of powers defined, has no constitution at all.

17. Since property is an inviolable and sacred right, no one shall be deprived thereof except where public necessity, legally determined, shall clearly demand it, and then only on condition that the owner shall have been previously and equitably indemnified.

Mary Wollstonecraft, The Vindication of the Rights of Woman, 1792[10]

Contending for the rights of woman, my main argument is built on this simple principle, that if she be not prepared by education to become the companion of man, she will stop the progress of knowledge and virtue; for truth must be common to all, or it will be inefficacious with respect to its influence on general practice. And how can woman be expected to cooperate unless she know why she ought to be virtuous? Unless freedom strengthen her reason till she comprehend her duty, and see in what manner it is connected with her real good? If children are to be educated to understand the true principle of patriotism, their mother must be a patriot; and the love of mankind, from which an orderly train of virtues spring, can only be produced by considering the moral and civil interest of mankind; but the education and situation of woman, at present, shuts her out from such investigations.

In this work I have produced many arguments, which to me were conclusive, to prove that the prevailing notion respecting a sexual character was subversive of morality, and I have contended, that to render the human body and mind more perfect, chastity must more universally prevail, and that chastity will never be respected in the male world till the person of woman is not, as it were, idolized, when little virtue sense embellish it with the grand traces of mental beauty, or the interesting simplicity of affection.

Consider, sir, dispassionately, these observations—for a glimpse of this truth seemed to open before you when you observed, "that to see one half of the human race excluded by the other from all participation of government, was a political phenomenon that, according to abstract principles, it was impossible to explain." If so, on what does your constitution rest? If the abstract rights of man will bear discussion and explanation, those of woman, by a parity of reasoning, will not shrink from the same test: though a different opinion prevails in this country, built on the very arguments which you use to justify the oppression of woman—prescription.

Consider—I address you as a legislator—whether, when men contend for their freedom, and to be allowed to judge for themselves respecting their own happiness, it be not inconsistent and unjust to subjugate women, even though you firmly believe that you are acting in the manner best calculated to promote their happiness? Who made man the exclusive judge, if woman partake with him the gift of reason?

But, if women are to be excluded, without having a voice, from a participation of the natural rights of mankind, prove first, to ward off the charge of injustice and inconsistency, that they want reason—else this flaw in your NEW CONSTITUTION will ever show that man must, in some shape, act like a tyrant; and tyranny, in whatever part of society it rears its brazen front, will ever undermine morality.

I have repeatedly asserted, and produced what appeared to me irrefragable arguments drawn from matters of fact, to prove my assertion, that women cannot, by force, be confined to domestic concerns; for they will, however ignorant, intermeddle with more weighty affairs, neglecting private duties only to disturb, by cunning tricks, the orderly plans of reason which rise above their comprehension.

Besides, whilst they are only made to acquire personal accomplishments, men will seek for pleasure in variety, and faithless husbands will make faithless wives: such ignorant beings, indeed, will be very excusable when, not taught to respect public good, nor allowed any civil rights, they attempt to do themselves justice by retaliation.

The box of mischief thus opened in society, what is to preserve private virtue, the only security of public freedom and universal happiness?

---

[10] *Source:* Mary Wollstonecraft, from the Dedication of the first edition, *The Vindication of the Rights of Woman* (1792).

Let there be then no coercion established in society, and the common law of gravity prevailing, the sexes will fall into their proper places. And, now that more equitable laws are forming your citizens, marriage may become more sacred: your young men may choose wives from motives of affection, and your maidens allow love to root out vanity.

The father of a family will not then weaken his constitution and debase his sentiments by visiting the harlot, nor forget, in obeying the call of appetite, the purpose for which it was implanted. And, the mother will not neglect her children to practise the arts of coquetry, when sense and modesty secure her the friendship of her husband.

But, till men become attentive to the duty of a father, it is vain to expect women to spend that time in their nursery which they, "wise in their generation," choose to spend at their glass; for this exertion of cunning is only an instinct of nature to enable them to obtain indirectly a little of that power of which they are unjustly denied a share: for, if women are not permitted to enjoy legitimate rights, they will render both men and themselves vicious, to obtain illicit privileges.

I wish, sir, to set some investigations of this kind afloat in France; and should they lead to a confirmation of my principles, when your constitution is revised the Rights of Women may be respected, if it be fully proved that reason calls for this respect, and loudly demands JUSTICE for one half of the human race.—I am, sir, yours respectfully,

M. W.

ADDRESSES FOR AUDIOVISUAL MATERIALS

Instructional Resources Corporation
1819 Bay Ridge Avenue
Annapolis, MD 21403
301-263-0025

American Historical Association
400 A Street, SE
Washington, DC 20003

The Social Studies Development Center
Indiana University
2805 East Tenth Street
Bloomington, IN 47405

National Council for the Social Studies
3501 Newark Street, NW
Washington, DC 20016

Learning Services
P.O. Box 10636
Eugene, OR 97440

Britannica
Encyclopedia Britannica Educational
Corporation
310 South Michigan Avenue
Chicago, IL 60604-9839

Society for Visual Education, Inc.
Department TD
1345 W. Diversey Pkwy.
Chicago, IL 60614-1299

Films for the Humanities and Sciences
P.O. Box 2053
Princeton, NJ 08543-2053

National Audio Visual Supply
1 Madison Street
East Rutherford, NJ 07073-0422

National Geographic Society
Education Services
Washington, DC 20036

Grolier Electronic Publishing
Sherman Turnpike
Danbury, CT 06816

National School Products
101 East Broadway
Maryville, TN 37804-2498

Cambridge Development Laboratory, Inc.
86 West Street
Waltham, MA 02154

Outline Map of the Ancient Near East

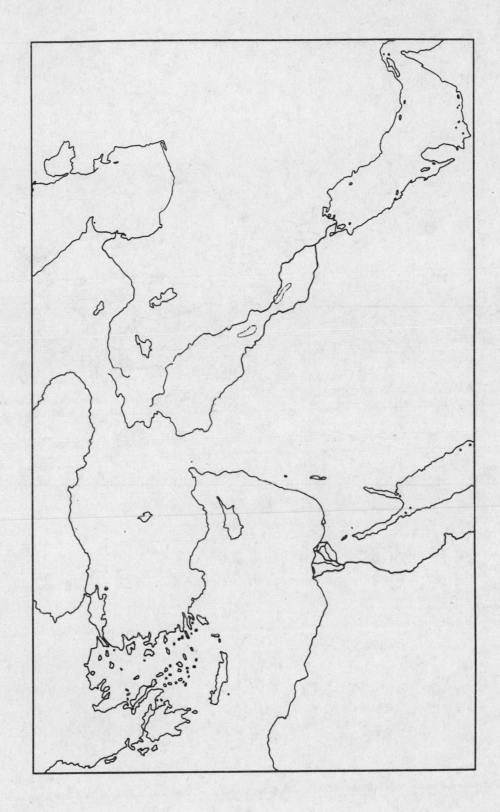

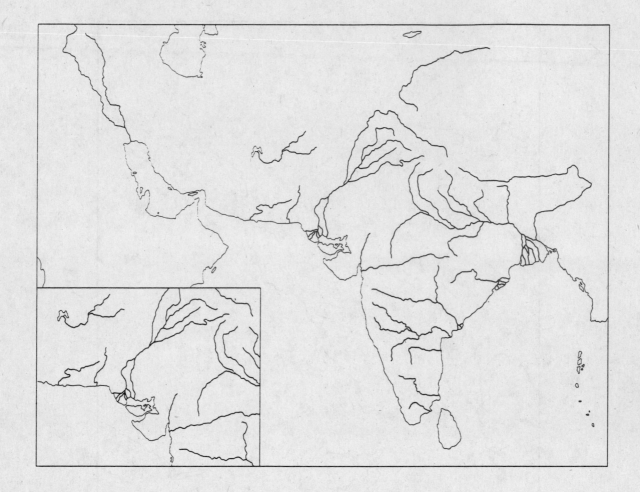

OUTLINE MAP OF CHINA AND JAPAN

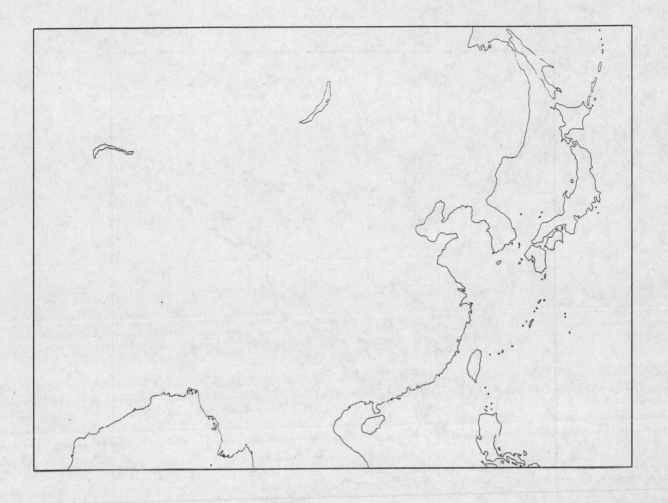

Outline Map of Greece
AND THE EASTERN MEDITERRANEAN

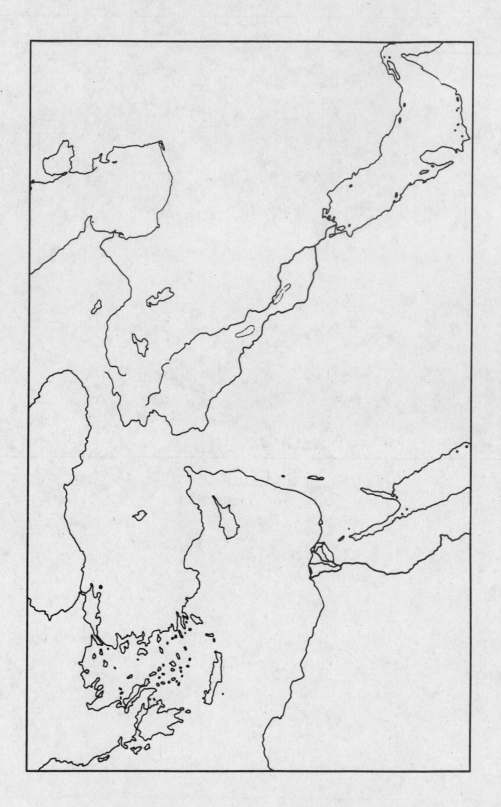

OUTLINE MAP OF THE WORLD

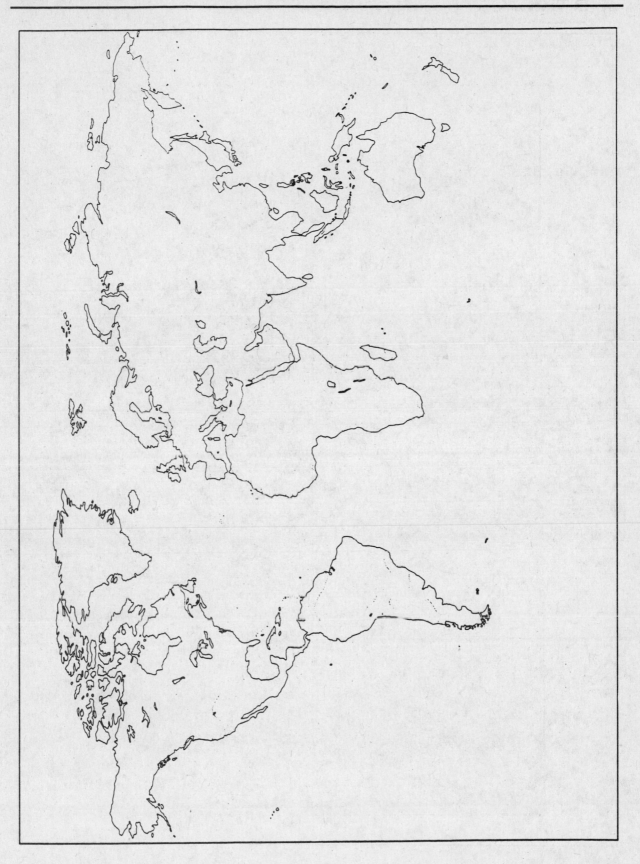

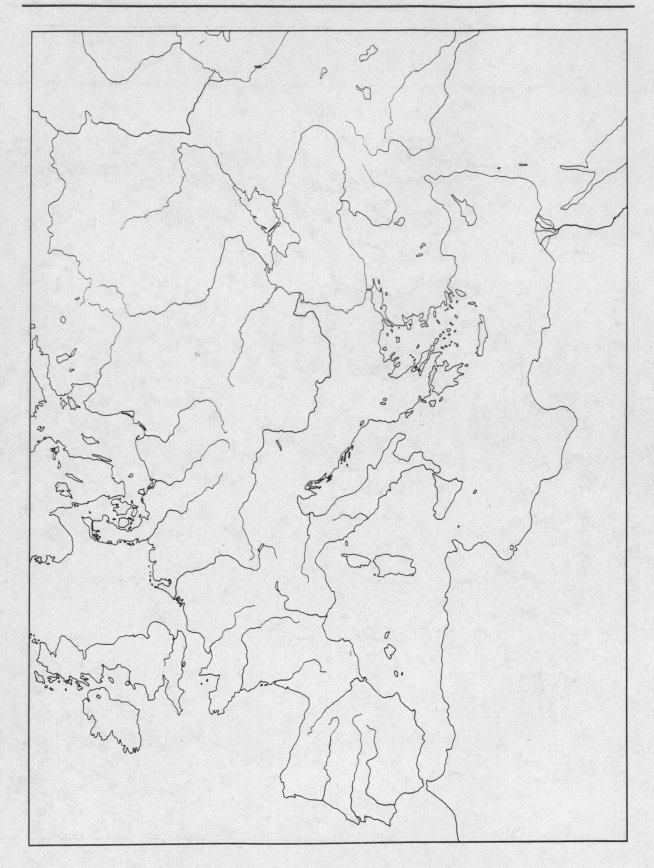

OUTLINE MAP OF EUROPE

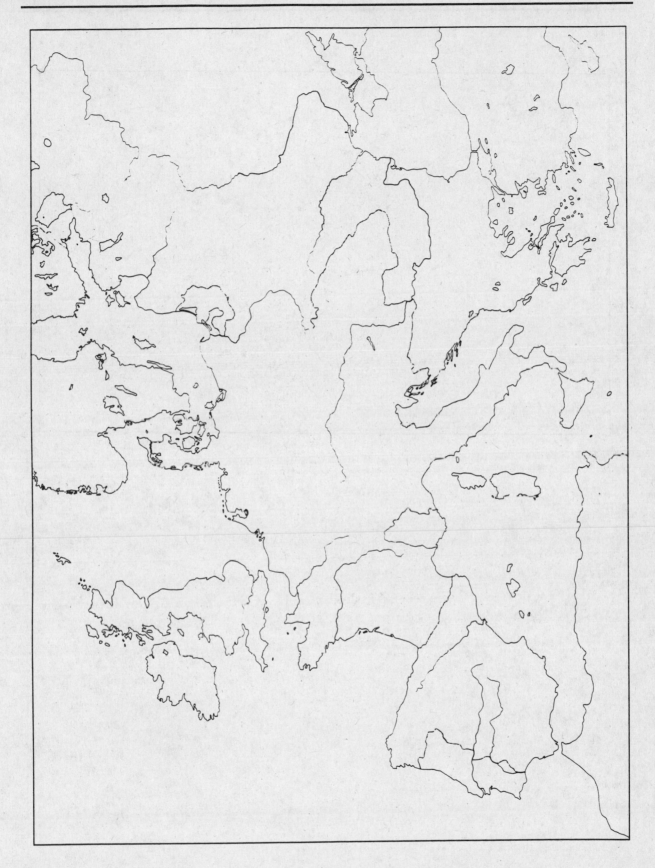

OUTLINE MAP OF EUROPE AND THE MIDDLE EAST

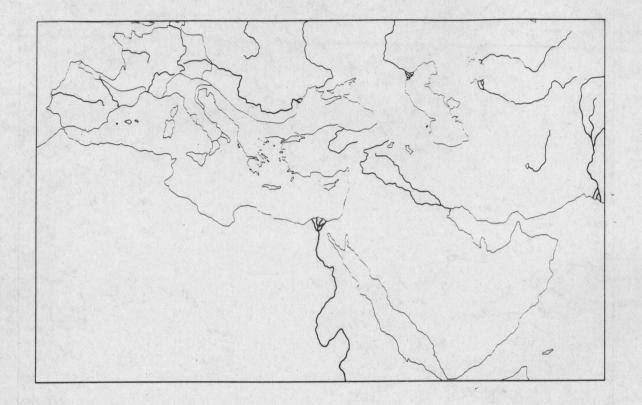

Outline Map of Africa

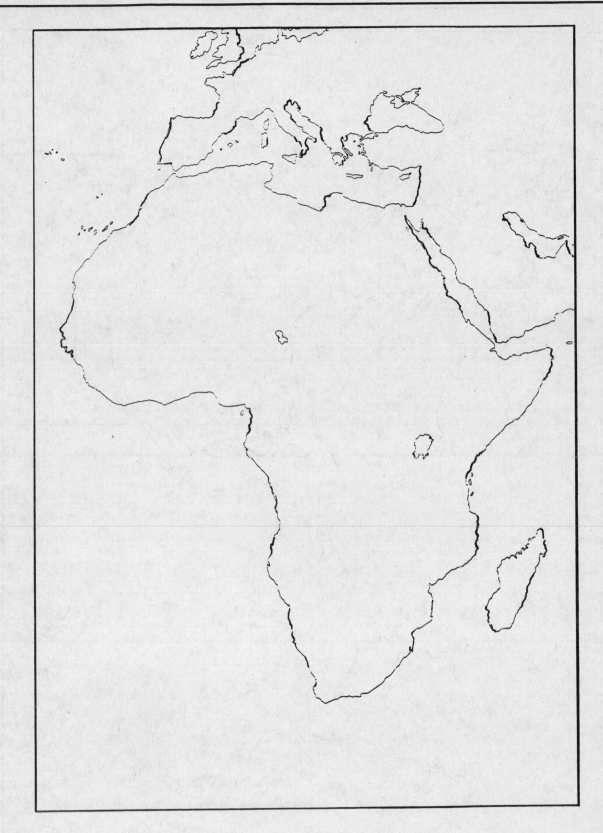

OUTLINE MAP OF NORTH AND SOUTH AMERICA